WANDERING DIXIE

WANDERING DIXIE

Dispatches from the Lost Jewish South

Sue Eisenfeld

MAD CREEK BOOKS, AN IMPRINT OF
THE OHIO STATE UNIVERSITY PRESS
COLUMBUS

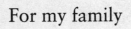

For my family

It is not your responsibility to finish the work of perfecting the world, but neither are you free to desist from it.

—RABBI TARFON, ETHICS OF THE FATHERS

CONTENTS

JEWS, THE CONFEDERACY, RACE, THE SOUTH, AND ME

A Prologue

A stream of slumped-shouldered, butternut-clad Rebel infantrymen march up a gravel road lined by Federals. When they arrive near the McLean House, the site of Lee and Grant's grand handshake the day before, they lay down their rifles in orderly tripods. It's the stacking of arms ceremony. After four years of brutal war, the men are forced to surrender. Their canteens jingle as their only worldly possessions—musical instruments, battered bags, battle flags—slough off onto the ground, and a Union band plays "Auld Lang Syne" and "Dixie." And then the most remarkable thing happens at Appomattox Court House, Virginia: this liberal, Yankee-born city girl starts to cry.

Oh yes, back on April 12, 2015, the last day of the five-day event commemorating the sesquicentennial of the Civil War—in the few months before the Charleston, South Carolina, shooting, when a young Rebel flag–toting white man shot and killed nine black churchgoers inside their house of worship, and two years before the deadly protest in Charlottesville, Virginia, when neo-Confederates and neo-Nazis marched and rallied to protest the city's decision to remove a Robert E. Lee statue—I was as caught up as ever in the *Confederate fever* of Virginia. The fever had been building in me for more than twenty years as I resided in the Old Dominion.

I'd been thinking about a road trip to the Deep South, with the goal of expanding my Civil War geography. I was going to make my way from Andersonville, Georgia, to Vicksburg, Mississippi, and learn more about the landscape of where this sprawling war had taken place. I hadn't yet decided to change my plans to focus on the "lost" Jewish South. I hadn't yet realized I'd be driving the route between Selma and Montgomery, through the heart of the Civil Rights Movement and that I'd hijack my own trip and turn it into an exploration of the history of America with slavery at its roots and realize my own lack of awareness. That gradual transformation would come later.

At this point, I was still caught up in ingesting the history that (white) Virginia had laid out for me.

I had spent my childhood in Philadelphia, visiting the homes and tombstones of our nation's founding fathers, learning about Colonial days, Quakers, the Revolutionary War, and the Underground Railroad in school. But in Virginia, I had spent my adult years and decades visiting the mansions, plantations, and gardens of former presidents and slaveholders; the cabins and cemeteries of enslaved people; battlefields with victories both blue and gray—Fredericksburg, the Wilderness, Antietam, Monocacy, and Gettysburg (where I spent a New Year's Eve); and small, dusty museums where Confederate letters were written on wallpaper during paper shortages and minié balls were mined from backyards. I had often stopped to see the curious Confederate monuments in the small Virginia towns my husband, Neil, and I would pass through on our travels—Abingdon, Amherst, Floyd, Washington—and attended reenactments at Manassas, Middleburg, and New Market. Neil and I had even gotten married at a bed and breakfast where a portrait of Stonewall Jackson hung over the mantelpiece, near where three brick slave dwellings still stand, spotlighted by sunset.

I routinely traveled in Virginia on roads named for leaders and history deemed most important here: Lee Highway, Jefferson Davis Highway, John Mosby Highway; passing Rebel Run and Plantation Parkway, reminded on Gallows Road that history is not that far away.

Even a freedom-and-justice-for-all Center City Philadelphian can get sucked into the general one-sidedness of Civil War commemoration in the South. I had, in fact, become fascinated with Confederates, with the seeming contradictions tied up in their positions and personalities, like Jefferson Davis—US secretary of war and US senator from Mississippi—who called his resignation from the senate to become the president of the Confederacy "the saddest day of my life." I was sad, of course, for the 597,000 Federals who were killed, wounded, captured, or missing, but I also felt empathy for the 490,000 southerners who found the same fate—friends, fathers, brothers, and sons, and the women left back home to manage somehow, fending off northern soldiers who'd come to take their potatoes and beans and destroy their homes, to break them; and the kids, too—many of whom became orphans. At a Battle of Spotsylvania reenactment and encampment I attended, all the white southerners (many wearing "Heritage Not Hate" T-shirts) were shouting a call-and-response chant in unison—

What do we do now?
Kill Yankees!
How many?
All of 'em!

—like a song remembered from childhood, making me feel afraid and wonder how long I'd be able to pass as a southerner. But I still felt an open-minded person's understanding of the pride people felt in their soldier ancestors—the whispered-down-the-lane heroes of family trees from a war that, generally speaking, the North has forgotten.

But I had always thought about the war as being between the blue and the gray. I never considered it to be about the enslaved. Virginia filled my vacuum of Civil War knowledge with Confederate history. I accepted white southerners on their own terms. I absorbed the narrative that mostly non-wealthy, non-slave-owning southerners fought for state's rights and against a northern invader—against a region imposing its rules on a place that didn't want to be governed. "What are you fighting for anyhow?" one northerner supposedly asked a captured

Confederate. "I'm fighting because you're down here," the Virginia private said.

Before Virginia, all I thought about the South, if I had spent any northern moments thinking about the region, which I probably hadn't, was that it was a strange, faraway place; racist, anti-Semitic, and godforsaken. Any northerner knew that. They had the Ku Klux Klan down there. They had enslaved and segregated and lynched people there. One historian even says that the Nazis got their blueprint for what to do with Jews from what the southerners did to blacks.

I ended up there because of a job, and Virginia was a different kind of interesting for a person who grew up on history. It was a slice of America that wasn't really *my* America; I was always an outsider, inhabiting and embracing a history and legacy that belonged to others, people with long histories in this country—people who had come early enough to have fought in the Revolution, the War of 1812, and the Civil War.

My great-grandparents had come to America via Ellis Island and the Port of Philadelphia around 1900 from Eastern Europe and had settled, like many Jews, in New York or New Jersey or Philadelphia. Everyone I knew in most of my younger life—my Irish, Italian, Indian, and Korean classmates and friends—seemed to have roughly the same history. Our shared experiences made up the seemingly vast urban, northeastern view of the country that I carried with me far into adulthood.

Then one day, fourteen years after moving to Virginia, Neil and I made our way to Richmond for the first time, and everything changed. That was the day I homed in on the one thing that seemed most incongruous for Richmond yet most natural for me to visit as a culturally Jewish historic-cemetery lover from childhood: the Hebrew cemetery on Shockoe Hill, once on the outskirts of the city and now next to a quiet area of low-rise housing. It dated from 1816.

Apparently there were Jews in America before 1900. In the South.

Thirty graves were separated from the others by an ornamental black iron fence decorated with muskets, swords, sabers, and a soldier's cap.

M. Levy, Mississippi, killed May 31, 1862
S. Weiss, Ga.
Henry Cohen, S. C. killed June 29, 1864
S. Bachrach, Lynchburg, Va.
Jonathan Sheuer, La.

It was the Confederate soldier section, with a monument erected by the Hebrew Ladies' Memorial Association of Richmond, 1866. They were Jewish Confederates, as foreign a concept as I'd ever encountered.

The premise of the place did not compute, and I shelved the idea in a far corner of my brain, shell-shocked, in a file perhaps called Denial.

Years later, when the *New York Times* was running a column during the four years of the 150th anniversary of the war, I needed a topic to write about that none of the other two hundred authors and one thousand articles had already covered. I thought back to my day in Richmond. There were questions that had swirled around my mind at the cemetery that I hadn't yet answered. This one above all: how could the Jews, who celebrate their freedom from slavery in Egypt each year at Passover, have fought for the South, for the side of slavery?

As I do with all my writing, I discussed the topic with my mother, Philadelphia born and bred, the person who nurtured my interest in history, whom I'd always considered a wise person providing excellent guidance throughout my life, but whose only experience in the South may have been limited to northern Virginia and Jewish Florida. She did not believe there were Jewish Confederates or other early Jews or that the South could have been a hub of Jewish life. None of her friends had ever heard of Jewish southerners or Jewish Confederates. She questioned me about my research and findings, pointing out that I'm not really a historian or scholar; maybe my sources were wrong, maybe I misunderstood the information.

The Jews started coming from Eastern Europe around 1900, she argued. They were often Socialists, like her grandfather, who had left Russia and escaped being sent to Siberia as punishment for his beliefs and activism in distributing anti-czarist literature. They believed in the little people, the underdog, human rights for all, she explained. They related closely to blacks because both groups were oppressed. Jews went down South during the civil rights era and *died* for blacks, she emphasized. Our cousin, she told me (really, our cousin's cousin) went down to Mississippi during Freedom Summer and was lynched by the KKK. She was referring to our New York cousin through marriage, Andrew Goodman, whose death had made her afraid of the Deep South all her life. We debated over email for weeks.

But I persisted. I began talking to and reading the work of scholars, seeing exhibits about Jews in the Civil War, interviewing a rabbi in Philly who is a Civil War buff and southern Jewish history expert, and talking to a descendant of Jewish Confederates from Baltimore. Then I took a trip to Savannah, Georgia, to visit the church-looking building of Congregation Mickve Israel, which dates back to 1733, when some of the first Jews on the continent had come through Savannah's port. The next year, I took a quick trip to Charleston, and I toured Kahal Kadosh Beth Elohim (KKBE), a synagogue organized in 1749, and the Coming Street Cemetery, established in 1764, the largest and oldest surviving Jewish burial ground in the South. It was full of Revolutionary War soldiers and War of 1812 soldiers, and—seen with my own eyes yet again—the graves of Civil War soldiers: Jewish Confederates. Anita Moïse Rosefield Rosenberg, president of the KKBE Reform temple, gave me a tour, and these weren't unknown men to Rosenberg: they were her relatives. And she was no anomaly; in Charleston, I learned from a tour guide at the temple, when the Civil War broke out, every able-bodied man who was a member of KKBE enlisted in the army of the Confederacy.

I learned, ultimately, that Jews had begun coming to America as early as 1654 and through the 1700s in the first "wave" of Jewish immigration to this country—a fact neither my mother, nor I, nor most other northern Jews we know ever realized. They were mostly Sephardic Jews from Spain and Portugal. After establishing a community in 1655 in what is now New York City and in 1678 in Newport, Rhode Island, they created a settlement in Charleston in 1695, which became the largest Jewish community in North America through the 1830s—with about five hundred Jewish people, compared to only about four hundred in New York. In 1841 the leader of the Charleston congregation, Reverend Gustavus Poznanski, speaking of America and the South as he spoke of his house of worship, summed up what many Jewish southerners felt: "This synagogue is our *temple,* this city our *Jerusalem,* this happy land our *Palestine.*"

So, why did the Jews love and fight for the South, this supposedly racist, anti-Semitic place that northern Jews like my mother still fear? Because after thousands of years of wandering, exiled and expelled from countries all over the world, the US South allowed Jews to become citizens and vote, own land, hold public office, live their lives in relative safety and peace, and practice their religion. According to Rabbi Bertram Korn, the highest-ranking Jewish chaplain in the US armed forces and the man who wrote the first notable book about Jews and the Civil War, "Nowhere else in America—certainly not in the antebellum North—had Jews been accorded such an opportunity to be complete equals as in the old South." What a country!

In Europe, Africa, the Middle East, and South America, on the other hand, Jews were imprisoned, tortured, enslaved, kicked out, and massacred. Governments and churches and fellow residents and neighbors seized their properties, banned them from land ownership, destroyed their villages, forced them into ghettos, burned down their synagogues, restricted how they could trade and marry, stole their money and investments, stole their children to raise them Christian, unfairly taxed them, required them to convert to Christianity, prevented their employment, barred them from holding public office, denied them citizenship, and forced them to assimilate again and again wherever they resettled in the world.

Here in America, the Jews kind of blended in. Although they were not considered white per se, they were white enough (in southern cemeteries, people were buried in either the black cemetery, the Jewish cemetery, the unlabeled white Protestant cemetery, or the white Catholic cemetery). Jews were, for the most part, accepted by and assimilated with other whites, just as long as they went to church—and "the Jewish church" was as good as any. With hard work, they could rise in social status, drawing on skills they had perfected over the centuries in occupations they had been allowed to pursue, becoming business owners, financial brokers, lawyers, slave owners and politicians like other whites. In fact, as one retired rabbi in Charleston told me, Jews became so instrumental in the development of some southern cities and so integral in society as business owners and community leaders, that they were "like the mortar in the bricks."

The South was home for these people, their Promised Land. The land of my tribe, as it turns out.

And so, my mother's disbelief notwithstanding, I finished my research and published my article about Jewish Confederates. I overcame my mother's doubts. Three years later, she and I would take the train together to New York City to visit the exhibit "The First Jewish Americans: Freedom and Culture in the New World" at the New York Historical Society, where all the fun facts I had tried to convince her of about Jews in the South were on display in the center of Yankeedom. I felt vindicated.

I needed to go to the Deep South because I'd never been to most of the eleven Confederate states even after twenty-three years of living in Virginia, the heart of the Confederacy. Reading about it is one thing, but going there and walking the ground myself is another. Aside from the general din of scary exoticness I expected, I wanted to know what this giant region would have to teach me about history and culture, people and life.

In addition to wanting to know more about the region the Confederates had fought for—its agricultural, rural, and independently minded ways—I wanted to know how the sky appeared in the South, how hot it really was, how people in the Deep South behaved and what they sounded like, and why so many people have been inspired to write about that region.

And, I realized, I wanted to learn about the Jews there. I didn't know much about Jewish life. I had never gone to religious school, never learned Hebrew, never had a bat mitzvah, nor had I ever been a member of a synagogue or voluntarily attended services. Rather, as a child, I had been dragged by my dad and stepmother to services at their temple out in the suburbs during the High Holy Days of Rosh Hashanah and Yom Kippur. As an adult, I'd always been a "should-I-go-to-work-on-Yom-Kippur?" kind of Jew, one who lights candles in my home at Hanukkah with my latke-making, non-Jewish atheist husband and who partakes of Passover Seders in other people's homes but who has never attended a proper Shabbat service in my own community. In fact, I have never been connected to a Jewish community. My Jewish friends are mostly nonpracticing and married to non-Jews, and I had never been interested in practicing my religion anyway: it felt oppressive and patriarchal with its rituals and rules.

My mother had told me when I was young that I might find my way to Judaism on my own terms someday. When I learned that the rural places I wanted to go to in the South—those less populous, off-the-beaten track towns I believed to be the most authentic southern locales—were some of the pre–Civil War and Civil War-era places Jews and their kin had called home, I thought maybe I had found my connection to Judaism after all.

Would the Jews there seem different to me, and would I feel any connection to them? Do they eat different foods for the Jewish holidays than I had been accustomed to? How did the Jews manage the intersection of their ways and world-views with this strange place, once nearly a country unto itself? I wanted to visit the towns southern Jews had inhabited, the temples in which they worshipped, and the sacred places where they found their final rest.

I knew I'd be doing mostly fly-by types of journeys, and what I'd come to know and feel about the region would be somewhat cursory. But curiosity can't be quashed, and a travel writer goes to the places she wants to know and walks those grounds with her own two feet. I wanted to go to the South as a pseudo-southernized Jewish Yankee and see where my compass would point me.

It pointed me in a different direction than I expected.

Four months after the Appomattox reenactment, and two months after the 2015 Charleston shooting, I set off. The nation was reeling over the shooting. I hadn't had much formal or informal education about African American history or the Civil Rights Movement—not much more advanced than slavery, discrimination, civil rights, then Obama!—and I had not been active in many conversations about race and privilege. At that time, I lacked nearly any self-awareness of my personal intersection with or responsibility for these issues. Black Lives Matter and the issues the movement stemmed from had not yet attracted my attention enough to influence my travel goals. And so this latest tragic shooting of African Americans, of what really has been an unending series of unjust crises, had not yet affected how I planned my trip. I was living my white privileged life the same way I always had.

I was taking with me what felt obvious but was an unexamined belief that I was a non-racist, open-minded, "color blind" person with progressive views about acceptance, cultural sensitivity, and everything else that's politically correct, or as I like to see it: respectful. I had attended integrated public schools in Philadelphia from first grade through high school—at least as many students and teachers of color as white people had been in classes, after-school activities, and leadership positions; my school environment seemed to epitomize equal respect for and acknowledgment of all people in society. I had been part of some South African anti-apartheid/divestment and anti-racism activism in high school, and later in life when I visited South Africa after the fall of apartheid, I made it a point to visit Soweto and Nelson Mandela's childhood home. I'd always believed in reparations for slavery and affirmative action, and I'd also been welcoming of cultural differences, having lived as an adult for more than two decades in a community where more than 130 languages are spoken in my zip code.

The way the South worked its magic on me was that even as I embarked on a "Civil War journey" and a "southern culture journey" and an "American Jewish journey," with my I'm-not-a-racist attitude, I also found myself on an African American history journey—or really an unabridged American history journey. In traveling the geography of "all the great battle-grounds of the civil rights movement," as civil rights activist and Georgia congressman John Lewis wrote in his memoir of the places I was going, these events and people and moments began to educate me, influence me, and change my viewpoint on the trip—and on America. My interests morphed, plans changed. Even from my first day in Alabama, exploring Jewish and southern life in a small town no one's ever heard of, I began seeing my journey in the South in an entirely new light.

And America began unfolding in a more uncertain light. As time went on, my travels coincided with the 2016 presidential election in which civil rights themes from the 1960s began replaying themselves before my eyes. By the time my travels ended in the spring of 2018, the nation had become distinctly divided, which to me seemed like a fast, precipitous plunge back—perhaps as far as the 1860s.

In the end, I returned home to a different Virginia, and I was different, too. My four-plus years of travel in and research about the South turned out to be a personal reckoning—not only about my own religion but about the lesser-known, hidden, abandoned, lost, forgotten, ignored, and refused African American history and culture and the role of enslaved people as the builders and backbone of America. This journey into the unknown forced me to explore my own culpability in our troubled American story.

In knowingly and unknowingly packing with me all my decades of sheltered ignorance, I never thought to consider how the South might change me—and that has been the greatest surprise.

This book is my journey.

PART 1

ROAD TRIP

THE PEANUT LADY OF EUFAULA

"A person from New York could not possibly understand what it takes to get a peanut into a Snickers bar." Thus says the peanut lady of Eufaula, Alabama, a small town on the Alabama–Georgia border, 150 miles south of Atlanta. "Most people don't even know that peanuts are grown in the ground, not in a tree." Though not a New Yorker, I admit I have no idea where they come from. This is my first lesson in the Deep South.

Sara Hamm is as warm as she is brash. Standing outside the Reeves Peanut Company warehouse on East Broad Street in Eufaula, where she is the plant manager and buying-point agent, on my first real day of my first trip to the Deep South, she smiles and pivots from Snickers bars to Jimmy Carter once I tell her we've just come from Plains, Georgia. She calls the former president an anti-Semite and points her finger in my face as she says it. Grasshopper that I am, I'm freshly wowed by the guy, straight from visiting his high school and boyhood home at the Jimmy Carter National Historic Site. I had gotten misty-eyed when learning about the Carter Center's mission to "wage peace" in the world. But Hamm, who talks openly with me like we've been friends for years, is filled with strong opinions about his darker side. "He's superficial," she says. "He's not a superstar. He has never been favorable to the Jewish people."

But peanuts—not Carter—are really what occupies Hamm's mind. Long-haired, pony-tailed in salt and pepper with a sweet, smooth face, Hamm, in her fifties, is a lone female in a man's world of peanuts, which, in Reeves's business, includes the

15

Black Belt—which I learn is named for its rich soil as well as its people, from below Selma, Alabama, to Columbus, Georgia, and into northern Florida. Hamm worked her way up from secretary to office manager to the role she holds now (attending half a dozen peanut-industry functions where Carter spoke as a peanut farmer, not as a president), and she's the only full-time employee of a business that handles about four thousand tons of peanuts a year, about four million dollars annually. Peanuts are, essentially, her life. And I happen to be a big peanut butter fan.

I met up with Hamm on a lark. I was holed up at a lakefront cabin at Lakepoint Resort State Park, facing Lake Eufaula (pronounced "you-fall-uh"), while Neil took the car to go birding at the Eufaula National Wildlife Refuge. All the prime waterfowl one might come to see were out of season, but we were in Alabama for the first time in our lives, and he wanted to see what he could find.

This was part of our agreement when we decided to take a three-week summer road trip through the Deep South: if we could hit all the Civil War, southern, and Jewish history sites on my agenda, then I'd be a dutiful birder's wife as well, all by my lonesome for a few select days. On this day, I lounged on the sofa in the cabin facing the lake and read the latest *New York Times Magazine* cover article, which happened to be "A Dream Undone: Inside the 50-Year Campaign to Roll Back the Voting Rights Act," written to commemorate the act's fifty-year anniversary. I learned that although the fifteenth amendment guaranteed African American males the right to vote in 1870, whites have been laying down state and local roadblocks to making that right a reality in all the years since. Meanwhile, out in the field, Neil wound up seeing his first-ever gray rat snake and amassing a pretty good bird list despite the season: forty-three species in four hours, including several, like the white ibis and loggerhead shrike, that are unusual or impossible to see in Virginia. Plus some alligators to boot.

While surfing the website of the Institute of Southern Jewish Life (ISJL) in the cabin that morning, I came across this fact:

"Sara Hamm . . . and her family . . . are now the last Jews left in Eufaula." Given that I was on a southern Jewish historical pilgrimage of sorts, this tidbit is what I latched onto. In the first time ever that I sought someone out specifically because they are Jewish, I gave Hamm a call—which is how Neil and I ended up, after he returned from birding, being invited over for a tour of the peanut warehouse, a guided drive around town to Eufaula's hidden Jewish sites, and a visit to the home of Hamm's mother (Me-maw)—confirming everything I'd ever heard about southern hospitality.

Neil and I had actually begun our visit the day before on the banks of the Chattahoochee River at the Jewish cemetery, a rear section of the East Fairview Cemetery. Marking the place is a black iron archway, erected in 1989 by Hamm's grandmother, Jennie Rudderman, to commemorate the burials that began in 1845 when Jews acquired the land. The town was settled in 1816, and according to the ISJL, Jews began arriving in Eufaula in the mid-1800s, immigrants from Germany who had started their American journey elsewhere in the country first. They had come to America in the second "wave" of Jewish immigration to America, beginning in the 1840s. Like most Jewish settlers of that era, they were predominantly store owners—clothiers and grocers and purveyors of "gents' furnishing goods" and "ladies underwear, collars, cuffs, rufflings, corsets, hosiery, trimmings, and ladies ready-made suits"—and had such a hard-to-believe large presence in Eufaula that the "town wore a rather lonesome look on the main business street" during Yom Kippur when all their businesses were closed, according to an 1899 newspaper article.

Hamm tells us that her grandfather was one of those Jews. "Jews would find a place where there weren't any other Jewish businesses, and they set up shop," she explains, like in Eufaula; Albany, Georgia, to the southeast; and Panama City, Florida, on the panhandle. "My grandparents came here out of sheer business necessity." Born in Atlanta and Birmingham, they moved to Eufaula in the 1930s and opened a family business selling clothing, which had buyers in New York, distributors in Birmingham, and shop locations in five different towns in and around Dothan, Alabama, including Eufaula. Hamm's uncle helped found Temple Emanu-El in Dothan, the strategic center of this ingenious wheel-and-spoke arrangement of places within an hour's drive of where her family members decided to settle, a plan the family devised so that "they could work together and pray together," according to Hamm.

The Eufaula Jewish cemetery that Hamm's grandmother twice rehabilitated was not in great condition, with once-upright stones now lying on the ground, broken marble, and acid rain-stained and smeared engravings, not that different from many historic cemeteries I've seen. Eighty-two graves—Bernsteins, Cohns, Sterns, and Lewys among them, including several Confederate soldiers with their white marble stones just like in the Confederate circle in Arlington National Cemetery I was familiar with, and many inscriptions written in Hebrew—are set enchantingly against a quiet edge of the Chattahoochee River. The land is owned by the city of Eufaula, "but the city quit tending to it," Hamm says. "The Jewish community is responsible for it, but they're gone." Weather, vandalism, and deterioration, including downed oak trees, have taken their toll on the place, and Hamm estimates it would require at least fifty thousand dollars to rehabilitate. Distant family members often contact Hamm to ask questions about their ancestors and the burial ground, but "no one wants to pay," she says.

Our Jewish tour of Eufaula had also included a brief hunt for the synagogue, the temple of B'nai Israel, a congregation established after the Civil War when enough people started to amass. In 1872 the group bought a building on the corner of Livingston and Barbour Streets, which once served as the Eufaula First United Methodist Church, and "re-fashioned it . . . at considerable expense . . . [into] a beautiful synagogue," according to an eyewitness in 1875, "which reflects much credit upon their good taste and liberality, and is an ornament to the city." A local merchant led lay services because, like many small congregations then and now, they could not afford a full-time rabbi. One hundred and five Jews in 1878 turned into fifty-six Jews in 1905. By 1911 the congregation sold the building, and now it's a weedy empty lot—what I did not yet know was a metaphor for much of Jewish life in today's small-town South. In 1919 only six households remained as part of the official congregation, and they salvaged what they could of their Jewish life by meeting at people's homes rather than at a formal building. There were twenty-five Jews in 1937, and sometime in the 1930s the congregation disbanded altogether.

Now there's Hamm as the spokesperson for the Old Testament and the keeper of Jewish history in this twelve-thousand-person town (50 percent black, 44 percent white, 6 percent other). She's the one who keeps the town's Jewish memorabilia, fields phone calls, and gives interviews when asked. And nearly every Passover and Easter for about thirty-five years, she says, various churches have invited her to come explain the Old Testament and her faith. When her son comes along too—with his long brown hair, yarmulke, and fringed, satin tallit (a prayer shawl)—the wide-eyed church kids think he is Jesus.

When her son was growing up, she says, his friends were always interested in him, as he was the only person they ever knew who had a bar mitzvah. This situation is in complete contrast to my own coming of age, where I was one of the few Jews of my mixed-religion friends not to have a bat mitzvah. In a large metropolitan area like Philadelphia, and in a generally nonpracticing family—none of my grandparents went to synagogue, and my parents didn't freak out when I dated non-Jews or married one—it was easy for me to choose not to "be" Jewish. Other people in the community kept the Jewish faith running; I could just decide to jump onboard anytime. I could acknowledge it as a cultural heritage, connected to geography, food, and stories, without much action. Here, in this dearth of Judaism, Hamm and her husband had to work hard to make sure their son was imbued with a strong connection to Judaism by driving him to a synagogue in Columbus, Georgia, about an hour each way, three times a week for three years to prepare for his bar mitzvah, an experience that led Hamm's husband, born a Baptist, to convert to Judaism.

Inside the peanut warehouse—a 1903 brick building with numerous ballroom-sized rooms that are either completely empty or filled with humongous bags of peanuts—Hamm is running around from office to office collecting paperwork and finishing loose ends for the day. Dressed in blue jeans, a black Future Farmers of America T-shirt, and sneakers, Hamm is in charge of purchasing peanuts from nearby Eufaula farmers— which used to include twenty-five or thirty within a hundred-mile radius, but now include only six or seven. They bring their loads on trailers or wagons, and the Alabama Federal State Inspection Service, which sets up shop here for four months of the year, inspects and grades each load of peanuts as it comes in during harvest. The agency determines the level of moisture content and debris, as well as weight, density, and other quality parameters.

Hamm explains that peanuts that are deemed "good" go immediately into storage in the warehouse, which can hold nine thousand tons; we observed a room filled with hay bale–sized bags of goobers. After the peanuts are bailed, they are sent out for shelling and then returned to Reeves for cold storage. For the past several years, Eufaula's good ones have ended up in one of my favorite snacks: Lance Sandwich Crackers, my go-to product for afternoon pick-me-ups and emergency caches. Hamm is also in charge of ensuring buyers for those peanuts—manufacturers like Lance, which in turn pay Reeves for the product and its storage.

The "bad" peanuts, those that don't meet the state and federal standards, end up being sold for peanut oil, and the mash left after pressing that oil is used for animal feed. Hulls from the good and the bad are used as beds for chicken farming or burned as fuel. Peanuts may be one of the original no-waste products.

In the high season, September and October, when peanuts are harvested, she and her seasonal employees work sixteen hours a day "in dust and dirt," she says, educating this Yankee in agricultural ways. Some of her employees are convicted felons. "I help them try to make a change in their lives," she says. "I have to lecture them not to get drunk and come in late after getting their first thousand-dollar paycheck [during harvest season], or I'll fire them." One Thursday in October when I happened to talk to her on the phone, she said she had already put in eighty hours that week, and there would be two more weeks of madness.

But Eufaula in August is where Hamm gives me the peanut lesson. Though peanuts grow in the ground, she explains, they are not a usual seed or root. The peanut plant—a legume—flowers aboveground, then the flower grows down away from the plant, forming a small peg and stem that extends several inches into the soil, which matures into a peanut. They are harvested by digging them out. In addition to not having a clue about how Snickers bars are made, most people also do not know that the whims of the weather can make or break an entire year's income for these farmers, and possibly the access to or price of our favorite peanut butter—in my case, an organic brand, creamy, no salt, no sugar. "We live on a prayer," says Hamm.

In fact, most people I know don't know much about the life of someone like Sara Hamm. She is the first peanut industry representative Neil and I have ever met, and certainly the first female peanut warehouse manager and most definitely the first southern Jew in the Deep South we have encountered. And by that, I mean the first I've known to work in a truly southern industry and the first to speak in a no-holds-barred pure and true janglingly syllabic southern accent, with no trace of New York, New Jersey, Philadelphia, Baltimore, the Midwest, or any of the northeastern or northern places where all the Jews I'd ever known were from.

There's no getting around the fact that Neil and I are real northerners because the twang from her mouth reverberates in our ears like a tuning fork. Being raised in New York State and Pennsylvania, respectively, Neil and I didn't grow up hearing these kinds of sounds, not from non-Jews and not from Jews especially. We've lived in Virginia for the last twenty-three years, though—a helpful fact while traveling as tourists in the South, constantly being asked where we're from; it gives us street cred. I personally have now lived more of my life in the South than in the North, which of course doesn't make me a southerner but gives me a feeling of insiderness. All this inner pondering on how unfamiliar her accent sounds feels kind of disrespectful and steeped in stereotypes, but then she winds up calling us "foreigners," so maybe we're even-Steven.

I find Hamm interesting—what with her female peanut power and southern Jewish background—and I tell her so. This sparks her to declare, "I'm just a normal person." But then she mentions how, by the way, she survived two brain surgeries to remove a benign tumor the size of an egg, she had to learn to walk again afterward, and she felt survivor's guilt because other people in the brain surgery ward didn't make it. She doesn't come right out and say it, but it seems that her gratitude in being alive and being well is part of the reason she likes to hire people "who can't get jobs in lots of places." It seems she mothers them back into society.

I'm so focused on Hamm and the Jewish history here and her peanut southernness that nearly as an afterthought, given our good conversation, does it occur to me to ask Hamm about race. I figure we are in the South, and it's a stereotypical and perhaps fraught topic of discussion among liberal white visitors wanting to understand everything. Luckily, I don't have to vomit out an ungraceful question about it outright, as she provides the entrée by telling me she grew up with the Wallace family—as in, Alabama Governor George C. Wallace—when she was a child in Clayton, Alabama. Like so much of what Hamm has spoken about today, so far from my small northern world, this casual reveal of her connection to Real History leaves me stupefied.

I don't know much about Wallace, but I know he is an infamous figure in American history. He is, in fact, the man "who became known as the embodiment of resistance to the civil rights movement," as his *Washington Post* obituary in

1998 stated; whose "campaign of racial oppression . . . burned him into the nation's consciousness as the Deep South's most forceful political brawler," according to the obituary in the *New York Times*; and who was a "white-hot segregationist," according to Kenneth Mullinax, former aide to Wallace in his fourth term as Alabama governor. He was the guy who would be remembered forever for advocating, "Segregation now, segregation tomorrow, and segregation forever." But to Hamm, he and his wife and kids "were just a local family."

"I knew George all my life," she says. "They were just normal people we knew growing up." Hamm says she was seven when the first two black children integrated her elementary school. "Based on what I know, and from talking to his son, I'll never believe he was an actual racist," she says. She's flummoxing me, as this sounds shockingly wrong, but later I learn that Wallace actually started his career in the early 1950s as a progressive judge who treated the black lawyers and clients who came before him as respectfully as whites. "Judge George Wallace was the most liberal judge that I had ever practiced law in front of," the first black attorney in Selma, Alabama, J. L. Chestnut Jr., once said. "He was the first judge in Alabama to call me 'Mister' in a courtroom." Wallace was also a member of the board of trustees of the all-black Tuskegee University. But since he was fourteen, his life's goal was to become Alabama's governor; and being interested in helping the poor, many of whom were black, became politically unpopular.

"He was always a politician, and he would do anything to get elected," Hamm said, including making a "Faustian bargain" of selling his soul for power, as described by many who knew him—biographers, historians, civil rights lawyers, and even his children. After losing his first run for governor—which he attributed to not being an anti-segregationist and to not gaining the support of the KKK like his opponent (instead, being supported by the NAACP)—he vowed to never be "outsegged" again. "He loved the power that came with winning," Hamm said.

I don't even have to prompt Hamm to dig deeper; she keeps on talking. "Not that what he did wasn't horrible," referring to the day in June 1963 when, in his first term as governor, he literally stood in a schoolhouse doorway, flanked by armed state troopers, to bar the path of two black students attempting to attend the University of Alabama. President Kennedy ordered the National Guard to the campus. Later that year, Wallace ordered state police to four locations to prevent public schools from opening after a federal integration court order, and the civil disturbances that erupted resulted in at least one death.

Some believe his lack of enforcement of civil rights—lawlessness, really—led to the bombing of the 16th Street Baptist Church in Birmingham, which killed four young black girls. In fact, when asked on the Friday before the Sunday, September 15, 1963, bombing what needed to happen for the civil rights problems to end in Alabama, he reportedly said, "What we need are a couple of first-class funerals."

"It's disgusting to think he'd have any part of keeping blacks down. But I didn't know him like that. I don't know if he was a racist, but the person I knew was real down-to-earth. I see him as a human being, a person." Some say the true, original Wallace came out again by 1982 at age sixty-three. After being paralyzed by an assassination attempt a decade earlier, he admitted to being wrong about race and was elected for his fourth and final term as governor, supported by a coalition of blacks and carrying all ten of the state's counties with a majority black population. "We thought [segregation] was in the best interests of all concerned," he said then. "We were mistaken."

An employee drops in at the peanut warehouse for a moment, and Hamm jokes around with him. Despite the fact that white planters in Barbour County, where Eufaula is located, owned twelve thousand slaves in the mid-1800s, as far as blacks and whites are concerned today, Hamm tells us, "Nobody will look twice at an interracial couple," and everyone treats everyone equally. Like this employee, she says, who is black. "He's as dear to me as my own kin." Of course she's the manager and he's the worker, but I keep my mouth shut.

When bringing us outside and showing us the new trailers that the large farms bring their peanuts in on, she mentions that the poorer farmers can't afford the new trailers, and they use the older wagons, half the size and pulled by a farm tractor rather than a tractor-trailer. *Who are the poor farmers?* I ask. Well, they are mostly black, she says, and their farms are smaller. Neither she nor I dive deeper into this disparity.

Hamm harkens back to when she was a kid, when her family ran a clothing store as well as a grocery store and a gas station, serving whites as well as the black community that made up 70 percent of the 1,500-person town of Clayton.

"My whole life, being Jewish, the color of someone's skin . . . we just didn't do that. We knew what it was like to be different. We were the only Jewish family in that small town. As a Jewish kid, racism was not in our realm of thinking. We weren't like that. We felt kinship. We were always on their side.

"It would kill me to say the N-word," she says.

When Hamm takes a break from talking, we follow her outside and she puts us in her black SUV and drives down the main east–west avenue. In 1875, it was reported, "There are over fifty brick stores in the city, besides three handsome drug stores, one carriage factory and many small shops; a handsome opera house . . . ; [and] the largest and finest dancing saloon in the State."

One could easily drive through Eufaula and never see some of the hidden signs of the Jewish community here, though; to our eyes, there is absolutely nothing left. So Neil and I are grateful for Hamm as our guide to the secret past. She brings us to an eye doctor's office along the small Broad Street commercial district, a circa 1865 one-and-a-half-story restored brick building. It appears to have three small circular windows upstairs, over the awning. Only with the telephoto lens of my camera can I see that the dark, black iron grillwork is covering what are actually attic vents, and they're in the shape of

Stars of David. Nearby, Hamm shows us a brick building with Corinthian flair, circa 1895, marked with "Lewy Brothers" in two places in tile, which recalls the Lewy gravestones we saw in the Jewish cemetery the day before, in addition to the 1879 Italianate "Lewy-Mixon House" that we walked past on the main avenue of fancy houses.

Having already seen the ornate antebellum homes that had been recommended to us by a southern friend and that were originally the sole reason we decided to come to Eufaula—the flowering trees and beautiful houses and grounds were once described as "almost like fairy land"—I asked Hamm if the town is segregated. Of course, towns in the more northern South and even in the North are historically segregated as well, by policy or otherwise (certainly my hometown of Philadelphia has segregated areas, as does my current town of Arlington, Virginia). But still, I wanted to know. Hamm brushes off any suggestion that there's a racial divide in Eufaula; she suggests it's quite harmonious. She says that area in the center of town is "mixed."

But then she drives us to the other side of town—literally, the other side of the street from the old-money grand antebellum mansions we'd seen yesterday, to show us where the Shorter cemetery is, the burial site of Alabama Civil War governor John Gill Shorter—a prominent member of the Eufaula Regency, a group of local lawyers that pushed for secession—and his family and slaves. She also mentions that this area is where the employee we were talking to in the warehouse lives.

"This is the black community," she says—or whispers—as Neil will point out later. The houses are certainly smaller, squatter, and less fancy than the grand old pillared homes across the boulevard. I notice later that this neighborhood barely appears on the Eufaula Chamber of Commerce's tour map we had picked up. The town doesn't promote the area, and I hadn't thought to seek out the black community, so without Hamm, we wouldn't have even known it existed.

"There's the black Masons," she indicates as we drive by a plain building. Ignorant of everything Mason, including that "white masonry" has been around since possibly the Middle Ages but "colored masonry," as it was known, became a thing in Alabama only in 1867, I ask, "What's the difference between the black Masons and the white Masons?" "Oh, the white Masons refuse to acknowledge that there are any black Masons," she says curtly. If Neil and I were side by side, we might be sharing confused looks about what race relations are really like here.

Next stop on Hamm's tour is Me-maw's house, an 1845 cottage orné, or decorated rustic cottage, the oldest house in Eufaula, once owned by the first mayor, a fellow Philadelphian. I can't believe real Jews live in a place like this—it's so . . . well, southern. It's a white, three-gabled, wide-verandaed house with Doric columns that I somehow didn't even notice when we walked by it the day before; nor did I notice the Star of David stained-glass transom window over the front door, which would have stopped me in my tracks. Hamm pulls into the driveway, and unlike all the other historic mansions we observed from the outside, this time we get to walk up the front stairs.

When we do, we are welcomed by Mrs. Sandra Gulledge, a smiling, kind-hearted, stocky woman wearing a T-shirt, shorts, and sneakers with ankle socks. She doesn't seem at all fazed that her daughter has brought over two strangers for an intimate tour of her home. Hamm apparently has done this before. Plus, Gulledge opens her house up for the annual Pilgrimage, an event that happens in the spring in small towns all over the South, when, according to promotional materials, "beautiful historic homes, built in the days when 'cotton was king,' [are] open to visitors during this nostalgic return to the Old South." Women dress up in period gowns, hoop skirts and all, and Gulledge shows off the place Jefferson Davis once visited and that has been in her family since 1939.

The combination of *Gone With the Wind* grandeur, the twenty-five-step curving staircase in the entry hall, the cathedral parlor doors imported from England, the golden patterned wallpaper and drapery, the red glass cordial finery, and a center fountain in the front yard—along with the could-be-in-any-Jewish-home étagère full of menorahs, Seder plates, and other Jewish artifacts—produces a cross-cultural explosion in my head: these really are my people. I see telltale signs and feel a kinship, but this house is so different from anything I've ever seen. When Gulledge leads us into the less showy, where-we-actually-live part of the house with wood paneling, easy chairs, a modest kitchen addition, and TV den, the familiar chickeny, briskety scent wafts out of the oven and instantly takes me back to my Grandma Myrt's Cherry Hill, New Jersey, split-level house when I was a pre-vegetarian child at a Jewish holiday meal. With the extra helpings of hospitality that this family is lavishing upon us—introducing us to Hamm's sister and her two kids, showing us the gigantic thirty-by-thirty-foot bedrooms with sixteen-foot ceilings—I am half expecting they are going to ask us to dinner. I feel at home here, related, even: like I've met these people long ago.

When we ask Gulledge why most Jews have left Eufaula, she says straightforwardly, "Because we send them off to college and educate them and they don't want to come back," embracing the same value on education that my family and other Jewish families always seem to espouse. From the looks of real estate offerings in town, though—including a circa 1895 five-bedroom, 6,400-square-foot Queen Anne–style home with double parlors on two acres, selling for $299,999, lower than any starter home in my region of metropolitan DC—it seems that others besides the Jews have fled this small town as well.

After taking a few photos of the family on the front portico and saying thank you and a long goodbye, Hamm delivers us back to the warehouse. It's dinnertime. We've been together like newfound cousins for several hours, with me unwittingly receiving my greatest education to date about the South with this fortuitous meeting. She stuffs my arms full of two canvas sacks of raw peanuts, which taste like raw peas. To Neil, whom she learned is a teacher, she gives fat packets of student activity sheets, workbooks, and newsletters from the American Peanut Council's Education Services Department. She wants him to pass on her excitement that the peanut is the most unique plant in all of America and that eating peanut butter is healthy and can help one lose weight.

When we tell her we'll be making our way to Mississippi in a few days, she shakes her head, lets out a deep breath, and says in all seriousness, "Now that's the Deep South. They're real southern there." Because she was the most colorful southern person we had ever met, with the most syrupy southern drawl we'd ever heard, living what seemed to us to be a very southern kind of life, the idea that there could be something more southern leaves Neil and me, once we return to our car, in heaving, befuddled, gusset-busting, Yankee hysterics.

And yet, when we wind up making our way out of peanut country and west into the soybean, sorghum, and cotton country of Mississippi—a state that civil rights activist and later Georgia congressman John Lewis once called "the belly of the segregated beast"; where the farms really do turn into plantations, so vast and flat in all directions it is like being on a ship at sea, and the horizon of green is laced with delicate white and pink blossoms that turn into cotton bolls, the crop that started the Civil War and is still the most important plant in the South—we realize after all that Hamm was right.

THE GEOGRAPHY OF HOPE

Neil and I have driven to Tuskegee, Alabama, the poorest place in the state, to see bricks. Red bricks, made from the red clay of Alabama. Hundreds of thousands—even millions—of bricks. They were made in the late 1800s and early 1900s by motivated young hands, digging out the material from the ground, combining it with straw, molding the thick mixture into slabs or setting it into molds, smoothing it by hand, and baking it in a handmade kiln. Hundreds and thousands of formerly enslaved people and their kin built the school that Booker T. Washington created for freed slaves on the grounds of an abandoned plantation near the town of Tuskegee: the Tuskegee Normal School for Colored Teachers, later the Tuskegee Normal and Industrial School, and then the Tuskegee Institute. Now it's Tuskegee University and the Tuskegee Institute National Historic Site, part of the National Park Service that encompasses a section of campus, Washington's enviable brick home, and the George Washington Carver Museum, the latter of which tells of the stunning innovations and successes of this enslaved man turned world-famous chemist, agricultural researcher, botanist, inventor, and professor—introducing the concept of crop rotation and developing three hundred products made from peanuts! The Tuskegee school has educated generations of black students since 1881. After I read Washington's book, *Up from Slavery,* I wanted to see those bricks.

Years ago, while renting a rustic one-room cabin in the Blue Ridge Mountains of Virginia, I went to the county library nearby to access the internet and find a book to read. I planted my stuff down at a table and took a peek at the immediate nearby shelves. The first book that caught my eye, at the very end of a row with its cover facing out, was *Up from Slavery,* a book I'd heard of but had never read. A book I certainly ought to have read. Booker T. Washington was someone I didn't know much about; he was never taught in any of my schools or discussed among people in my community.

"I was born a slave on a plantation in Franklin County, Virginia. I am not quite sure of the exact place or exact date of my birth, but at any rate I suspect I must have been born somewhere at some time," Washington wrote. I knew I was in the hands of a competent writer within the first paragraph. I devoured the book, and because it was located in my own state, I went to that plantation the first chance I got.

When I saw it on a frigid January morning, the land was the same rolling Virginia farmland as it had been in the book, crunching under my feet. The eastern red cedar was the same tree, more than a hundred years older now, with more resistance in tornadic storms, greater reach in the summer sun. The red clay, used as chinking in the tobacco barn and the big house and the slave cabins, was the same mud dug up from the earth that kept the wind out from between the timbers even in 1856, when Booker T. Washington was born enslaved on that plantation, and in 1865, when he was freed.

In fact, the 239 acres of the Booker T. Washington National Monument, near Hale's Ford in southern Virginia, run by the National Park Service, encompass most of the original 207 acres of the small farm James and Elizabeth Burroughs once owned. It was there that the Burroughses owned a boy who lived in a one-room log cabin, slept on a pile of filthy rags on a dirt floor, and was not allowed to learn but would carry the Burroughs daughter's books to school. It was there that the boy thought that "to get into a schoolhouse and study would be about the same as getting into paradise." It was there that a government official came and gathered the family and slaves around to impart the important news of emancipation, and then Washington, that young boy, would go on to become the foremost black educator in the nation. With a Jewish colleague, he would lead the way to education for hundreds of thousands—maybe millions—of black students in the dark days before, during, and after the Jim Crow segregated South.

Through Washington's book, I traveled with him on his journey of teaching himself to read, finding his own education at a school for freedmen, and doggedly pursuing the goal of setting up schools for black youth—not waiting for the long, late train of desegregation to find its way to the station. Due to the power of his own words, I wanted to know him more, so I found myself on that land where Washington said he never played as a child, where he suffered in the cold all winter, and where meals were found rather than served, but where he noticed that "the slaves, in many cases, had mastered some handicraft, and none were ashamed, and few unwilling, to labor." And so "when freedom came, the slaves were almost as well fitted to begin life anew as the master."

At Tuskegee, Washington vowed to provide education "of the hand, head, and heart" to show students "not only the utility in labor, but beauty and dignity." "It was not a disgrace to labor," he wrote of his time at Hampton Normal and Agriculture Institute of Virginia, the school he attended and that became the model for Tuskegee. "[I] learned to love labor . . . for the independence and self-reliance." Because we were already in Alabama, and I thought we may never be there again, and because Tuskegee was only about sixty miles from Eufaula, I wanted to see the place for myself.

Our travel plans were easily adjustable to accommodate this detour, but I came unprepared. I had not thought about and was not expecting to confront some of the uncomfortable realities of America that Tuskegee would teach me. For example, to put Washington and his students' achievements in perspective, I realize that the all-white colleges and universities up North, the future Ivy League schools, were founded as early as 1636, giving those students as much as a 229-year leg up on higher education and thus advantages in all aspects of life—from employment, networking, banking, investing, and home-ownership to the ability to vote, hold office, and accumulate and pass on wealth and pursue the American Dream. Shall I go on? These beneficiaries include, for example, Virginia slave owner and eventual president James Madison, who attended what is now Princeton. On the other hand, the property for Booker T. Washington's school of higher education for blacks in the South had nothing—no proper classrooms, dining halls, or dormitories—just an old cabin, a kitchen house, a stable, a henhouse, and one blind horse.

Embodying the opposite of most white college students' experience, like mine and Neil's at Cornell University, the black students eager for education at Tuskegee had to clear the land for cultivation so they could grow their own food. They had to collect pine needles and sew them into their own mattresses. They had to learn to craft their own furniture out of wood scraps for their bedrooms, lecture halls, and laboratories. In formal clothes, they had to dig out the earth for the founda-tions of buildings. Holding heads high, they even had to forge their own nails. And they made those bricks. Then they erected beautiful buildings designed by faculty architects in Greek Revival and Queen Anne styles on a campus now designated as a National Historic Landmark. Once I see the place, it's a wonder to me that the story of this man and his success goes so undiscussed. Or maybe I have simply never put myself in the way of those kinds of conversations.

Neil and I join a tour for prospective students, visiting the newly rebuilt chapel with its black biblical characters por-trayed in stained-glass windows. One mother of three on the tour, with two kids considering the university, asks me why we are here—standing out, as we are, for our whiteness and childlessness, I presume. I explain it's because of my inter-est in Washington, because I wanted to see the bricks that his students made by hand, the buildings they erected for the promise of their education, and his final resting site. Once the words leave my lips, she turns away with no reply, making me feel there was something wrong with my answer in her mind. Later, much later in my journey, I'll ponder that while I was there for historical interest, she was there, perhaps, out of necessity: black student acceptance rates at top-tier colleges and universities have dropped over the past decades, which could make historically black colleges and universities— once called the "main artery connecting to the heart of black America"—some of the best places for smart black students to feel welcome, first, and best in an ongoing legacy of inequality.

Neil and I break away for our own walk around campus, finding a quad surrounded by four turn-of-the-century brick buildings, as grand as any Ivy League buildings. We walk up close to one hall as if approaching a castle, examining the wide swaths of brick walls as if dermatologists looking at skin, running our fingers over the charming irregularities like a lover's first touch.

The bricks and the mortar have a pink hue but are made of tiny points of multi-sized, multicolored grains like a pointillism painting, with smears of orange, red, rust, burnt sienna, and even patina green. They are pock-marked with black, burnt holes like bullet wounds from the kiln-firing process and a rough surface like the top crust of fresh-baked bread. The bricks, in fact, look like something baked, a hearty red-clay pastry.

From a distance, the bricks are an assortment of candy stacked in rows, black licorice, cherry, orange, and raspberry, the variety of individualistic color tones and imperfections together forming a canvas of striking beauty, a display of the variegation of Alabama's rural red clay, forming the structure of the place where, starting in 1881, "a whole race . . . [went] to school for the first time"—after centuries of white slave owners' fear of insurrection keeping education out of reach.

The day becomes the tiniest opening into a portal of a history I never knew. What I always saw as color-blind equality, like all my high school classmates' seemingly equal success in school and life, has actually occurred against a backdrop of inequality, measured by the access and privilege gained or not gained over the course of generations.

Fifteen miles away from Tuskegee (population 8,800; 97 percent black, 2 percent white, 1 percent other), in even more rural Notasulga, Alabama (population 1,000; 48 percent black, 52 percent white), the birthplace of author Zora Neale Hurston, I am being hugged by two sisters who are strangers to me, Felecia Chandler and Shirley Johnson. The former is wearing a summery calf-length skirt and dressy sandals, and the latter is dressed in a black pantsuit and black straw hat adorned with sequins. The sisters have met us here on Highway 81, a country lane in a rural community that perhaps isn't much more developed than it was in the 1950s and '60s when Chandler was a child. Most of the people who had lived there then were poor sharecroppers, tenant farmers, or hired workers for white landowners, and they lived below the poverty line in shacks with dirt floors and no plumbing. The sisters have met us here to teach us about their past.

Neil and I are standing in front of Shiloh School, their refurbished schoolhouse, a school for black people, built in 1922 after the original, built in 1913, burned down. The school feels so familiar, with its long tin roof; its two-room design, separated by pocket doors; its platform stage and some side rooms for canning and other vocational arts and home economics. We are welcomed by familiar dark-stained wood floors, wooden bead board walls with wainscoting, and extra-large, double-hung paned windows letting in bright, filtered daylight.

Neil and I stood in a similar rehabilitated school in Scrabble, or Woodville, Virginia, one afternoon years ago when we took a day trip from the weekend cabin. The Scrabble School, also built in 1922, is now a senior center and an African American heritage center with a multimedia display showcasing oral histories of former students and teachers.

"We walked from Woodville to Scrabble School, which was approximately three miles, every day," said Charles Wallace, who attended that school in Virginia from 1931 to 1941, in an oral history video. "There was a school about a hundred yards from my house, a white school, but we had to walk three miles to get to the black school." Even in the heart of winter in deep snow, it is said that the students never missed a day.

Before these beautiful schools were built, in the deeply segregated South, where separate did not mean equal, black students were educated in underfunded, falling-down, leaking buildings with dilapidated furniture and scant supplies, if any. In Alabama in the early 1900s, for example, the state might give two million dollars to white schools per year, and $350,000 to black schools, even though the ratio of children was fifty-fifty. These new schools for black children were one of Booker T. Washington's quiet but radical ideas. They came to fruition because he partnered with a new member of the Tuskegee board of trustees, a man who had grown up in a house across from Abraham Lincoln's home in Springfield, Illinois, and whose uncles had clothed Lincoln and escorted Lincoln's casket back to Springfield. He was a man who had already demonstrated interest in advancing African Americans by offering matching grants to build black YMCAs, and he was a man who, as president of Sears, Roebuck and Company, headed the Amazon of its day. He was Julius Rosenwald, a Jewish Yankee who came down South to do good.

As a Jew, Rosenwald appreciated the plight of blacks trying to pull themselves up against all odds. "The horrors that are due to race prejudice come home to the Jew more forcefully than to others of the white race, on account of the centuries of persecution which they have suffered and still suffer," he wrote in 1911. He set up the Rosenwald Fund for "the well-being of mankind" and agreed to fund the cost of one-third of each of these new schools, with another third coming from white county governments, and the last third from the black communities the schools would serve. The community often provided land for the schools, sweat equity in building the structures, and supplies, as part of a philosophy that gave the people a stake in their own school and led to the Rosenwald schools becoming the centers of their communities. Rosenwald schools became known as "schools of hope."

The Shiloh Rosenwald School in Notasulga was the second of all the 4,977 Rosenwald schools built in fifteen southern states from 1912 to 1932, along with 217 teachers' homes and 163 shop buildings serving the schools. There were 389 Rosenwald schools in Alabama alone. For first through sixth or eighth grade, black students like Felecia Chandler and Shirley Johnson were the beneficiaries of some of the latest innovations in rural school design, like the bright, natural lighting from the batteries of tall double-hung windows that stretched from the wainscoting to the eaves; foundations built on piers for building ventilation; proper heating and sanitation systems; and rooms for instruction and vocational work. The students also benefited from progressive best practices regarding instructional needs and educational space, including planning for enough land to allow for a practice garden, farm plots, and landscaping.

Imagining the Shiloh School and the other thousands of schools that followed plotted on a map in chronological time lapse, it is as if a spark in central Alabama ignites a wildfire that engulfs the entire southeastern United States—a fire of goodness and kindness and righteousness as it spread through nearly 30 percent of the country. The schools' importance to black children and families in that era was notable, as by 1928 one in every five rural schools in the South was a Rosenwald school. There was a Rosenwald school in every county in the South with significant black population, and the schools educated one-third of the region's rural black children: 663,625 students in all. As a testament to their effectiveness, one gentleman, a former Rosenwald school student said, after a Washington, DC, viewing of the documentary film *Rosenwald,* "If Rosenwald hadn't been here, we'd be a hundred years behind now."

"The parents of the students at the Rosenwald schools understood the need for education. They knew that education was the key to a better life," Chandler, vice chair of the board of directors for the Shiloh Community Restoration Foundation, explains. "Before I even entered the Shiloh School in first grade, my parents had already taught me the ABCs, numbers, how to recite things from memory, and this was also reinforced at church, by having us memorize speeches and plays, and the parents' active participation in the PTA."

While talking with the sisters, I take note of the fact that Chandler and my husband, Neil, are both fifty-seven but have life experiences that are worlds apart. For a suburban, upper-middle-class northern white kid like Neil, the default setting was to attend well-funded and well-supplied, mostly white suburban public schools. But Chandler, having been born with black skin in the South, would have no guarantee of an education if it weren't for Rosenwald, and even then, she was required to attend a segregated school that was inherently unequal. Despite its lovely natural light and other innovations, like most other Rosenwald schools, the Shiloh School had no electricity and no running water (thus, outhouses rather than bathrooms) and was heated with a potbelly stove. Johnson said students were responsible for cleaning the blackboards and sweeping the wood floors—"There were no such things as janitors!" she says. Girls were responsible for getting water from the well with a bucket, and boys filled buckets of coal from under the building and kept the heat going all day.

Chandler was there only one semester when the school closed in September 1964 because of integration. Johnson, thirteen years older, attended the school from first to sixth grade and then was bussed to all-black Tuskegee Junior High and Tuskegee Institute High School.

By sitting and talking with the sisters and receiving a tour of their school, my path is crossing with this history. I'm receiving the gift of a brief window into a time and place that would otherwise never be part of my world. Johnson recalls the Shiloh School with great adoration. She recalls playing on a swing set, attending fish fries at the school, having parents put on plays—with a ten-cent admission price—on Friday nights to raise money for the school. There were movies shown, a Coke machine, May Day celebrations, Easter egg hunts, field trips to Birmingham, and Friday devotional services. "We had used books and used desks, but they were fine. Parents and teachers worked together at this school to give us everything we needed," Johnson said. "I never once wished I could go to another school."

Civil rights activist and Georgia congressman John Lewis also remembers his Rosenwald school fondly, with fish fries and many of the same activities. "I loved school," he writes in his memoir. But in his case, family farming duties in Troy, Alabama, often forced him to miss classes. "I wasn't the only one," he says. "This was true for almost every child in our school. It was a southern tradition, just part of the way of life, that a black child's school year was dictated by the farm rhythms of planting and harvesting. You went to school when you could."

A few months after Notasulga, I will walk the unmown grass around the 1922 one-room Cairo Rosenwald School, located in Ziegler's Station, Tennessee, a rural area more than an hour outside of Nashville. It is similar to the Scrabble and Shiloh Schools but much smaller, like a small country church. Rehabilitated, it is now used as a community center and listed on the National Register of Historic Places. Above the inside front doorway, like in many of the Rosenwald schools throughout the South in their heyday, hangs a black-and-white portrait of Julius Rosenwald, dark-haired in a dark suit, mustachioed, with a receding hairline and frameless spectacles, looking relaxed and comfortable in his own skin.

Integration ended the era of Rosenwald schools. Cairo closed in 1959 after consolidating with other schools. Shiloh locked its doors in December 1964 with the passage of the Civil Rights Act, which prohibits discrimination based on race, color, religion, sex, or national origin, including racial segregation in schools. And Scrabble shuttered later, in 1968, when Virginia—a commonwealth in which one county closed down all the public schools out of protest rather than integrate them—finally complied with the federal law after the Supreme

Court ordered states to dismantle segregated school systems "root and branch."

In Notasulga, the two acres once sold to the school's board of trustees by the sisters' great-grandfather, the Reverend Sam Moss, who owned more than eighty acres in the 1860s—"good land along the highway, not the swampland and forest most black people owned," Chandler said—was deeded to the Shiloh Missionary Baptist Church. According to the National Trust for Historic Preservation, which has listed abandoned Rosenwald schools as some of the most endangered historic properties in the nation, the schools were generally unneeded after school integration, and most have disintegrated; there are only five hundred to six hundred left in the country—in various stages of preservation or decay, taking all their precious, lost American stories with them as they molder away.

I had called on Chandler and Johnson to give me a tour of the Rosenwald school because Rosenwald was part of my southern and Jewish history tour and agenda. But when the sisters lead me and Neil across the hot grass to the right of the school and up a small hill toward the Shiloh Missionary Baptist Church next door, we are heading off into the unknown. It is a clear, bright day, with tropical humidity, but it becomes suddenly no ordinary day, no ordinary place. Crossing onto more land that Sam Moss donated, we find ourselves walking on the site of a former crime scene, an era in American history of medical malfeasance that rivals Nazi medical experiments, something I had heard about only in passing.

This is not hyperbole. On this church property, Neil and I stand under the very tree where the US Public Health Service recruited six hundred poor black farmers to be part of a study. Of those, 399 had syphilis and were a part of the experimental group to be treated for their "bad blood"—a euphemism people used at that time for syphilis, anemia, and other ailments—and 201 were control subjects. This spot is where these men—churchgoers—over a period of forty years, lined up to wait for a black woman known as Nurse Rivers, the Shiloh School nurse, to come and either administer treatment or transport the men to Tuskegee Institute for treatment. It is the epicenter of where they were all unknowingly part of the "Study of Untreated Syphilis in Negro Males in Macon County, Alabama," a secret study with lofty origins that went awry, unknown to the public from 1934 to 1972.

The nation's largest and longest-enduring medical bioethics disaster—the infamous "Tuskegee Syphilis Study"—was led by a US federal agency.

The study began innocuously and legitimately with the Rosenwald Fund striving to support health care and education for poor African Americans in the rural South. The US government was involved with a general movement to manage venereal disease, and target areas tended to be urban. The Alabama State Board of Health operated fourteen free clinics that treated ten thousand venereal disease patients in urban areas. But, as Fred D. Gray, a Tuskegee native and attorney for Rosa Parks, Martin Luther King Jr., and the syphilis-study men who ultimately brought and won a class-action suit against the federal government in 1973, recounts, the people in the rural areas weren't included in that benefit and had to pay private doctors for treatment, which most could not afford.

Already helping to build hospitals and clinics in the rural South, the Rosenwald Fund connected with the US Public Health Service to expand treatment services to the poorest African Americans there, with the ultimate goal of finding a way to administer mass treatment. The Rosenwald Fund's medical director was assigned as the US Public Health Service adviser to the Rosenwald efforts in the South, and the fund gave a one-year grant to provide follow-up treatment to African Americans infected with syphilis, as identified in a different study in Mississippi.

Due to the project's success in providing treatment up to this point, the Public Health Service asked for additional Rosenwald money to support similar projects in other areas. The fund then provided more money for legitimate syphilis testing projects in six counties in six states, including Macon County, Alabama, home of Notasulga and Tuskegee, which was found to have the highest prevalence of the disease of any of the six. The Rosenwald money was used to test forty thousand people for syphilis, and one quarter were found to have the disease. When the Depression hit, however, the Rosenwald Fund could not continue its financial support for these programs, and Rosenwald's connection to the syphilis studies ended.

Instead of simply closing up shop, however, sending the people with syphilis back home, the US Public Health Service decided to take advantage of the good will the men had felt toward those they believed were helping them. The agency offered these men treatment for their bad blood, giving them "what most Negroes could only dream of in terms of medical care and survivors insurance . . . medical exams, rides to and from the clinics, meals on examination days, free treatment for minor ailments, and guarantees that provisions would be made after their deaths in terms of burial stipends paid to their survivors," according to Tuskegee University's National Center for Bioethics in Research and Health Care. The Public Health Service wanted to embark on a new kind of study, an "observation study" initially, with the limited funds it had: to find out the effects of *untreated* syphilis on black people, which was posited to be a different reaction than untreated syphilis on whites and would thus assist in providing appropriate treatment in the future.

The sisters don't tell us all this on the spot, but I'll learn later that a white man named Dr. Taliaferro Clark, head of the US Public Health Service's Venereal Disease Division, proposed a study period of six to eight months, bringing the local and state authorities on board as well the Tuskegee Institute's hospital, which would provide exams, X-rays, and spinal taps as part of the study. The president of Tuskegee agreed to support the study if "Tuskegee Institute gets its full share of the credit" and black doctors and a black nurse would tend to the participants and be part of the research. The Public Health Service roped in these authorities by saying it would provide some level of treatment to the people known to have syphilis. Things seemed above board at this time.

In fact, no treatment was provided; the intent was to follow the sick until their deaths and then autopsy them. The government went to great lengths to prevent the study subjects from receiving treatment—prevented them from being drafted in 1940 where the military would have found them to have syphilis and treated them; prevented them from receiving the cure for the disease, penicillin, once it was discovered in 1945; prevented them from using the Public Health Service's Rapid Treatment Centers, established in 1947 to treat syphilis. The study continued year after year, decade after decade, with various reputable groups like the American Medical Association and the National Medical Association approving it along the way, either in the dark about the details or fully aware. They gave this approval, despite the fact that the men never knew they had the disease or never knew they weren't being treated for it, never gave informed consent for the procedures being done to them or for being in a study at all, and never knew they could quit participating at any time.

Meanwhile, men with syphilis were passing along the disease—which can cause deafness, blindness, mental disabilities, neurological issues, cardiovascular disorders, skin and bone lesions, paralysis, aneurysms, and other devastating effects—to their wives through sexual contact as well as to their children while in utero.

A reporter broke the story on the front page of the *New York Times* in 1972, which ended the study due to public outcry. A federal government advisory panel called it "ethically unjustified." When it ended, only 74 of the 399 test subjects were alive; 28 of the original 399 men had died of syphilis, and 100 were dead of related complications. Forty of their wives had been infected, and 19 of their children were born with the disease.

These women, standing before me in their fine clothes in the sunshine, are the descendants of one of the Tuskegee Syphilis Study subjects, putting me face to face with three of the darkest chapters of American history: slaveholding, segregation, and the Tuskegee syphilis study. Chandler and Johnson's grandfather, Julius Mott, was part of the study but died before either of them knew him. "My mother used to tell us how he had to stay sitting up in a chair because lying down was so uncomfortable after undergoing the spinal taps," Chandler says. Another participant told of having to stay in bed for ten days after that procedure.

From these survivors of some of that torment, I want to know how this community reacted to the revelation of the truth of this study, the deceit of this study, as Chandler and Johnson are my only real links to that place and time. "People were hurt. Upset. Angry," Chandler says. "But not surprised. This was during the Jim Crow era. These people thought of us to be less than human, or not even human. The community was definitely hurting, but not surprised."

Knowing that many African Americans still do not trust the medical establishment due to the syphilis study and other medical transgressions against the black community, I also ask how a community can move forward after such a tragedy. How did the sisters' family move on? Johnson answers straightfor-wardly with rhetorical questions: "Who do you blame? Who do you punish? What can you do? After so much time and after the study subjects and the study creators have moved on, I can't hold grudges in a general respect," she says.

As for Chandler: "We were thankful that we had enough faith in God to know that even though this happened, some-thing good will come of it."

In 1974 attorney Gray's class-action suit against the US government—which excluded from fault the Tuskegee Insti-tute and Nurse Rivers, whom he felt had been conned right along with the study subjects—resulted in a ten-million-dollar out-of-court settlement, and the government promised to give lifetime medical benefits and burial services to all living par-ticipants as well as their wives, widows, and offspring via the Tuskegee Health Benefit Program it established. But it was not until twenty-three years later that the government formally apologized for the study.

On May 16, 1997, President Bill Clinton—who grew up a poor, white southerner, whom Toni Morrison referred to as "our first black president" because of the similarity of some of his experiences and his connection to the black community—presided over a ceremony at the White House attended by Charlie Pollard and seven other syphilis survivors. Clinton talked of "a time when our nation failed to live up to its ideals, when our nation broke the trust with our people that is the very foundation of our democracy . . . [and] the United States government did something that was wrong—deeply, profoundly, morally wrong. It was an outrage to our commitment to integrity and equality for all our citizens."

I wonder what else our government has done or is currently doing that is exacerbating, prolonging, ignoring, denying, or actively not rectifying some injustice that its citizens don't even know about. And what am I doing to open my eyes to and protest overt and masked racial injustice? What am I doing to help open doors for others to all the opportunities and benefits my ancestors in this country and I have been granted because of the color of our skin? I hear words like *institutional racism,* and I know I'm against it, but, truthfully, I am not always sure I know what it means or looks like.

This newfound information is a weight that will gnaw on me, a spark that has lit in my consciousness—and an opening, but to what, I don't yet know.

The Shiloh School is where the men who participated in the study had gone to learn, and the church is where they prayed, and down the road, where we follow the sisters in separate cars, is the Shiloh Missionary Baptist Church Cemetery, where many of those men were laid to rest.

The sisters bring us to the burial site of Charlie Pollard, the man who brought the syphilis study to the attention of lawyers, a Shiloh School student, a member of the Shiloh Missionary Baptist Church, and a landowner of a large acreage in Macon County who lived until age ninety-four. Here, too, is the sisters' great-grandfather, who died in 1918. It is a quiet place on a bluff, with few cars passing by, in a tiny African American hamlet far from where decisions about these men's fates were made, far from the lives and worldview of so many Americans in power throughout the ages. Has any president ever visited the people of Notasulga, Alabama? No. Not even Obama.

More ghosts that Neil and I will explore later in the day are the Tuskegee Airmen, the first African American soldiers to enter the Army Air Corps, with nearly one thousand aviators who became America's first African American military pilots, and more than ten thousand military and civilian men and women who served as technicians, radio operators, parachute riggers, mechanics, bombardiers, navigators, meteorologists, control tower operators/dispatchers, and other related roles during World War II. Just like in the syphilis study, the airmen—who trained at the airfield in Tuskegee, originally funded by the Julius Rosenwald Fund and later another National Park Service site—were considered experimental subjects. The idea was to see if African Americans had the intellectual capacity to become successful fighter pilots. That this was even a question was absurd. The Tuskegee Airmen went on to fight the Nazis and were so successful that white bomber pilots often requested them as escorts into enemy territory. The Tuskegee Airmen were hailed as heroes in Europe and North Africa.

During their training in the United States and when they came home to the Jim Crow South, though, they were relegated to second-class citizenship and were denied full access to hotels, gas stations, restaurants, movie theaters, train and bus stations, public transportation, schools, and public facilities; they were not permitted to vote or receive any protection against violence and intimidation. In fact, they were treated worse than the Germans treated those they shot down and took as prisoners of war. "The slave went free; stood a brief moment in the sun; then moved back again toward slavery," said W. E. B. Du Bois, historian, civil rights activist, and author.

The history of this place is flabbergasting to me—flabbergasting to my sense of how recent these publicly endorsed policies were happening, just one generation ago. Of the syphilis atrocities—and perhaps the whole era of injustice—Chandler tells me, "We have to forgive. You can't hold hatred in your heart, or it affects you." Living and working in such sacred land—a nexus of suffering, triumph, and recovery—she reiterates how important it is to tell these stories and to have hope for the future. It's the reason she and her sister give tours of the Shiloh School, church, and cemetery to as many as seventy people per month. They tell their stories to ninth- and tenth-grade white kids from a Hebrew academy who come to learn the history of their black brothers and sisters, to college students celebrating Black History Month and looking for knowledge about the struggles African Americans have overcome, and to adult relatives of descendants of the Tuskegee Study who don't even know the story of their own families. And they tell it to outsiders like Neil and me—who have come to walk in the footsteps of history, to work our way out of the ignorance of the people and places we don't know and all that we don't even know we don't know, to grapple with the shadowy backstories of our nation, the ones hidden far away on the dark roads so close to disappearing into the night—who walk away wanting to be agents of light.

DEFENDERS OF SELMA

Ronnie Leet, mid-sixties, a trim, balding, third-generation Sel-manian, meets me at the 1899 red-brick Temple Mishkan Israel where he's the president of the congregation of the last seven Jews of Selma, Alabama. He is now the second Deep South Jewish person I've met, and the first Jew with a pickup truck.

We came to Selma (population 19,000; 80 percent black, 17 percent white, 3 percent other) somewhat at the last minute because in plotting a Civil War route across the Deep South, I realized we would be driving through the heart of the Civil Rights Movement. We started our trip essentially at the infamous Andersonville prison in Georgia, a former Confederate prisoner-of-war camp from the last year of the war that highlights how horrid humans can be, where the Rebels enabled such ghastly overcrowding conditions that most Union prisoners died of scurvy, diarrhea, or dysentery rather than from battle injuries. Eventually, we will make our way to Vicksburg National Military Park on the far side of Mississippi, a place where the South surrendered after a long Union siege that had cut off food and supplies to the town for more than forty days. In the light of the June 17, 2015, Charleston shootings and with the thrum of Wallace, Washington, and Rosenwald history coursing through my mind, highlighting the connection among slavery, the Civil War, and racism today, I couldn't ignore the Civil Rights Movement embedded in the South's landscape. And so, although I didn't originally envision the trip this way, I maneuver the itinerary and make way for the Civil War/southern/Jewish theme to cover this geography as well.

I emailed Leet in the evening from the hotel, where Neil and I had the new experience of seemingly being the only white guests, which feels a little like walking around naked but no one says anything; I don't even think to consider the fear or uncomfortableness the reverse situation can engender. *I'm a writer traveling through the lost Jewish communities of the South,* I had said to Leet. *I know this is last minute, but any chance you could talk to me and show me the temple?* Again the southern hospitality of a complete stranger eager to help surprises me, and we make a date for 10:00 a.m. As the synagogue has no regular hours, isn't open for weekly services, has no rabbi, and has a congregation of less than a minyan (a group of ten Jewish adults normally needed to conduct public prayer services), it remains locked until someone wants to visit. It isn't even on the circuit for a once-in-a-while traveling rabbi anymore. It is, in some ways, a relic—a museum to what once was in Selma: four hundred to five hundred Jews in the 1920s and a congregation of 140 families, having settled in the city in the 1830s.

"The temple is focused on the past rather than the future," Leet says when we meet, though he hopes that with preservation—if funds ever materialize—Mishkan Israel will provide a future for any potential Jewish resurgence in Selma. Leet acknowledges that this is "not reasonable thinking," but he holds out hope.

Leet walks us up the side steps of this striking Romanesque Revival, which has two symmetrical towers, a raised octagonal roofed sanctuary, and stained-glass windows, and into the more recently built social hall. The room is set up with rows of chairs from the last speaker, who came to talk to a group of Jewish and black kids as part of Operation Understanding, fostering respect, cooperation, and understanding about each other's group's history and culture. Leet plants us in that room to talk to and teach us for a while, as it is the only area of the building with even meager air conditioning and thus even partially tolerable in the August heat and humidity. The sanctuary—where just a few months ago, on March 8,

2015, whites and blacks, Jews and Christians, filled the hall in a moving tribute of song and prayer for the fiftieth anniversary of Bloody Sunday—is intolerably hot, he says. Months later he'll tell me the roof is leaking in that sacred space, and the walls are crawling with mold, which to me, as a supporter of historic preservation, is heartbreaking.

Leet is a former automotive parts man, just like his father and grandfather, both of whom operated companies that recycled scrap iron and sold welding supplies and equipment. That's what Jewish people did in Selma, as throughout the South; they ran small businesses, like department stores and dry goods stores, or they were tailors or provided other necessary services. (When there was only one such store in town, it was often called "the Jew store," not necessarily insultingly so.) They tended to offer lower-priced merchandise rather than fancy boutique items. In Selma, department stores included Tepper's and Kayser's. Simon Maas was a dry goods retailer. Benjamin Schuster was a hardware merchant. Then there was Bendersky's, Liepold's, and Rothchild's merchandise companies; the Siegel Automotive Company; Benish and Meyer Tobacco; Richard Thalheimer liqueurs; and Morris Hohenber's cotton business. M. J. Meyer had a Stable and Harness Company. Selma had three Jewish mayors in the late 1800s and early 1900s as well as Jewish city council and school board members. Selma was no exception to Jews' belief that being involved in making a better community overall also meant a better community for Jews.

Now that I'm in this famous—or infamous—place, I figure I should ask what it was like to be there during the civil rights era. Growing up, I'd heard few stories from the white people of that era up North. My mom was busy with women's rights issues, and there was just one anecdote from my dad, from a business trip that took him south in 1966 or '67. "I was in Columbus, Georgia, when I first saw 'whites only' and 'colored' signs on the public bathrooms," he recounted again for me recently. "For sure I didn't go into the whites' bathroom. I wouldn't do that. I was a northerner and we just didn't have that up North. I waited until I got to bathrooms that didn't have those designations. It made me angry that this was happening. I had taken trips to Birmingham, Montgomery, and Dothan, Alabama; Columbus and Valdosta, Georgia; and Nashville, Tennessee. And Columbus was the only place I saw segregated bathrooms."

Maybe I'd never gotten stories because I'd never asked the questions. Maybe it has taken me more than forty years to understand that the idea of race is one of the central threads of American history, one that shouldn't be ignored but constantly is. And so at age forty-five, I am meeting the first person and first southerner—and the first southern Jew—who can tell me what being alive in the center of civil rights activities during that era was like. Leet was fourteen in 1965 when activists first attempted to march from Selma to Montgomery as part of the voting rights movement centered in Selma. Less than 1 percent of the 57 percent of black citizens in Dallas County were registered to vote there due to whites' intentional roadblocks preventing them from doing so, exactly 100 years after the end of the Civil War that was supposed to emancipate them into America's welcoming arms, and 105 years after white Dallas County landowners had enslaved 76.8 percent of their population.

I knew that a civil rights march happened in the South, but I never knew the details of it. I learn that the march was held in part as a response to the death of a twenty-six-year-old man, Jimmie Lee Jackson, a US Army veteran who was African American and had been beaten to death at a peaceful voting rights march in Alabama in protest of the poll tax and literacy test to prevent black people from voting. Literally, a low-level white worker in charge of voter registration could impose a fee at will or demand that blacks undergo some kind of demonstration of literacy, as a way to deny them their right to vote; these exclusion tools were instituted and used in Alabama and all southern states beginning in 1890. Sometimes the literacy test meant having to recite the preamble of the Constitution, or, as in Dallas County, having to name all sixty-seven county judges in the state. Would any person of any color have been able to do that? After politics put an end to Reconstruction—a period of policies, constitutional amendments, and other federal government actions after the Civil War (1865–1877) to bring the South and freed blacks back into the fold of a reunified United States—white southerners began the re-disenfranchisement of black citizens in all the ways they knew how. The policies were random, discriminatory, and allowed.

The march was meant to be a news-flash type of pivotal event that couldn't be ignored, couldn't be hushed up, to bring attention to and then eradicate the legal and illegal restrictions that county officials and the (White) Citizens' Council imposed on black people to keep them from voting. The Citizens' Councils were a network of white supremacist organizations throughout the South fixated on "pursuing the agenda of the Klan with the demeanor of the Rotary Club," as sociologist Charles M. Payne describes it, or the "coat-and-tie version of the Ku Klux Klan," according to civil rights activist and Georgia congressman John Lewis. (Even fictional hero Atticus Finch was a member, revealed in Harper Lee's *Go Set a Watchman*.) They threatened people's jobs, imposed economic boycotts of black-owned businesses, restricted voter registration hours, cut off access to a federal program that supplied surplus food to poor people, denied people loans, increased their rents, unleashed violence against those trying to register to vote, and sometimes killed them with direct attacks.

(This drive to deny voting access hasn't ended. A few months after my visit to Selma in 2015, about a year ahead of the 2016 presidential election, the state of Alabama closed driver's license bureaus in eight of the ten counties of the state where African Americans make up more than 75 percent of the population. In Alabama a driver's license or special photo ID is required for voting. The state's justification was to save money in underpopulated areas.)

Leet remembers one night in 1965 when his father drove him, his mother, and sister into town to see what was going on at the Brown Chapel African Methodist Episcopal Church.

This church was to be the starting point from which John Lewis—who was born to sharecroppers, grew up in segregated Alabama, and would become the representative for the Fifth Congressional District in Georgia in the US Congress—would lead the marchers on what became known as "Bloody Sunday," March 7, 1965, despite Governor Wallace forbidding protest marches.

The first of the events started with "young folks with bedrolls and backpacks . . . milling about. Veterans of the movement train[ing] newcomers in the tactics of non-violence; the right way to protect yourself when attacked. A doctor described what tear gas does to the body, while marchers scribbled down instructions for contacting their loved ones. The air was thick with doubt, anticipation, and fear." Then six hundred protestors crossed the Edmund Pettus Bridge—named for a Confederate brigadier general and Grand Dragon of the Alabama KKK. When the marchers came off the high crest of the bridge onto the other side, state troopers and county posse men began beating them with nightsticks, swinging bullwhips and rubber tubing wrapped in barbed wire, firing tear gas, and charging the crowd on horseback. By the end of the attack, more than ninety men and women had to be treated for broken ribs, wrists, jaws, and other injuries. Lewis, who by then had been deemed "one of the Big Six leaders of the Civil Rights Movement" and would continue to fight for civil rights even through the forty-fifth president's administration, had his skull cracked.

"What I remember is the quantity of police cars that night," Leet says, taking me back in time to the night he saw activity at the church. "They lined the street, bumper to bumper on both sides of the street, one end of the street to the other." Even Joseph Smitherman, the mayor of Selma during the civil rights years, recalled in a 1985 interview, "I remember at one time I had 400 state troopers, conservation officers, and game and wildlife, everything, ABC agents, under my direction, and we ringed around that 16-block area."

Anything I had ever heard about the Civil Rights Movement was so clearly delineated: there were the good guys and the bad

guys; there were the people fighting for justice, and there were
those seeking the continuance of injustice. I had never heard
about an in-between.

But then Leet begins to share with me how he lived in
the gray area, the unacknowledged points of southern Jewish
history. No one knew what would happen, he says, and Jews
were scared. "At home, we locked doors, and we stayed inside."
Given the church bombing in Birmingham in September 1963
and the KKK murders of civil rights workers Andrew Goodman and Michael Schwerner, both Jewish, and James Earl
Chaney, who was black, in June 1964, he says, "We were worried about the family business, worried about our safety. We
were worried about buildings burning, looting. We were afraid
of what might get out of hand." He mentions that his aunt got
a call from a friend in Europe, who had heard about the civil
rights–related violence in the South, asking if they were OK.
Knowing that the world was terrified for Selma fueled the fire
of fear in his family.

Most of all, they were worried about who would get blamed
if things got out of control, if people died because of outside
influences by northern agitators, and, specifically, northern
Jews, who had come down South to do good. Not only were
eventually about 90 percent of the civil rights lawyers in Mississippi northern Jews, but northern Jews made up a third to
a half of the young activists who went South during Freedom
Summer 1964, the voter-registration drive. "How would that
reflect on us?" Leet remembered the Jewish community asking.

"We supported voting rights," he says. "Jews generally came
out on the side of fairness, given what happened in World War II
with Hitler. But our main issue has always been our survival."
Jews had carved out a life in Selma and were accepted in the
fragile trust of both whites and blacks. But "the Jewish community's stand, in general, was not to take a stand. Our businesses were our livelihood, and we didn't know which way
this would fall," Leet says. If Jews had worked for other
people rather than themselves, Leet suggests, maybe they
would have been more willing to stick their necks out. Scholars

in southern Jewish history in the 1970s—which became a serious discipline of study in that era—supported what Leet lived: "It is rare for a Jew to support publicly controversial issues for fear of exciting latent bigotry."

These are the defenders of Jewish Selma, a place that was apparently socially and culturally distinctly different from its brethren Jewish communities in the North, where people didn't have as much to fear or as much at stake. "We had two priorities in life: our families and our businesses," Leet said, a view confirmed by a 1966 survey of Selma's Jews by student Marshall Bloom (cofounder of the Liberation News Service, which disseminated underground, or counterculture, news). It wasn't that the southern Jews didn't support civil rights, people say, but they knew it could be difficult or dangerous to do so.

Northern Jews, on the other hand, didn't have the same concerns, didn't risk losing their livelihoods, didn't even yet absorb that they could lose their lives. Many of the northerners fighting for civil rights at events and protests felt that risks on behalf of the cause would be worth inconvenience or potential injury. They could go home afterward and not be left to live in a community hostile to them. But southern Jews had to calculate a daily risk of living inside the battleground. In terms of business risks, if Jews sided with their white, racist neighbors and customers, and their many black customers boycotted white stores—many Jews sold to blacks while other white people would not—business could go down substantially. One Selmanian in the mid-1960s expressed the "willingness to concede whatever is necessary to the Negroes to insure that business conditions are not upset."

Then again, if southern Jews were too vocal in their beliefs of equality for all people, they could face repercussions from their white neighbors, which meant that "those relations may have been less solid than had been acknowledged, that the equilibrium was more precarious than even the most defiantly southern of southern Jews would have liked to believe," in the words of one scholar. One southern Jewish couple in Selma voiced their support for voting rights to people they knew, and the Citizens' Council got word of it and launched a boycott of their business. "I would feel more free to speak my mind if I knew it wouldn't jeopardize my father's position in the community," Hermene Cohen said in the survey in the 1960s.

Even in areas where Jews weren't politically active, the KKK had to "give permission" for them to stick around, and the two groups had to come to a sort of understanding. A man I talk to in the Washington, DC, area, Nat Finkelstein, who grew up in Opp, Alabama, tells me that when his father opened up the Economy Store in the 1920s, the only Jewish clothing and notions store in town, the Klan came in and flooded the place with fire hoses. Instead of allowing the Klan to drive him out, however, his father decided to hold a "damaged merchandise sale," and then restocked. "They probably figured he was a force stronger than them," Finkelstein says of his father's resistance. The Klan never bothered him again.

In some places, support for blacks led to synagogue and house bombings, such as the September 1967 KKK bombing of Beth Israel Congregation in Jackson, Mississippi, where Rabbi Perry Nussbaum was an avid anti-segregationist and whose home was bombed as well. The KKK bombing of Congregation Beth Israel in Meridian, Mississippi, occurred in May 1968, along with the attack on the home of a leader of the Jewish community, Meyer Davidson, who had been outspoken in his objection to attacks on black churches. So afraid were members of the Jewish community, it seemed, that as early as 1956, members of the Selma B'nai Brith Lodge urged the American Jewish Committee and other Jewish groups to "avoid intervening in affairs outside of the Jewish community, particularly on the issue of civil rights."

It was a refrain that harkened back to the old "We don't want northerners telling us how to run our plantation" kind of thinking about states' rights, which, some argue, is what the Civil War was all about. But it was also a matter of life and death, and Jews, for all they had suffered throughout the ages and around the world, wanted to choose life. In some ways, I could understand that. Jews have always done whatever they could to live and produce another generation, a generation whose lives would be better.

"It is hard to know how the Jewish people really feel—perhaps fear and self-preservation have somewhat warped their ideas," said one respondent in the survey, a forty-year Jewish resident of Selma in the 1960s.

As I ponder what I would have done, as a concerned citizen and as a Jew, I'm also forced to consider what I'm doing now, what I could still do once I get back home to help ensure voting rights and voting access for those who still don't have it. So I ask Leet what he thought of northern Jews coming to Selma and other places in the South to help register black people to vote. Leet's answer sounds shocking, but John Lewis said the same thing in the 1960s about northern students untrained in nonviolent protest coming down South, as did civil rights activist Medgar Evers about activists like John Lewis who wanted to integrate a Mississippi that Evers thought wasn't ready for change: "We didn't want them to come."

My cousin's cousin, Andrew Goodman, had come from New York for Freedom Summer, also known as the Mississippi Summer Project. He believed in leveling the playing field, according to his brother, David Goodman. Andrew was one "who dared, who had the courage to go to the lion's den and try to scrub the lion's teeth," as Maya Angelou put it, and he was lynched when attempting to investigate the firebombing of Mount Zion Methodist Church in rural Neshoba County's all-black community of Longdale. I called David Goodman, who is president of the Andrew Goodman Foundation, which aims to inspire young people to vote and get involved with democracy, to ask him what kind of attitude from whites Andrew expected to find in the South. Goodman told me that prior to Andy going south, the Goodman family "had no general consciousness of Mississippi and had no concept of the southern way." He compared their familiarity with Mississippi at that time with what mine might have been growing up in

Philadelphia—which was zilch. He suggested that the Good-
mans knew as much about the lives and intricacies of Mississippians as Mississippians knew about lives and ways of New
Yorkers. Thus, it seems that Andy went south with no concept
of the lion's den he would find or the southern Jews' perspective. The southern Jews also may have been taught in the same
ways of *tzedakah* (acting justly in all dealings and engaging in
charity toward and caring for neighbors in need) and *tikkun
olam* (repairing the world), but he did not know they would
not welcome eager, young activists like him. "I hate northern
Jews," one Jewish Selmanian said in the 1960s. "They threw
us to the wolves."

Goodman's mother, Carolyn, wrote in her memoir that
"Andy didn't go to Mississippi expecting to die."

"We were concerned for their safety," Ronnie Leet explains
of those activists. "We just didn't feel that they understood the
situation they were coming into."

Mayor Smitherman recounts, "We had Jewish Rabbis from
up East [come to Selma and] embarrassed the local Jewish
community here. . . . We wouldn't arrest them, we put 'em in
the courtroom and let 'em sit there and call the local Jewish
people down to talk 'em into going back home."

Some southern Jews tried to help the Civil Rights Movement "in quiet ways," according to Hanna Berger, another
one of Selma's remaining seven Jews. Her parents fled the
Holocaust in Germany in 1938 and were resettled in Selma
by the National Refugee Service, based in New York City.
These tactics were sometimes considered quite subversive at the
time, she said, such as inviting activists to stay at their homes
or speaking on the radio about how people should get along.
Others covertly made financial contributions to civil rights
organizations.

After chatting for about an hour, Leet escorts us to the Jewish section of the Live Oak Cemetery so I can continue my pilgrimage to visit the living and the dead. Neil and I shake hands
with Leet to say goodbye and then walk the pea-gravel paths
with Spanish moss dripping from stately live oaks. There are

more than five hundred Jewish burials here—including Bambergers, Cohens, Eichenbergs, Goldsmiths, Herzfelds, Meyers, Weils, and Yaretzkys—a wide expanse of mostly flat slab markers in the largest southern Jewish cemetery I've seen, with people interred as early as 1812 (the earliest Jews came to Alabama in 1785).

But it's the Confederate Memorial Circle we amble over to that becomes the story here. Not just the towering 1878 Confederate monument obelisk—"There is grandeur in graves / There is glory in gloom," it declares. Not just the Confederate gravestones, decorated with their Confederate battle flags, like S. B. McCary, "The Last Surviving Confederate Veteran of Dallas County" in 1938. Not just the memorial stone chair for Jefferson Davis (who southern Jews remember as "the first chief executive on the North American continent to appoint a Jew to his cabinet, and he did it not once but confirmed it three times"), where I sit in the shade to try to evaporate some of my sweat and near which we are surprised to discover a hidden video surveillance camera. Nor just the pedestal-mounted cannon with memorial pavers. It's the new granite monument with a brass bust on top that we are drawn to, inscribed as follows:

Defender of Selma
Wizard of the Saddle
Untutored Genius
The First with the Most

We have unknowingly come face-to-face with the monument to Nathan Bedford Forrest, whom I only know as a "prominent figure," or Grand Wizard, in the foundation of the original KKK that started in 1865. He was also a slave owner, slave trader, and a commissioned Confederate lieutenant colonel whose call to arms in June 1861 implored, "Come on boys, if you want a heap of fun and to kill some Yankees." He reflected the same animosity toward the northern government as his state when it broke from the Union in January 1861 and declared that the Union was "avowedly hostile to the domestic institutions ... of the State of Alabama," and "is a political wrong of ... [an] insulting and menacing ... character." As major general, Forrest also commanded the massacre of the US Colored Troops at Fort Pillow after their clear surrender and then went on to deny any wrongdoing, claiming that "dastardly Yankee reporters" were making things up (which reminds me of the forty-fifth president's frequent and false allegations of "fake news"). He was, apparently, a military legend with so many Confederate victories that Union general William Tecumseh Sherman declared, "That devil Forrest must be hunted down and killed if it costs ten thousand lives and bankrupts the federal treasury." And he was the only man on either side of the war to rise to lieutenant general for his apparently brilliant military strategy.

It's surprising to me to find out from sources as varied as the American Battlefield Trust and the Mississippi Civil Rights Project that Forrest was also the man who eventually ordered the dissolution of the first iteration of the KKK in 1869. He apparently abolished his racism, advocated for the admission of black students into law school, volunteered to help "exterminate" the men responsible for continued violence against blacks, and said black people should be given full voting rights. He was, perhaps, one of those changed-my-tune reformed southern racists—after all the damage had been done.

Forrest is beloved by southerners for his self-education and solid military service, and particularly by Selmanians for his (unsuccessful) effort to save their city from invaders at the end of the Civil War. Selma is a city known for two things: the march from Selma to Montgomery and the Battle of Selma in April 1865. But the city became a battleground again when a group called the Friends of Forrest got approval from the city's mayor to erect a monument of the lieutenant general at a city-owned building in 2000 "as a testament of our perpetual devotion and respect ... to honor his unwavering defense of Selma, the great state of Alabama, and the Confederacy."

Years before the movement to take down Confederate flags began in 2015, citizens and civil rights supporters opposed this particular monument vehemently—"Jews would not tolerate a statue of Hitler in their neighborhood, and what they put up in our neighborhood . . . was pretty much the same thing," said civil rights lawyer Rose Sanders (also known as Faya Rose Toure). At the city building, people vandalized the statue, dumped garbage on it, and attacked it with cinder blocks.

After much public outcry on both sides, the city approved moving the monument to the Confederate Memorial Circle in this cemetery, whose debated ownership now lies with the United Daughters of the Confederacy and where the bust was ultimately stolen in 2012 by an unknown thief. The Daughters' video camera now keeps a watchful eye on its replacement, night and day, recording Neil and me as we circle the thing as gawking, curious Yanks, with its list of Forrest's twenty-four battles and its seemingly placid stance in a grassy area on this quiet, sunny day among his fellow men.

Our excursion in Selma ends by driving through downtown, a ghost town if I ever saw one, nearly an archaeological site with more than half its retail buildings shuttered, with peeling paint and boarded-up windows, a windswept, lost, and forgotten-looking place. Then we drive across the Edmund Pettus Bridge because I feel we must; John Lewis said at the fiftieth anniversary of Bloody Sunday: "Our country will never, ever be the same because of what happened on this bridge." I want to feel a part of that history. It was here, two days after Bloody Sunday, on March 9, 1965, that Martin Luther King Jr. and others organized a second march—a symbolic gesture, really, leading 3,200 people onto the bridge where they knelt and prayed within sight of a wall of Alabama State Troopers and then turned around, obeying a restraining order to not yet march.

It's the place where, finally, on Sunday March 21, 1965, eight thousand people—including Rabbi Abraham Heschel in the front row and at least nineteen other rabbis (nearly all northern, midwestern, or western, not southern)—crossed over, and some southern Jews, like Hanna Berger's father, came out to watch. A thousand military policemen and two thousand army troops sent by President Johnson as escorts assembled as the marchers took their first steps on the historic fifty-four-mile walk "across desolate valleys and trying hills," in the words of Dr. King, to Montgomery.

Neil and I make the journey as well, backward, from Montgomery, where we first entered this fraught geography. Highway 80—which passes through an area of majority-black counties where today less than 50 percent of the population is connected to a municipal sewer line, meaning some people have to drain their toilet waste into their yard—is now designated as the Selma to Montgomery National Historic Trail, administered by the National Park Service, with two visitor centers, both closed during our evening trip.

We miss Campsite 1 in our rush to avoid the approaching thunderstorms that evening, but this was where three hundred of the marchers stopped on the first night, an eighty-acre farm owned by a black man, David Hall, where he and his eight children resided. Volunteer security marshals patrolled the campgrounds, as marchers felt threatened by some of the Alabama National Guardsmen, federalized by President Johnson to ensure their safety. What we see now are the gathering clouds hovering over the silver ribbon of empty road: rolling green fields, a copse of trees, and wide sky, but no buildings, no towns, and no people.

On the second night, March 22, 1965, the marchers stopped at Campsite 2, the farm of Rosa Steele, which is marked now by a brown park service sign at the edge of someone's front yard along the highway. Soon after the march, in retaliation for her support of the protestors, her grocery store was burned to the ground.

On the third night, the marchers stopped at Campsite 3, the Robert Gardner Farm, where, on March 23, 1965, they were served barbecued chicken, hash, peas and carrots, and a candy bar for dinner, and heavy rains turned the farmer's field into "a soggy mess." I snap a picture of the nondescript grassy corner of the intersection near this site only after coming back around to it again, having been momentarily distracted by a sight I had never seen: a group of about two dozen African American cowboys on horseback, men and boys who seemed twenty feet tall from our perch, like bronze statues come alive. They take off from the same corner as the sign, making their way across the highway to a quiet country lane.

And on the fourth night, when several thousand marchers joined the core team, Campsite 4 found itself at the City of St. Jude, a Catholic social service complex, where Harry Belafonte, Tony Bennett, Peter, Paul, and Mary, Sammy Davis Jr., Joan Baez, and others performed at the "Stars for Freedom" rally, and a National Park Service sign marks it as the "Final stop before arrival at State Capitol."

By Day 5, on March 25, 1965, a crowd of more than twenty-five thousand arrived at the steps of the Alabama Capitol in Montgomery—some had walked more than fifty miles in five days but had come with "three centuries of suffering and hardship," as their petition to Governor Wallace stated—to demand the right to vote for black people. These civil rights activists were the other defenders of Selma, the city King specifically chose for this final phase of the movement's nonviolent work—"Picked . . . just like a movie producer would pick a set" because of "the right ingredients," according to Selma's Mayor Smitherman at that time: low voter registration in the black community and "the notorious brutality of local law enforcement under Sheriff Jim Clark [which] would attract national attention."

Of course, Governor Wallace was not present at the capitol to meet with the protestors, but five months later, after years of negotiation, the highest officer of the land, President Lyndon B. Johnson, signed the Voting Rights Act, which intended to prohibit discrimination in voting practices or procedures because of race and color. In fact, the number of registered voters who were black rose from 31 percent to 73 percent in the subsequent decades. Section 5 of the act required parts or all of sixteen states, including Alabama, Georgia, Louisiana, Mississippi, South Carolina, and Virginia—"those areas of the country where Congress believed the potential for discrimination to be the greatest"—to seek federal approval for any changes in statewide voting law.

But, alas, almost fifty years later, in 2013, three years before the 2016 presidential election, the US Supreme Court gutted Section 5, saying that these places "no longer need to seek preclearance for new voting changes," even though this act prohibited more than three thousand discriminatory practices from happening over its lifetime. Even with the law in place, after President Obama's election in 2008, 395 voting restrictions were introduced in 49 states. From the time of its gutting through May 2017, 31 states introduced at least 99 bills to restrict registration and voting.

We, too, make it to Montgomery, to the Alabama capitol building, the epicenter of everything the South is known for, hated for, revered for. Not only is this the place where King gave his famous "How Long, Not Long" speech in 1965 ("How long will prejudice blind the visions of men . . . .? Not long, because the arc of the moral universe is long, but it bends toward justice"), but it is also the place that served as the first Confederate capitol where Jefferson Davis took his presidential oath to the Confederacy. It is where Governor George Wallace ordered state troopers to encircle the exact spot on the floor where Davis once stood "so that a visitor, Attorney General Robert F. Kennedy, could not put a desecrating Yankee foot atop it," as one reporter put it.

It is the place where, at the Confederate Memorial Monument on the capitol grounds, four iterations of the Confederate flag once flew as recently as May 2015—the First, Second, and Third National Confederate flags and the Confederate battle flag—but which Alabama Governor Robert J. Bentley quietly instructed state workers to remove, seven days after the Charleston shootings, so state employees would not be distracted by controversy. (Nearly two years later, Bentley would resign due to allegations that he used public resources to conduct and conceal an affair, pleading guilty to two misdemeanors, with state lawmakers beginning the process of impeachment against him; but, hey, at least he wasn't Governor Wallace, who decided to erect the Confederate flag over the capitol on the day of Kennedy's visit.)

The scene is so quiet now; no sign of discord here, out of sight of the Montgomery Greyhound bus terminal where in 1961 mobs attacked Freedom Riders like John Lewis who rode buses into the cities of the segregated South to test and bring attention to the nonenforcement of the nation's laws desegregating interstate bus lines and bus stations; the riders were clubbed with baseball bats, bricks, chains, and tire irons until they were knocked unconscious.

Today the streets are clean, few people walk about this late weekend afternoon, and Neil and I hold hands and practically skip around the grounds, freed from the constraints of our car. The sky is a clear, sunny cerulean blue. Rivulets of sweat are not making their way down our backs and necks; it is only 95 degrees. We walk the Avenue of Flags, a crescent of state flags of the United States in front of the capitol building. To the south, a memorial signpost commemorates King's journey to this spot.

I come home changed from this journey. A portal into the other world of American history is opening for me. What hasn't been part of my world is now part of my world. I want to be like the Freedom Summer Jews and help overcome obstacles to voting. So for the first time, I volunteer to drive the elderly and disabled to the polls, starting in the November 2015 presidential primary in my community of Arlington, Virginia. I drive mostly the residents of a fixed-income and low-income retirement-community apartment building near my house. Among the people I drive to cast their ballots is an African American woman in her eighties wearing a wild wig, fancy jewelry, a flowy skirt, and an Obama T-shirt; she tells me what a great feeling it is for an African American woman to vote in America. Another passenger, an African American man in his seventies, who doesn't talk much, says he has never voted in his life and asks me to help him fill out the ballot, for he does not appear confident in reading or writing. And when I think back on this day in Montgomery, what I'll remember most is that in 2015, across the street from the crescent of state flags, in full view of the grand, Greek Revival–style capitol, at the First White House of the Confederacy where Davis lived and worked for the first half of 1861, now a museum listed on the National Register of Historic Places—the First National Confederate flag, with the seven stars of the first seceding states of the Deep South, still flies high.

PART 2

MEETUPS

A NIGHT IN NATCHEZ

It's Friday night, and I'm at The Temple in Nashville, a congregation that began in 1851, located on the property of an old plantation that belonged to one of the largest slaveholding families here. To my left is an Orthodox couple, extremely learned; to my right is a professor of Judaic studies. Before me, bathed in the soft evening light cascading in from the upper windows of the contemporary great room, are the musicians who accompany this evening's Shabbat service—a flutist, four guitar players, and a banjo player—a sextet, rather than the traditional lone organ or piano player or even a single fringed, long-haired guitar player that I've seen at my friends' kids' bar and bat mitzvah services recently.

It is "Blue Jean Friday" at this Reform synagogue, we are told, and the rabbi and cantor are wearing, well, blue jeans. They are the most casually dressed religious figures I have ever witnessed on official duty. Their voices also aren't of the northeastern variety to which I am accustomed or that I expect to hear at synagogue from the days of my youth when I went to services begrudgingly on the High Holy Days; their words sound slow and syrupy and relaxed and lulling. They welcome us with kindness and graciousness, strangers and fellow members of the tribe—our group of eighty or so, hailing from twelve southern states, as well as some expats living up North.

We are joined here through our common interest in southern Jewish history. It's the second day of the fortieth annual conference of the Southern Jewish Historical Society (SJHS). I decided to join this organization to dig deeper into my interest in southern Jews, and it's my first conference with the group. I'm at the conference on my own; no traveling companion to soften the anxieties of travel. It's the first conference I have ever attended voluntarily based on a personal interest rather than a required event related to work. And it is the first time since I attended a Jewish day camp from ages six to eleven that I've been part of an all-Jewish group.

So I'm a little nervous here, feeling a bit like an imposter, like I'm not as Jewish as everyone else. But now in my mid-forties, I have been gravitating toward Jewish friends the past few years, feeling a kinship that hadn't mattered to me before, and as a history lover I have started to value more the attachment I inevitably have through my bloodline to the people and traditions born thousands of years ago, a connection that far precedes my parents, my grandparents, my greats, and my great-greats. I don't know all the words to the songs sung here tonight, literally or figuratively, but I realize that the sounds resonate inside me in rhythm with my own heartbeat.

We're five days out from CMA (or, the Country Music Association awards, for those of y'all not from around here) in early November. At this holy site of unusual and unfamiliar meet-ups of music, religion, and southern and Jewish culture, sitting here in this semicircle of cushioned wooden seats in a light-filled modern chapel, some of the hymns I recognize from my youth and now-and-then bat and bar mitzvahs I've attended are sung not in the traditional or typical tune that I've ever heard. Rather, they have been reimagined into a country music rhythm. Over the next few days, when my dad, step-mother, and sister will arrive for a brief family trip, we'll take in the Grand Ole Opry and other country and folk music concerts at the Bluebird and a honky-tonk in town where we'll hear generally non-Jewish themes of pickup trucks, guns, the devil, and Jesus, but much of it will sound like this.

Tonight I'm a newbie to country and western music, and the cantor's voice could just as well be Carrie Underwood's or Faith Hill's for all I know. *Shelter us beneath Your wings,* we sing. *Guard us from all harmful things. Keep us safe through-*

out the night, 'til we wake with morning's light. Teach us, God, wrong from right. Ahhh-mein. It's our own little Jewish opry, and part of my introduction to Music City.

Yesterday, a group of about fifty of us arrived in Nashville to spend a preconference day on a Julius Rosenwald field trip. It included a bus trip to the Cairo Rosenwald School (that's pronounced "cay-row"), a small, white, empty, one-room, wasp-filled, church-looking building out in the country. We also traveled to Fisk University, one of the nation's historically black colleges and universities. Aside from famous graduates—like the writer and historian W. E. B. Du Bois, the journalist and civil rights/anti-lynching activist Ida B. Wells, the civil rights activist and politician Marion Barry, and John Lewis—Fisk is best known for its Fisk Jubilee Singers. The ensemble introduced the world to slave songs, or Negro spirituals, when they traveled the globe, starting in 1871, singing for kings and queens in Europe. For me, traveling to places like Fisk and Tuskegee University makes me realize there's a whole branch of American history related to art, science, and leadership that's not taught in most American schools, overridden by the white narrative of presidents and wars. But on the Fisk campus, walking from building to building along charmingly manicured paths with a small group of interested Jews from all across the South, I got a tiny taste of it.

Fisk is also the repository of the archives of the Rosenwald Fund, which gave grants to African American artists and intellectuals, including Ralph Ellison, W. E. B. Du Bois, Maya Angelou, and James Baldwin. On a private tour, our group hovered over tables in dim light to see a sampling from the collection the librarians set out for us: Langston Hughes's original application for a Rosenwald Grant, which he received in 1941; old blueprints from Frederick Law Olmstead for some of the Rosenwald Schools he designed; and photographs of children in Rosenwald's state-of-the-art schoolhouses across the South.

As seemingly the lone single person at the conference and clearly a newcomer to the group, perhaps one of the youngest in attendance, I became a magnet for polite and inquiring minds. "What brought you to this conference?" many people asked as way of introduction and welcome.

And as we walked and talked, and I moved in and out of conversation with various lay historians, history buffs, experts in Jewish history, I began to feel at home, even as I felt at a distance. As an adjunct faculty instructor in creative nonfiction and science writing at a university, I was an outsider to the PhD academics in whose Jewish or history fields they write and publish and lecture. As a nonreligious Jew, unaffiliated with a congregation, I was an outsider to the Orthodox, the Conservatives, the Reconstructionists, and even the practicing Reforms. As a lay historian, new to the field of Jewish history—and especially southern Jewish history, which is not my background—I was an outsider to those who have been coming to this annual meeting in various southern cities for years or decades. Even as a writer, in the very early anarchy stages of writing this book, I was an outsider to this very well-published group.

But as a member of the Jewish bloodline hailing back to Abraham, I realized I felt part of the family. I felt I belonged. Despite my northern heritage and because of my great curiosity, unspoken ties bound us before we even met and would bind us forever, the history of our shared worldly struggle, the experiences of our common forebears, the desire to press on and continue our heritage, no matter what the challenges or geography. Best of all, and most surprising, everyone knew how to spell and pronounce my last name. Normally I have to say "Eisenfeld, with an 'E,'" or even spell it out—"E-I-S-E-N-F-as-in-Frank-E-L-D" as I often get "Izenfield" and various other spellings, despite the presumably familiar name of President Eisenhower. The people were warm with welcome, even as I went off on my own for dinner that first night. The next day, when I arrived in the morning for the first official day of the conference, I already felt quite connected to this charming group.

A year later, in November 2016, I am attending my second SJHS annual conference, this time with my stepmother, Marci. This year, the final destination is Natchez, Mississippi (population 15,000; 60 percent black, 36 percent white, 4 percent other), the oldest settlement on the Mississippi River, just north of the Louisiana state line. It's my second time in Natchez. Last summer, I came to Natchez with Neil on the Natchez Trace Parkway, a ribbon of road that starts in Nashville and follows a historic traveling route—the Natchez Trace, used by the Choctaw, Chickasaw, Natchez, and prehistoric Native Americans, now a national scenic trail, where numerous large spiders' webs stretch across the path. We liked Natchez so much, we stayed for several days. Neil went birding in the nearby St. Catherine Creek National Wildlife Refuge and saw seventy-five giant wood storks, while I toured some astonishingly ostentatious in-town mansions, including Longwood, an octagonal Oriental villa designed by a Philly architect.

These types of places were where plantation owners lived in order to conduct business, while leaving their massive plantation landholdings and slaves in the hands of overseers across the river in Louisiana. At one such place—Frogmore, still a working cotton plantation and gin from 1815 whose Civil War–era owner was a Union sympathizer and yet owned 159 slaves—my tour guide explained some of the terminology for enslaved field hands: "full hands" or "prime hands" were prime-age males who were expected to produce a large amount of work per day; "three-quarter hands" were expected to produce slightly less work; "half hands," such as pregnant women, half as much; and "quarter hands," half that. The guide explained matter-of-factly, "If you take the inhumanity out of it, a slave was like a piece of machinery." One daughter of a planter described it exactly like that in 1886: "Negroes

were but pieces of machinery" and the role of the wife of a
southern planter was to be "the master hand that set them in
motion."

From those Greek Revival homes that took up entire city
blocks, afforded by working humans like machinery, I learned
that planter families sent their children to boarding schools in
Europe or up North; summered in northern spas like my own
childhood vacation place, the Jersey Shore; and imported their
marble mantelpieces from New York, their intricate "gasoliers"
(gas chandeliers) from Philadelphia, their ornate gold mirrors
from France, and their furniture and draperies from various
places on the continent. Those massive manors were where
I learned about "prie-dieux," "watchdogs," and "petticoat tables."
From my experience of being in those high-ceilinged spaces and
reading *Gone With the Wind* for the first time during the trip,
I fed my mind with both contextual fact and fanciful fiction and
developed a real "Are-you-kidding-me?" attitude about the Old
South. The way of life that Confederates fought for was insanely
royal.

One morning during that trip with Neil, I tried to coun-
terbalance the immersion in white wealth by visiting the
Natchez Museum of African American History and Culture.
Unfortunately, I had only about an hour to look around this
detailed and complicated place, and I was forced to join a tour
in French because that's what was happening when I arrived
(I understood a few words). But I was chastised for leaving
early. "We are not an appetizer!" a man scolded me on the way
out, referring to the museum and the town's African American
history, I'm sure, which may be accustomed to being passed
up in favor of Natchez's white history.

A big draw for Natchez tourists is Pilgrimage, visiting the
grand mansions and experiencing "the way of life" of the South.
These tourists are not, perhaps, also venturing off the beaten
path to see the humble home of writer Richard Wright. They
may not even visit the center-of-town home of William Johnson, who was born a slave but became a prominent citizen
in the free black community as a barber, landowner, and slave

owner; his residence is now operated by the National Park Service. Nor are they necessarily driving out to see the roadside historical marker for "Forks of the Road," which was the second-largest slave market in the South, located in what was "unquestionably the state's most active slave trading city." Nor are they likely studying up on how antebellum Natchez was home to the largest community of free people of color in Mississippi. So I can understand how the African American museum—located on a prominent central street—wanted to ensure that visitors know that black lives matter(ed) here.

Before the Natchez conference with my stepmother, I had been looking forward to getting together with this Jewish group again. I felt surprisingly reinvigorated after the Nashville conference, and I came home and celebrated Rosh Hashanah with a Jewish friend for the first time in years and then fasted on Yom Kippur for one of the only times of my life. This year, before the conference, after conjuring an image of Jews all over the globe breaking their fast and after considering the many small southern Jewish towns that were fading away, I hosted a break-fast at my house on Yom Kippur for the first time. I wanted to be part of our tradition in my own small way. The closeness of small-town southern Jews had been inspiring me. Maybe being a little more Jewish wouldn't hurt.

On our first night in Mississippi, after flying in to Jackson, Marci and I follow the recommendation from fellow conference attendees to eat dinner at a seafood restaurant next door to our hotel and order its free blackened oyster appetizer. Marci does so, as does the table next to us, a group of Jewish attendees of the conference. Marci also orders an enormous fried oyster po'boy, marveling at the size and eating nearly all of it. This meal, it turns out, is the beginning of nearly all the conference goers' descent into "trayf" territory—that is, forbidden, nonkosher foods that even nonobservant Jews often shun due to stigma or custom. In a nutshell, kosher means no pork, no shellfish or any sea creature without fins and scales, and no mixing of meat and milk in the same meal, as well as a variety of other rules and preparations to meet Jewish dietary law.

Our group is no different from any other Jews embracing the South, however: they eat it all. Since their arrival in the South, Jews have been eating "regional foods that are among the *most* delectable dishes in the world but also the *most* forbidden by Jewish standards," according to researcher Marcie Cohen Ferris. Jews have always wanted to—needed to—assimilate, to try to belong in whatever area they ended up. "Eating like one's Gentile neighbors affirmed both solidarity with white society and loyalty to the segregated South," Ferris says. That means southern Jews generally don't avoid southern favorites such as deviled crabs, oysters Rockefeller, shrimp creole, shrimp mousse, and ham soufflé—"the elegant heart of the diet of the lower Mississippi River." In addition, Jews southernize some traditional foods—instead of matzo balls in chicken soup for Passover, some southerners make fried matzo balls as a side dish, or matzo balls covered in turkey gravy. Some make matzo charlotte for dessert.

Unrecognizable in a northern Jewish diet but common in the South is lox and grits (instead of bagels) or sweet potato or peach kugel (instead of plain kugel or kugel with apples and raisins). Foods that are just not a thing up North at all include Sabbath fried chicken; Rosh Hashanah hoppin' John, a black-eyed pea dish; and the addition of okra, pecans, or butter beans to any dish. Some foods and behaviors that observant and non-observant northern Jews would consider to be downright scandalous include serving ham biscuits at a synagogue luncheon or breaking the fast of Yom Kippur—the holiest day of the year—with pork roast, as one Natchez family did. "Jewish food culture in Natchez defies kosher law in a way that dazzles and surprises," Jewish radio journalist Robin Amer says.

When we arrive in Natchez a few nights hence, Robin Amer, whose family has lived in Natchez for more than 160 years and whose ancestors fought for the Confederacy, will regale us with a story about a "traditional" Natchez Jewish meal planned for some northern visitors at the mansion Staunton Hall in 1994. This now-famous Natchez Jewish homecoming meal included shrimp mousse, crab dip, and ham biscuits, and a brouhaha ensued when planners and visitors got wind of "the greatest trayf buffet one could ever imagine." Ironically, this tale will foreshadow our own conference luncheon one day later, also at Staunton Hall. Meant to be as kosher as a nonkosher restaurant can be in a town with no kosher butchers or kosher kitchens, what will be served mistakenly is a meal of catfish topped with shrimp, green beans cooked with bacon, lima beans with ham, dirty rice with pork sausage, and other unmentionables. (As further irony, I'll learn later that in 1883, a similar accidental "treyfa banquet" occurred in Cincinnati when the first four American-ordained rabbis graduated from the new Hebrew Union College. "The event turned into a faux pas heard round the Jewish world.") But will I hear any member of our Jewish group complain or see anyone not clean their plate? No, I will not.

I have been vegetarian since 1992 and stick with the portobello po'boy that first night in Jackson with Marci. While she devours the oysters, I try to swallow the lump in my throat that has formed from acid reflux, sparked by weeks or even months of anxiety due to the upcoming presidential election in five days. This year, I took another baby step toward more voting-rights activism and volunteered to do a voter registration event, and I am signed up as a driver to take the same elderly people to the polls on Election Day. There's so much at stake this time; two days ago in Greenville, Mississippi, someone tried to burn down a black church and graffitied "Vote Trump" on an exterior wall, which feels like a descent back into the 1960s, a period I thought we'd escaped.

Most northern people I know think that the South is and always has been anti-Semitic and racist—more so than the North. But I hear and read many stories that indicate a messy, more complex zone there as well. For example, the first iteration of the Klan—established in Tennessee just after the Civil War, intended to frighten the newly freed slaves and northerners who had come down to help rule the South—included Jews among its members, such as Simon Baruch, a Confederate surgeon. According to scholars, the early twentieth-century revival of the Klan was actually more anti-Semitic up North than in the South. In the South, "its members did not bother to boycott the Jewish retailers on Main Street"—"Who else would have sold Klansmen their denims, their shoes, and even their sheets?" Many sources tell the story of southern Jewish storeowners recognizing men under white hoods by the shoes they had sold them. "Most of the Klan's anti-Semitism was discharged against the shadowy, imaginary Jew who lived far away in the big cities. Klansmen felt a little guilty and ashamed at picking on the Jews whom they had known as good neighbors their whole lives," according to one scholar.

From my research, I've learned that southern church-going people of all faiths have been good to southern Jews throughout the centuries, and so generally, in my heart, I had no qualms about coming to the South again, even in this more hostile climate. Macy Hart, president and CEO of the Institute for Southern Jewish Life (ISJL), for example, who grew up in the only Jewish family in Winona, Mississippi, says, "We were revered as a Jewish family" because—as he and many others have noted—Christians often considered Jews the "chosen ones" and the "people of the Book" for their serious worship of God. Many stories tell about when early Jews in a community could not yet afford to build their temple, Christians helped them raise money because they felt Jews ought to have a place of worship.

But intellectually, I did fear the concept of a large group of Jews publicly announcing their presence in the new atmosphere of hate that surfaced during the 2016 presidential campaigns. Fifteen days from the start of this trip, only ten days after the presidential election, 867 reported cases of hate crimes against Jews, blacks, immigrants, Muslims, women, LGBTQ people, and others would amass, including nooses hung in people's front yards, references to lynching written in public places, and swastikas drawn on people's front doors or cars with written threats. By 2017 anti-Semitic incidents would rise 57 percent in a year, the largest single-year growth on record, including at least one incident in each state. A dam of hatred unleashed.

On the ground, though, here, on the Southern Jewish Historical Society trip in Mississippi, all the hate and fear feels very
"somewhere else" in our group of 150, banded together as we
are as Jews, historians, information seekers, and advocates of
truth and justice.

The SJHS tour of Mississippi makes me feel, in fact, like all of
Mississippi was and is Jewish, which is so far from the truth;
there are only about 1,500 Jews there today, though they
arrived in the state in the 1700s and were integral in establishing towns and infrastructure. After leaving Jackson, our
first stop on the bus trip is Vicksburg, Mississippi (population
23,000; 71 percent black, 27 percent white, 2 percent other),
where twenty Jewish families lived by 1825. We are treated to
a luncheon at the old B'nai Brith Literary Club, or the BB Club,
established as a social club for Jews in 1871, with 650 members
and the city's first indoor swimming pool. Then we head to
Temple Anshed Chesed, which holds the oldest Torah in the
South, brought over by Russian immigrants.

Inside the temple, we hear from Richard Marcus, one of the
last eleven Jews of Vicksburg, down from nearly five hundred
in the 1870s and again in the 1920s. When this eighty-seven-
year-old tells us that they haven't had a rabbi since 1980 and
have had laymen leading the services instead, with no children
in the religious school for twenty-five years, the conference
goers expel an audible gasp. We walk the adjacent grounds of
the Jewish cemetery, next to Vicksburg National Military Park,
a place of old trenches and monuments. Here, General Grant
surrounded and bombarded the city and trapped a Confederate army, blockading the city in a forty-seven-day siege while
residents starved, even eating rats and shoe leather for lack of
supplies, before the Confederacy surrendered on July 4, 1863.
The cemetery dates from 1864 and was the site of a Confederate fortification from which "Federals were slaughtered in
droves" during the siege.

Civil War history is as alive here as anywhere in the southern United States. Vicksburg is considered a significant win for the Union because "with the Mississippi River now firmly in Union hands, the Confederacy's fate was all but sealed," according to the American Battlefield Trust, but the days of the Jewish congregation are numbered. We may have been the last private tour of the temple, as the congregation is working on partnering with a nonprofit organization to preserve the building and the history of the Jewish community as it essentially folds. In exchange for ownership and use of the temple for office space after it is deconsecrated, the organization will ensure perpetual care of the Jewish burial ground, home to 1,300 souls.

Our second stop on the way to Natchez—on what could be called a Jewish ghost tour because most of what we're learning about is already dead and gone—is Port Gibson (population 1,700; 91 percent black, 7 percent white, 2 percent other), a town that General Grant called "too beautiful to burn" on his northward trek to Vicksburg. Temple Gemiluth Chassed, the oldest temple in Mississippi, which has had no rabbi since 1908, found another way to save itself after the once-thriving Jewish community dissipated to Memphis, New Orleans, and Baton Rouge and the building was about to become a parking lot: the congregation sold the temple to private buyers, Bill and Martha Lum. They turned it into a Messianic Jewish church, a group with one branch better known as "Jews for Jesus." This is a concept that does not compute for most Jews but is an interesting subject to ponder given that Jesus was Jewish. Jews agree Jesus was a good and influential man; they just don't believe he was the messiah. Jews generally believe the messiah is still coming—and therein lies the rub. Bill Lum welcomes the conference goers inside to examine the dramatic red-brick, Moorish-Byzantine style architecture, with its keyhole-style doorway, a Russian-style dome, a turret, and a horseshoe arc inside, and he does not mention religion at all. Two glistening glass chandeliers shine down on the dusty pews, and we're all grateful for his preservation of the place.

Though there are no Jews left in Port Gibson now, which consists mostly of Methodists and Catholics, "A lot of people here have Jewish ancestry," Lum tells us. "That's where we all come from, after all, back to Abraham." Before the boll weevil and jobs elsewhere compelled Jews to leave, Port Gibson was home to sixty Jewish families, and they were considered a "lauded group," Lum says.

The Jackson-Vicksburg-Port Gibson bus trip finally culminates in Natchez, located high on a bluff overlooking the Mississippi River. A place originally inhabited by the Natchez tribe, then colonized by the French, ceded to Spain after the French lost the French-Indian War, and then acquired by the British, Jews first settled here in 1798, and about a third of all businesses once were Jewish-owned, with storefront windows facing popular streets in town. Jews here and throughout the South were known to sell merchandise to blacks, unlike many white-owned stores. "They stayed open on Saturdays until one or two in the morning, because the black workers didn't come in until eight or nine at night," according to one long-time Natchez resident.

Though it was considered a backwater fort in 1717, within a hundred years Natchez became a place of refinement, a cultural oasis of opera, music, and culture, even back in the days when New Orleans was "nothing more than a whorehouse town," as one person told me. Saved from destruction by surrendering to the Union during the Civil War, Natchez does feel comparatively cosmopolitan, with many blocks of boutiques, antique shops, cafes, and restaurants; a lovely riverside walk and park; a grand city cemetery overlooking the river; and even international tourists. But it's also dead enough that even during its three hundredth anniversary, Marci and I can find no festivities to attend.

Feeling like we just arrived in a quaint European town, Marci and I dress for dinner and then walk a few blocks on narrow streets to the neoclassical Temple B'nai Israel for an entertaining trayf food talk by Robin Amer and then Shabbat services. We sit beneath a soaring dome ceiling, before an arc of Italian marble, among approximately two hundred other conference participants and community members.

Rabbi Jeremy Simons, a traveling rabbi for ISJL, leads the service. He is one of two rabbis who in 2016 journeyed as a "virtual synagogue" to make sixty visits to twenty-three congregations in ten southern states where there are too few Jews for full- or even part-time rabbis. The support these traveling rabbis provide has prevented some small rural congregations from closing. On this night, Rabbi Simons recounts how it has been so long since the Natchez temple had a full house of worshippers that he had to reach out to congregations in other states to amass enough prayer books for the evening. Natchez has only fifteen Jewish residents, down from a high of 145 families in 1907. It was a good problem to have, he says, even if for just one remarkable night.

The lights of the temple twinkle in the silence, and the stained-glass windows still shine a muted evening luminescence into the sanctuary. The wooden pews that had seemed so hard during our conference now are warm with hips pressing against hips during the packed service. Next to me is a lifelong Natchezian who is not Jewish. She says she first began coming to services and events at the temple years ago because, "I delighted in the space." The group is led in a hopeful Shabbat service, praying, singing, renewing, or affirming faith in God and, in a sense, each other, in what is likely the last large religious service this congregation will ever host, after 145 years.

The rabbi does not speak overtly about raising funds to save the temple, or tzedakah, what some might define as giving to charity, a way to enable righteousness, justice, or fairness—such an important part of Jewish life. He speaks of a different kind of giving. He tells us to do our part in saving these places by joining them as members, to sit in the pews of dwindling congregations, to *be* the lifeblood—or the defibrillator—to keep something valued from slipping away.

Go, be Jewish!, he seems to be saying directly to me. *Partake.* Though I've always lived in large northeastern or mid-Atlantic metropolitan areas with plenty of practicing and nonpracticing Jews and many synagogues to choose from, I had never felt the call to join one, as it was never part of my upbringing. Now, though, I've visited more temples and in quicker succession than ever before in my life, places barely getting by with hardly any members, making me think that if I lived in one of these small towns, I'd definitely attend. The big question as I sit in this moribund synagogue is: will I join one at home? Will my travels in the South lead me to embrace practicing Judaism? The message I hear here is, *Don't take anything for granted; it won't last forever.*

On the final night of the conference, Marci and I enjoy a warm November evening stroll through town to the Merrill House, an Italianate mansion circa 1869. Hosts graciously welcome us through the large front door, which unveils a vast center hallway, leading through the house to a catered bar outside in the backyard. In the living room, a violinist massages our hearts with "Ashokan Farewell," that lovely Scottish lament made famous by Ken Burns's series on the Civil War, musical notes that sound like tears. Later, under a shimmering chandelier, the musician plucks at our heartstrings on a grand piano. We aren't wearing hoop skirts, but we waltz from room to room on the shiny wood floors, clacking our heels, holding small plates of (nonkosher) hors d'oeuvres.

I chat with Sam, a professor from Philly, and we discuss architecture and our youth in the city. I bend low to speak with Adele, a woman I met last year in Nashville, who has traveled to many countries and continents over her long, interesting life. We talk about art, love, philosophy, and politics while sipping cocktails and wine in crystal glasses, and later my stepmother, Marci, and I peruse books in the library, a floor-to-ceiling collection of novels and biographies.

From this middle-class northerner's point of view, this could have been 1860, the grand southern life of charm and extravagance, white folks living the high life right here in the river city of Natchez. I imagine a party like this at an abode of one of the 340 planters of Natchez, some of the richest men of the nation, benefitting from the proximity of the river to keep cotton and cash moving. I imagine them carefree, assured of their place in society, masters who might have ordered or carried out the branding, whipping, or torturing of their slaves—even cutting off their ears—with no compunction, while in the evening of the same day, enjoying a brandy or a bourbon. They thought the war would be short, and they thought it was worth the price. They were "ready to do almost anything to keep their negroes in the field," according to one scholar, and they could not envision the devastating numbers of southern dead, their own cities in ghastly ruin.

Or, I imagine, it could have been pre-1933 Berlin, in a Jewish intellectual's home. A home full of Jewish businessmen, politicians, artists, and scholars, just like this one, surrounded by oil paintings in gold frames and China finery.

In this home on this night, at a cocktail party to raise money to help support the dying Natchez synagogue, I find myself sensitive to every piano note, every swipe of the bow on violin strings, every moment of laughter, each warm smile and welcoming eye, strangers meeting strangers, old friends reuniting. Never have moments felt so precious in the light of history. In three days, I keep thinking to myself, everything could change. In three days, I will put on my black pantsuit to drive my people to the polls, and I will wind up saying to my husband, Neil, when I leave the house on the morning of Election Day that I am willing to die to defend the right to vote, that I'll throw my body in front of my voting ladies if I have to, in light of the threats of violence at polls throughout the nation. This joy that we feel tonight in Natchez, with the overhanging shadow of a new world order, is so tenuous in the lead-up to the 2016 presidential election. Will we or other minority groups be rounded up? Will our sacred places be ravaged? Will we be threatened by our own people, our neighbors and storekeepers, people we trust?

Macy Hart of ISJL, which organized this year's SJHS meeting, would say, after the election of the forty-fifth president and his rhetoric egging on anti-Semitic white nationalists, that

ISJL—which provides education and cultural programming for Jewish communities throughout the South—has not been impacted. "This president cannot stop us from continuing our work in social justice and education." I believe Hart was saying that the new president cannot stop Jews from following their faith. None of the atrocities thrown at Jewish people over the millennia ever really has.

But on this final November night in Natchez, against the backdrop of what has been the most contentious election year of my life and some of the most memorable few days I've ever experienced as a traveler and as a Jew, the merriment and freedom feel as fragile as a windowpane of glass—with a stone hurtling toward it.

ALL MIXED UP IN GUMBO LAND

Kerlin Caspari Sutton is ninety years old and handsome, with combed-down white bangs and a chiseled jaw and cheekbones, wearing a striped collared shirt. If not for his aged body, now in a wheelchair from a stroke, he'd seem a spry seventy-five. He's wide-eyed and excited to have guests and to talk about history, as his son says he is bored 90 percent of the time. Sutton laughs as he tells me that he and his friends wonder about how they have gotten so old—and conclude they have no idea.

I am in Sutton's living room in Natchitoches (pronounced "nack-a-tish"), Louisiana, founded in 1714 on what was once the Red River, which was a good corridor for cotton commerce to New Orleans before the river changed course and left the town stranded on an oxbow lake. Natchitoches (population 18,000; 58 percent black, 38 percent white, 4 percent other) was the first permanent European settlement in the Louisiana Purchase. And in Louisiana, historic events are described as happening either before or after the Louisiana Purchase; all time is marked by 1803, the year that the United States, under President Thomas Jefferson, acquired land from the French (a whole bunch of slaveholding territory) in what is now fifteen US states. As a former Philadelphian and a Virginian now, this year seems an unusually late-in-history benchmark. My early points of reference have always been years like 1607, when Jamestown, Virginia, was established, or 1681, when King Charles II gave William Penn the land to found Pennsylvania, or even 1742 when the first house in my current town of Arlington was built. But a variety of research contacts had encouraged

86

me to visit Natchitoches because "it's a town founded before the Louisiana Purchase, the oldest town in the Louisiana Purchase!" So I wound up here.

More specifically, I am here because Sutton is the great-grandson of Leopold Caspari, a German-speaking Frenchman from Alsace-Lorraine who became a Confederate captain, a member of the Louisiana House of Representatives, and a Louisiana State Senator for twenty-six years—and was among the first three Jews to settle this town in 1858. I was told first to visit Sutton's son, Mark Sutton, a real estate man in middle age, because he has taken on the role of maintaining the old Jewish cemetery, a task he inherited from his father. In a town of less than a handful of Jews now, the Suttons were to be my portal to the past.

Earlier this Sunday morning at a restaurant, when Neil and I first met up with Mark, he and his wife were dressed up for brunch (Mark in seersucker pants, this Yankee takes note), and Neil and I apologized that we were not. "That's OK," he said, in what to my northern ear sounded like the sweet, slow-drawling Bill Clinton. "We just came from church." An awkward silence followed, as the gears were grinding in my head and Neil's, as we both expected Mark to be Jewish. He then explained that after being raised in his parents' Baptist home, he became a Catholic when he married his wife.

Louisiana, we come to learn over our three-week trip, is a very Catholic state that's a mish-mash of cultures, having been settled, taken over, and influenced by the Native Americans, French, Spanish, British, Africans, and Jews who had come to the area in 1757, primarily from the Caribbean—Suriname, Curacao, British Jamaica, and Barbados—where they'd fled the Spanish and Portuguese Inquisitions as early as 1494 and through the late 1600s. The culture and identity is fluid, with few defining boundaries of "us" and "them." Even during slavery, many black people, especially in New Orleans, were free and owned property.

When we first arrived in Natchitoches, we saw the Carroll Jones House along the Cane River Lake, a Creole plantation home purchased by a free man of color who had married a Choctaw woman and became "one of the most successful plantation owners in Rapides and Natchitoches Parishes." Even before we showed up here, I spoke to a few local people who explained that it was not uncommon for plantation owners to marry their slaves after their wives had died and then live with them and leave their properties to them as equals. Likewise, even the French "Black Code" from 1685, decreeing that Jews should be expelled from any French territory, was rarely enforced in Louisiana under French rule (though the Spanish kicked the Jews out when they took over, based on a prohibition dating from the homeland from 1492). The Jews' own rules about keeping kosher were often ignored in this seafood-loving state. "There's always been a relaxed attitude about culture and religion in Louisiana," one Natchitoches resident told me.

So Jewish Captain Caspari married a Protestant and had seven children who became mostly Catholic and Protestant, and hardly anyone in the family ever took up being Jewish again. "If you are an extreme minority," Kerlin says of the Jews in Louisiana, "you just kind of melt away."

Kerlin tells me he was raised in a confused state of Protestant-ish with a Jewish twist. "My mother professed to being a Jew, though not openly. I presumed that I was a Jew, but I did not know exactly what that meant," he wrote in a paper called "Jew Boy." "[I knew] that this was a topic that was never to be discussed with my friends. I was never told why. I must have sensed that it was not a popular thing to be a Jew. [One time,] as we passed through [an area with many churches], all with crosses displayed, I said, 'Us Jews better get out of this place, quick.' Why did I fear non-Jews? I was taught by my mother to never cross a Christian."

The Suttons' only connection to their family's original faith is the old Jewish cemetery because the synagogue on Church Street dedicated in 1904 and disbanded in 1925—where a church choir used to provide music for the High Holy Days' services—is gone. The cemetery lies in what now appears to be a lower- to modest-income black community, outside of historic downtown Natchitoches. In-town Natchitoches is a mini-version of New Orleans with its Spanish-influenced, decorative wrought-iron balcony bannisters. It's a lovely place, with benches and gardens along a river walk, but it's a town where slave sales once "treated people just as important as tractors, plows, and harvesting equipment," in the words of one Jewish resident I spoke to who is descended from some of the original Natchitoches Jews, a family who owned a one-thousand-acre sugarcane plantation along the river and, thereby, I presume, slaves. It's where, even as recent as the 1970s, a statue still stood of an elderly, stooped-over black man with a plaque that read, "We love our darkies."

The Natchitoches Jews' final resting place consists of an acre of land donated in 1847 by the first Jewish member of the community, Samuel Myers Hyams, the town and parish's surveyor and engineer starting in 1837 and also a first cousin of future US senator Judah P. Benjamin—the first acknowledged Jewish person elected to the US Senate and, later, appointed as the secretary of war and secretary of state of the Confederacy. More than a hundred graves—Cohens, Kaffies, Nachmans, Nelkens, Lissos, Levys, and Littmans—keep company with Suttons and Casparis, though Captain Caspari is buried at the American cemetery nearby because at the time, non-Jews like his wife could not be buried in the Jewish cemetery. "Church rules shaped civil law more then than now," Kerlin explains, and by "church" he means "Jewish."

When Jews settled in a town, one of the first actions they took when amassing enough people to call a community was to buy a plot of land for a cemetery. Even before establishing a congregation or building a temple, the Jews consecrated a place to bury their dead. In Natchitoches, this plot follows the custom of other Jewish cemeteries as well: upright stones indicate Ashkenazic Jews, of Eastern and Central Europe descent, and stones laid flat are for the Sephardic Jews, those of Spanish, Portuguese, or Mediterranean descent. Most are engraved with both English and Hebrew. It is, in many ways, like so many other historic cemeteries I've seen: graves are cracked and fallen over, engraving has in some places worn away.

There, on a road once named Lee Street and now called Martin Luther King Drive (which Kerlin notes is a trend throughout the Deep South), Kerlin mowed grass, trimmed brush, collected trash, and tried to maintain a locked gate for sixteen years. He says the cemetery has faced an ongoing battle with the neighborhood, in which, he reports, residents sit on the headstones, pry open the locked gate, remove flowers that people bring to the graves, and leave soda cans and other trash behind. He says, too, that neighbors have complained that it is not as well kept up as other nearby cemeteries (although by my observation, I disagree; none of them look that great). Mark faces the same challenges—along with the ongoing and long-term need to repair broken and knocked-over headstones and upturned bricks from short walls surrounding family plots—without the expertise, connections, or funding to do so. Neither has attempted to engage the community that surrounds the property or the city, which owns land adjacent to it, in any kind of mutually beneficial partnership, and there are no Jewish young people left or any benefactors to care for the place in the future. The situation seems hopeless to father and son.

Both tell me there never was and still isn't any discrimination against Jews here in Natchitoches. In fact, it is said that "the mere fact of non-discrimination . . . was a motivating factor for assimilation," which, including intermarriage, was one of the reasons for the Jewish community's demise. But when I also suggest that the unused portion of the cemetery be offered for burials to non-Jewish whites or to the black residents nearby, Kerlin looks astonished. "No white Protestants want to be buried there. No way! No way!" he says. "Neither do the blacks."

I deduce he's ultimately not that confident in the harmony of the community. "It was Hitler time when I was young," he recalls, "and the sentiment in this country went along more with Hitler than with the Jews." He suggests that in their heart of hearts, some Christians were not supporters of Jews and perhaps still aren't. "Maybe you like one Jew, but not all."

Not being Jewish has not diminished the Suttons' fervor about trying to preserve their family's heritage, however. Back in 1965, the B'nai Israel Cemetery Association started a trust fund with the People's Bank and Trust in Natchitoches as a source of income for upkeep of the cemetery. Problem is, according to Mark, the fund never generated enough income to last for perpetuity. Six to eight people in the community make donations when asked, but they are all aging, and the fund only has five thousand dollars left, which is enough for no more than five years' worth of mowing and care and is tens of thousands of dollars short when it comes to any greater maintenance or repair. Mark is genuinely distraught that he and the few other descendants of original Jews in the town have no clear way to ensure that the cemetery will be preserved forever.

This is a town where people reported that every store was run by Jews, but now hardly anybody near or far knows it or ever will, and so the stakes are high for this small, weedy lot. Who will remember Mrs. C. Freedman (1847–1906), who was a dealer in "dry goods, groceries, boots, shoes, hats, clothing, hardware, and general plantation supplies"? Who will mourn S. Winbarg (1832–1910), who offered "fancy and staple groceries, wines, liquors, cigars, etc."? Who will ever walk the streets and know that Isaac Kahn was a butcher, and Abe Harris ran the Harris Hotel, and Caspari & Dietrich offered dry goods, groceries, hardware, clothing, and "cotton and country produce"? Even the Jewish Community Legacy Project—a nonprofit organization that provides free living-will services to small Jewish congregations going extinct for perpetual care of their cemetery and preservation of historic documents and sacred ritual objects—says that Natchitoches is too far gone to receive its assistance.

As our conversation begins to wind down and I privately vow to write an article about these small dying places as a way to bring attention to the sad state of affairs, Kerlin changes the topic of conversation and is eager to tell me about the controversy in Natchitoches about whether the Confederate flag should still fly in the town's annual Christmas Festival parade. He explains that flags of all the other governments that once owned the land still fly—France, Spain, Florida, and the United States. The mayor, however, decided to ban the Confederate flag from the Christmas parade in 2015 (although not from general public display) because, he said, "I am accountable to all citizens who live in our city, and for many the Confederate flag is a symbol of hate, bigotry, violence, and division." Members of the local Sons of Confederate Veterans were upset, as the group has participated in this annual parade for more than twenty years, and it has decided not to attend anymore.

Who knows what Kerlin assumes my views are about the issue. Maybe he sees me as an urban Yankee coming down South with views of social justice and civil rights for all and an advocate for change and atonement. Maybe he sees me as someone who understands that families may be earnestly confused by new challenges to their generations-old family traditions that they cannot imagine disowning. A push and pull I can't see giving up any ground anytime soon.

Kerlin asks what I think about the Christmas controversy. I tell him I understand both sides of the argument. But my answer seems to disappoint him. When I excuse myself to the restroom before taking our leave, Kerlin—who knows I am documenting my journeys and who, despite his vigorous mind, will pass away within the year—turns to Neil with zest and says as his final words to us, "Tell her to be kind to the South."

As a last gesture of respect and remembrance to the Jewish history of Natchitoches before hitting the road again, I make my way to the Kaffie-Frederick General Mercantile, the oldest general store in Louisiana. It's the only original Jewish business left in this town.

Like in most other places throughout the South, Jewish businessmen generally started off as peddlers, or "rolling store men," selling goods on foot or by horse and buggy, to black and white homes, from a pack on their back, a pushcart, or a horse, before the days of mail-order catalogs. They filled a niche where there generally was no other competition—in both merchandise sold and clientele served—and later opened their brick-and-mortar businesses. (Levi Strauss of Levi's jeans is one example of a peddler turned business owner.) After the Civil War, when farmers and sharecroppers needed help and many cotton brokerage firms had failed, these men extended what many believed was "life-saving credit" to big planters, to be paid at harvesting time, thus becoming "pivotal figures in cotton marketing and financing." Because of their networks of contacts of Jewish merchants in New York and other big cities in the East, Midwest, and South, these peddlers were able "to become conduits for funneling some much-needed cash into rural areas" and keep the cotton economy alive. By not always requiring cash payments, some posit that Jews got the reputation of being rich.

"They don't need the money," is how some people saw the lending of credit, according to Nat Finkelstein, whose father ran a store in the small town of Opp, Alabama. Finkelstein recalls that Jewish storeowners extended credit to African Americans and farmers, who "always paid their bills," though sometimes in the form of watermelons and tomatoes as well as cash.

Here in Natchitoches, Harris Kaffie from Germany (1845–1925) peddled and eventually opened up this general merchandise store with clothing, toys, farm tools, coffins, and more, also becoming a purveyor of goods to northern troops during the war. The store still features the two-story skylights that were the only source of light before electricity. I amble through tchotchkes and hardware in this time capsule, well-stocked and full of modern things, and then take Neil out for a famous Lasyone's Cajun Creole "meat pie," Natchitoches' only culinary specialty, advertised as "one of the 500 things to eat *before it's too late.*"

Back in Virginia, in the summer just before the 2016 presidential election, just before the gloom of the season coalesced at the Natchez cocktail party with Marci, we made the decision to go to Natchitoches to walk the landscape of its long-gone Jewish history, and for Kerlin. But more pressingly while in Louisiana, we decided to go to escape the storm.

Three days before arriving here in August 2016, Neil and I had decided to stroll through Cat Island National Wildlife Refuge in southern Louisiana to see the largest tree of any species east of the Sierra Nevada mountains: a bald cypress believed to be 1,500 years old with a huge root-like buttress, like a pair of hands holding it up with strong outstretched fingers.

We took a short walk on a trail through a muddy, flat bottomland hardwood forest, surrounded by a cypress-tupelo swamp. The refuge is a place prone to flooding, and the plant and animal species are all adapted to that periodic inundation; waterfowl and wading birds thrive there, and the alligators probably have the run of the place when the water comes in. We took the low-water road to the refuge because we could; it was dry and dusty and any misty rain we'd gotten that day had nearly evaporated before it reached the ground. Our map indicated that another road was available when the low-water bridge is closed due to high water.

The refuge website warned that access to the place becomes questionable when the Mississippi River reaches twenty feet on the Baton Rouge gauge and that visitors are advised to check the current river stages. None of that information really meant anything to us that afternoon.

As we walked, Neil looked up from the muddy grounds on either side of the dirt path, high into the trees, and pointed there. He told me to look at the white scum, which encircled each tree ten feet up, all along the half-mile route. He would tell me later that the sight of this mark made him uneasy, similar to how someone might feel in a slot canyon with a rainstorm coming. It was the high-water mark from previous floods, and we were essentially in the slot canyon, walking through the vast flash-flood zone without a care in the world.

In the six days since we left Virginia, it had rained on and off since we arrived in Louisiana on our road trip, and we had seen on the looping radar images on our cell phones the bands of precipitation emanating from four states and seeming to be headed to converge in southern Louisiana. We had learned, at the West Feliciana Historical Museum earlier that day, that near the current site of the Cat Island refuge was once a town called Bayou Sara, established in the 1790s, the largest antebellum Mississippi River port between New Orleans and Memphis for a time. The Great Flood of 1927 displaced nearly a million people throughout the state and flooded out Bayou Sara, when the river rose to its highest point ever and stayed that way for 153 days. That event was "the worst flood in the history of the United States"—though most people outside of the vicinity have never heard of it—overflowing the Mississippi River in eleven states and eventually leading Congress to pass the National Flood Control Act of 1928, which is what first authorized the US Army Corps of Engineers to construct projects to control flooding along the Mississippi and its tributaries. "Towns became deserts. Plantations became inland lakes," as it is remembered. And Bayou Sara's residents ultimately abandoned their town for the high ground of St. Francisville, New Orleans, or New York.

That evening, we returned for a second night to a simple cottage at the Butler Greenwood Plantation. By chance, we had chosen to stay in St. Francisville (population 2,300; 25 percent black, 74 percent white, 1 percent other), a half hour north of Baton Rouge in southern Louisiana, near a sharp bend of the Mississippi River. We didn't know at the time that St. Francisville was located on a narrow loess bluff, hills of wind-blown dust from the last glacial period, which had saved it during that 1927 flood. Several weeks after our visit, when maps were created to show where the water from the now-impending, no-name August storm had risen in southern Louisiana, St. Francisville would emerge as one of the only areas in West Feliciana Parish that remained unflooded. The innkeeper had placed us in a particular cottage, the Pool Pavilion—one of eight built in recent decades around the big house—because she said it was the best place to unload our car in the rain, which was falling when we arrived.

We spent the evening making plans for the next leg of our trip—south and west to Lafayette and then Lake Charles, where Neil would go birding closer to the Gulf Coast and I would try to visit synagogues. More rain was in the forecast, but no one knew that an "unprecedented," "deadly, record-setting flood," a once-in-a-thousand-year event was coming, as the news would report it (though not at the level of the 1927 flood). Hundreds of thousands of households—many of which had no flood insurance because their properties had never flooded but would wind up later registering with the Federal Emergency Management Agency (FEMA) for rental help or home repairs—were not preparing, worrying, or evacuating.

That night, for twelve hours, it rained with a vengeance. For six hours at least, flashes of nearby lightning tore through the windows; thunder vibrated the room like blasts of war. Rain pummeled the roof with an incessant beating. By midnight that night, the Baton Rouge gauge was up to almost eighteen feet. Two times during the night, each of our cell phones clanged with an emergency beacon that woke us up from our fitful slumber. The National Weather Service was warning us of flash flooding in our area.

I emailed the innkeeper at 7:00 a.m. the next morning to tell her: "Our phones are issuing emergency warnings. Is there something going on nearby?"

"Turn on the news," she said. "You might be able to get out if you leave now."

The day before the rain, we had planned to visit St. Francisville to meet a man who could tell us about a building that once was a temple and then wasn't and might be preserved. It was a vague arrangement. But upon meeting my contact and his wife, who traveled from Baton Rouge to have brunch with us, the day started falling into place.

After I discovered "sensation salad," a Baton Rouge specialty that would become my favorite dish in Louisiana, similar to Caesar salad, and Neil had his first crawfish étouffée, a common Cajun and Creole dish in these parts, the couple escorted us to meet a woman named Betsy Levasseur at an old, slate-roofed, giant brick high school.

Levasseur was a flash of light in bright pink and green silk against a backdrop of dark oak floors, wainscoting, and archways, waiting for us at the top of the inside front stairs. A huge divided stairway to the second floor rose up behind her. Dull, rusty, white pressed-tin ceilings; cracked plaster walls and their cascade of dust; and well-worn black chalkboards met us in each of eight giant rooms. Told by engineers that the building has "good bones" and could be renovated, Levasseur, who is president of the Freyhan Foundation, works toward the foundation's goal of restoring the Julius Freyhan High School, named for the town's Jewish benefactor, and turning it into a new cultural and conference center for the community. The renovated school will include the only museum in Louisiana to celebrate the history of Jewish families in this state. Beset by state budget troubles that are holding up the project's funding and without any large private donations, however, the only obvious renovation so far is the windows, installed by nearby inmates.

St. Francisville is nearly the classic-small-southern-town-with-Jews story, but on an even smaller scale than anywhere else we've been so far. In 1856 Julius Freyhan, originally from Germany in the second wave of Jewish immigration, was the first Jewish settler to arrive in St. Francisville, and he was like most other Jewish immigrants who came south: just a fellow looking to set up a business to fulfill the needs of the community. In this case and many cases throughout the Deep South, the need was to support the cotton trade.

He opened a dry goods store called Julius Freyhan & Co.; served in the Fourth Louisiana Infantry in the Civil War; then started a network of stores, cotton gins, and mills. As he made more money, he opened opera houses and saloons, donated funds toward levees and roads in the community, and helped struggling planters after the Civil War so they could get back on their feet. Ultimately, he left a sum of money upon his death to be used to build the parish's first public school: the place where we stood brainstorming about grants. The school, now listed on the National Register of Historic Places, was built in 1905 and operated until 1950—for white children only, as per custom.

St. Francisville is more than 70 percent white and located in a parish where nine families own 80 percent of the land. It's a small town with a few shops and restaurants on its one main street. Unlike most small, historic towns I have seen throughout Virginia, this community has no shuttered storefronts, no businesses that look like they had seen better days. Buildings are well maintained and businesses active, including a candy shop across the street from the historical society where Neil bought fudge during the off-season. The center of town is darling, with 146 well-preserved historic structures, including a densely packed grid of restored and colorful bungalows, cottages, and Greek Revival–style buildings. But it retains its legacy of segregation, because the black population, I am told, lives in the rural areas beyond the center of town, which, I am sad to say, I didn't even notice and where in the early part of the twentieth century, Julius Rosenwald had built the black residents a school.

A few steps from the Freyhan School is Temple Sinai, nearly all that's left from the once-thriving Jewish community. The temple is a compact, white, restored building reverberating with pyrotechnic color from its fourteen cathedral windows in an array of solid pinks, plums, greens, oranges, yellows, and royal blue, which looks very much like a small-town church I'd visited recently in the village of Norwood, Virginia. In the late 1800s and early 1900s, this was the place to be for the Jewish population in St. Francisville and Bayou Sara. The first congregation was recorded in 1892, with people gathering to worship in the Meyer Hotel and Julius Freyhan's opera house while they worked on getting this permanent building constructed.

The first generation of Jews got their wish when Temple Sinai was dedicated in St. Francisville in 1903, and the entire community celebrated it, Jewish and Christian alike. Rabbis, an Episcopal rector, and local judges presided over the opening event, with music and a children's procession. "It was an hour of rejoicing," the local paper reported. But by 1904, most members of the synagogue had left due to unsuccessful efforts to find a permanent rabbi, the tantalizing opportunities that could be found in bigger cities, and the damage wrought by the boll weevil on cotton crops, disrupting a critical link in the business webs of many Jewish businessmen. By 1921 the Presbyterian Church bought the building, and the temple is now owned by the Freyhan Foundation and used for weddings, concerts, and plays—and there's not a single Jewish person left. Visiting the temple felt like a birth and a death all at once.

That's when we made our way to the wildlife refuge, and it's a good thing we did because the point at which the low road met the high road (and the low-lying "black people area," as one white person told me) would wind up flooding from the storm, and the refuge would close indefinitely.

Before the storm, before our glimpse at the Great Flood of 1927, before our journey into the life and death of southern Jewish towns, there was the plantation tour. Neil opted out of this part of the trip, but I wanted to know more about plantation life, the cotton business, the root of the entire Civil War. So I spent a day at three of the remaining plantations along River Road between New Orleans and Baton Rouge, which snakes along the Mississippi River adjacent to the levee.

First there was Oak Alley, a multi-columned, white Greek Revival manor built in 1837, with its famous, giant live oak trees lining a walkway to the front door and where visitors trying to stay dry purchased white rain slickers with unfortunate pointed hoods. Then there was Laura, built in 1804, the yellow, baby blue, and red Louisiana-Creole-style manor of a sugar plantation once run by Creoles—white, native-born, French-speaking, Catholic, non-Anglo-Saxons, like Confederate general P. G. T. Beauregard, who ordered the first shots of the Civil War at Fort Sumter. Creoles blended influences from western Europeans, West Africans, and Native Americans and were discriminated against for their Frenchness by the Anglo Louisiana government. And finally there was the Whitney Plantation from 1790, a museum and memorial focused on the life of the enslaved people of Louisiana—the first museum in the United States dedicated solely to memorializing slavery, where the most staggering artifact is a slave pen, a rusted-out barred enclosure once used for overnighting or punishing up to twelve slaves while they awaited auction. The Whitney Plantation is planning to pay tribute to an 1811 armed slave revolt along River Road, known as the German Coast Uprising, with an installation of sixty-three severed-head sculptures; the leaders of the revolt were decapitated and their heads were then displayed on stakes as a warning to others.

In each southern town I visit, I still am blindsided by the legacy of white people who have justified slavery, segregation, the Holocaust, the KKK, lynchings, and all kinds of injustices toward people different than themselves, the opposite of what I imagine Jesus would do. But no place had more of a visceral effect on me than what we saw on River Road as we approached those plantations.

It's flat there, on the one side of River Road opposite the levee next to the river, like the ocean. Punctuating this landscape are run-down rural dwellings and junk heaps, areas of suburban sprawl, fancy new mansions built on fat concrete pillars that lift the homes two stories high to protect them from flooding, refineries and chemical plants with industrial loading docks, and some still-active plantations with their own private river ports to ship goods to market.

In 1827 River Road was described as "Everywhere thickly peopled by sugar planters, whose showy houses, gay piazzas, trim gardens, and numerous slave-villages, all clean and neat, gave an exceedingly thriving air to the river scenery." The area was once known as the "Gold Coast," home to five hundred plantations and two-thirds of the known millionaires in the United States in the decades prior to the Civil War. The place, therefore, also included parishes with some of the highest concentrations of enslaved people in the United States, one big area of oppression and violence on both sides of the river: St. Charles, 81.5 percent enslaved; Iberville, 73.8 percent; West Baton Rouge, 74.2 percent; West Feliciana, 83.5 percent; and Concordia, 91 percent, according to the 1860 census, all the way up to Arkansas and the Mississippi Delta. And yet, even while being the majority population, these black enslaved people were voiceless, voteless, landless, and rightsless.

In long, narrow rectangular- or pie-shaped wedges on tens of thousands of acres of land, emanating from both sides of the snaking river, these cotton, sugarcane, and indigo plantations were the engines of the southern economy and its precious "way of life"—all made possible by slavery. The slave owners, which were only about 25 percent of all white southerners, exerted their will on the entire region from positions of political and economic power. In fact, according to a Charleston historian I'll later meet, Robert Rosen, "in all the history of America, it is doubtful that a more absolutely powerful class or group ever ruled a city, colony, or state."

According to historian Bruce Levine, slave owners fell into several categories.

The largest group, possibly up to 75 percent of all slave owners, the ones merely considered "wealthy," owned four to six slaves. Even on this lowest rung, they were generally still not the people who fought in the Civil War. Those soldiers were some of the two-thirds to three-quarters of white southerners who were slaveless, the "Poor fellows . . . [who] did not understand in the least what they were fighting about," as a Charlestonian characterized them amid the ruins of that city after the war. Or, as one person wrote on the South Carolina Secessionist Party Facebook page, "Poor Southern White boys who never owned a slave but didn't want them being considered equal were led to death by Lee and Davis, traitors to the United States."

Next were the planters who owned at least twenty enslaved people (12 percent of all slave owners, or about 46,000 people), and these were the folks who owned most of the South's agricultural wealth. The "aristocracy" who owned fifty or more slaves (about 2.6 percent, or 10,000 people), who basically ran society, like Robert E. Lee and his wife, came next; and then the uber-aristocracy that owned at least a hundred humans (6.7 percent, or 3,000 people), like Jefferson Davis, who, after serving as a US congressman, US secretary of war, and US senator, became the president of the Confederacy.

The aristocracy (less than 1 percent of slave owners, or 300 people) followed in rank, which included some people who had served in the highest levels of the US government; they owned at least 250 enslaved people. At the Laura Creole plantation here, for example, more than 300 slaves once worked 12,000 acres of sugarcane. Finally, there's the insanely rich planters (way less than 1 percent, or about 50 individuals in the whole South), who owned at least 500 human beings; some owned 1,000 or 1,500 slaves. It's hard to imagine the mindset that would allow people to build their extreme wealth on the backs of the stolen labor of other humans who they treated worse than animals.

Neil and I had never seen sugarcane before, but on River Road we passed oceans of the bamboo-like plant as far as the eye could see, sloshing in the wind, sandwiching us against the levee. A grass, a reed, a crop that produces honey without bees, as the Persians once said many centuries ago. We had always heard that when slaves were sold "down the river," from the Upper South to Louisiana—like the people the Jesuits sold from Maryland to finance Georgetown University—it was the worst situation for them, the hardest and most dangerous work, and they dreaded it the most.

On some sugar plantations in this state, more than half the slaves died during childbirth due to their difficult lives. Slaves on sugarcane plantations were made to use broad, curved machetes to cut the cane and worked in the sugarcane mills and boiling houses that had slaves working in them around the clock. Scalding burns could disfigure or kill a person, fingers could be ground off, and arms could become trapped and have to be chopped off—although slave owners did try to keep their property alive, so they could keep producing. Sugarcane work "left an appalling legacy of death in its wake," according to the Whitney Plantation.

Aside from the dangers of the work itself, overseers or slave drivers were always feared as well. Although the French (and the Louisiana) Black Code seemed to prohibit the worst offenses against slaves—forbidding owners from torturing or mutilating them or separating married couples or mothers and children—white overseers, or white or black slave drivers working for absentee owners, had the run of those sugarcane plantations and were allowed to punish slaves harshly. Article 12 of the 1724 Louisiana Black Code, for example, allowed the whipping of slaves who were caught carrying weapons or heavy sticks, while Article 13 allowed slaves from different masters found gathering together to be whipped, branded, or even killed. First-offender runaway slaves could have their ears cut off and be branded; second offenders were hamstrung—literally, their hamstring would be cut—and were branded again. Three-time offenders were killed.

For twenty-five years while living in northern Virginia and visiting central and southwestern Virginia, I only have seen manor homes that no longer sit on huge acreages of land, no longer operate as working plantations. These buildings are tourist attractions now, museums and gardens, like George Washington's Mount Vernon (317 slaves at the time of his death), Thomas Jefferson's Monticello (607 slaves), and James Madison's Montpelier (100 slaves). They are event spaces, like Oatlands (133 slaves), where someone once suggested we hold our wedding; they are county parks; like Sully Plantation (40 slaves), where I took a watercolor class; they are national park sites, like Arlington House (200 slaves), the site of Arlington National Cemetery where my history-buff friend

Kim and I go walking. It's easy to see these sites as simply part of the current landscape. The lands around these former homes have been developed with strip malls and highways and other trappings of suburbia, erasing visual evidence of the history there. Tobacco, which once dominated the Virginia economy, is no longer farmed in any of these places. The land is not wide and vast.

By living in Virginia and being around rural people, I've become comfortable with the idea that poor whites didn't knowingly go fight to save the institution of slavery, even as their southern government decided to do so based on the economic benefit of preserving it. I can see how the idea of states' rights—and freedom from the overbearing industrial northern government that didn't respect the southern agricultural economy (even as it depended on it), the slower-paced and rural way of life, the customs and culture of a different region and a different people—is an alluring idea to rally around to preserve an ancestor's memory. I can also see how people who still celebrate their Confederate ancestry could feel misunderstood, especially by city people who generally do not relate to or value rural folk, their way of life, or the influences that shape their beliefs.

But there on River Road—with images reeling in my mind of lavish plantation mansions here in Natchez and other places I've visited, like the Kingsley Plantation and its twenty-five slave cabins made from oyster-shell concrete in St. Augustine, Florida—I saw those Louisiana plantations as *alive*—not as "living history" with docents but as real places of work. I observed with my own eyes land that revealed the large amount of work slaves had to perform in a day, and I felt the oppression of the blazing August sun. Hour after hour, day after day, year after year, generation after generation, these people, who happened to have black skin, would be forced under threat of violence, torture, separation of families, rape, deprivation, and death to work these fields, plantation after plantation, county after county, in all eleven states of the Confederacy. (Most northern states had abolished slavery during and following the American Revolution.) In their ordinances of secession, many states outlined outright, in clear, plain language, that slavery was their main reason for breaking away. Even among poor whites, an unacknowledged feeling of white superiority and not wanting to compete with blacks for work can underpin the whole states' rights crutch. Above all, looking at the Civil War from the point of view of a slave or a descendant of a slave, rather than a white person, can there have been any other reason for that war? When it was over, the slaves were free. The end.

On River Road, I felt the gears clicking back into place, righting themselves in my northern mind. That way of life, those states' rights I'd acceded to: they all boiled down to keeping slavery alive. Slavery drove banking, insurance, railroads, shipping—everything in the economy was powered by it, by "the human machines that worked to build the honor of someone else," as one historian put it. The Civil War—sometimes called the War Between the States, the War of Northern Aggression, the Second American Revolution, or the Great Unpleasantness by genteel southerners who euphemized the worst of their actions—would not have happened if the richer, more powerful white southerners hadn't insisted on keeping their slave-system alive, hadn't expected lives of such extreme decadence, hadn't put blinders on to finding options and opportunities for innovation for moving forward in a different way. It's not just that the history is written by the victors; there's just no other way to cover over the core truth of it once you witness the sheer size of these Deep South plantations in person and understand what humans did to one another here in support of their own greed and gluttony.

Many of the white people I speak with during these southern trips are descended from slave owners, and all around me are the ocean fields of crops where slave blood still runs through the soil.

There was one more element to this journey, some unfinished business to attend to from a previous trip. Before River Road, one other destination to keep it all real: the Andrew Goodman murder site—the murder I had grown up hearing about, the murder my mother taught me she felt symbolized the rage and evil inherent within the Deep South, a reason never to come here.

We detoured significantly from our path from Virginia to New Orleans—to Meridian, Mississippi, to follow Route 19 north toward Philadelphia, Mississippi, where on June 16, 1964, the Mt. Zion United Methodist Church, a place that hosted freedom meetings with the community and that was going to become a Freedom School that summer, had been fire-bombed in a case of KKK intimidation-arson. We took the route that Freedom Summer volunteer Andrew Goodman, my distant cousin, took with veteran Congress of Racial Equality (CORE) workers Michael Schwerner and James Chaney on June 21 to visit that church. This interracial group—a no-no in the South, especially with Chaney, a black man, riding in a car up front—left from the CORE office in Meridian and was arrested on the way out of Philadelphia, reportedly for speeding but more accurately because they were Jews and blacks engaging in black voter registration work. The local sheriff held the three men in jail until after dark and then released them to travel back to the office and to the KKK ambush the sheriff knew was waiting for them.

Neil and I followed that path—turning off the narrow, winding Route 19 onto what was once known as Rock Cut Road, where a historical marker now commemorates the martyrs. We had attempted this same journey last summer and had ended here, not realizing we had not driven far enough. This time, we continue on Rock Cut Road to an intersection of two sandy lanes now in a remote neighborhood of low-slung homes. The intersection is the murder site, where the three young men were shot at close range, a tragedy that horrified the nation—finally—because two of them were white and college educated. Then, like today—when white people like myself are starting to tune into the injustice of black deaths at the hands of whites—black injuries and deaths from slavery, segregation, and the fight for civil rights had yet not registered with the white-majority Americans.

The area is still wooded along the borders, with trashy, scraggly trees that are uninviting even on a sunny summer Sunday. And there, we would have found nothing of note, but thanks to a diligent blogger's scouting, we located what he reported: "A small cairn of stones, pine cones and flowers at the edge of the trees . . . [with] notes written to James, Michael and Andrew. Remembering them. Thanking them."

Weeks before he signed up for Freedom Summer, when segregationists in Congress attacked the Civil Rights Act, Goodman had written in a school paper, "The Senators could not persist in this polite debate over the future dignity of a human race if the white Northerners were not so shockingly apathetic." And then he went out and acted on his convictions. His memory demands that I keep asking myself what I will do to keep his mission alive.

Back inside in St. Francisville, dry and on high ground but anxious and stuck at the Butler Greenwood Plantation with no open road out, we became glued to the television and to our tablet searching for information on road conditions. All around us, the roads south to Baton Rouge and west to Lafayette and Lake Charles, where we had planned to go next, were flooded and closed. The road north, Route 61, was closed due to flooding at the Buffalo River. The unexpected storm brought unprecedented rainfall, flooding places that had not flooded in a generation, with waters rising faster than anyone expected, ruining lives for tens of thousands, including people who had started over after "the federal flood," which is what one person called Hurricane Katrina because of the belief that it was the fault of the US Army Corps of Engineers due to poor planning and engineering and "voodoo math."

By 5:00 p.m., the Baton Rouge gauge was at twenty feet. It had been raining all day and was expected to rain continuously for the next twenty-four hours. The pool next to our cottage overflowed onto the lawn where we were parked. The electricity flickered. I filled up the bathtub so that later, when our water pressure disappeared, we could use the water to flush toilets. The news said the storm was acting like a tropical depression, but it didn't originate from the tropics; it was homegrown, feeding itself off the intense humidity in the air and the water in the Gulf of Mexico, hovering steadily over southern Louisiana like a toilet that wouldn't stop flushing.

In St. Helena Parish, water reached the roofs. On the news, I heard people calling it a "FEMA-level event." The National Guard was out rescuing people in Youngsville. Alligators were swimming in the neighborhood streets and driveways of New Iberia and making their way into City Park in New Orleans. One man said it looked like a "horror movie." More than twenty inches of rain fell in the town of Central. The TV showed footage of SUVs getting washed away and disappearing into floodwaters. I texted my parents that I was OK and staying another night on high ground, but this disaster had not yet made national news, and so they didn't really know what I was talking about.

By midnight, the Baton Rouge gauge was at twenty-two feet. Since the rain began two nights before, twenty-two to twenty-six inches had fallen in towns nearby: Norwood, Livingston, Zachary.

At 6:00 a.m., the Baton Rouge gauge was at twenty-three feet, but the road conditions report showed an opening on Route 61 north. We dressed and packed quickly and steadily— me in my boots and raincoat and with my day pack that held a first-aid kit, food, water, money, identification, underwear, light fleeces, my yoga strap (for use as a rescue rope if necessary), and my waterproof cellphone case attached to me via carabiner (in the event our car became submerged and we needed to jump out and abandon everything). With Neil at the helm, we drove silently and tensely past the ditches on the Butler Greenwood Plantation that were dry the day before but then had filled with seven or eight feet of water, past the flooded

Buffalo River, like chocolate milk spilled out of its banks one mile wide, north to Natchez, Mississippi, where we crossed the Mississippi River and could finally let out our breath. Then we drove to the northwest part of Louisiana to Natchitoches and took a calm drive around the skinny, still waters of Cane River Lake, an old arm of the Red River, now an oxbow lake, far away from the disaster.

When I had come calling in Natchitoches—an outsider interested in that faraway and unknown place brimming with history, a northerner who had already traveled to ten other old Jewish communities of the South, places where either the temple is gone or in need of funds for maintenance and preservation, or the tombstones of pioneers, soldiers, and salesmen are broken, fallen, or faded from time and the elements—Mark Sutton seemed to see me as a spark of hope. Maybe I could find a way to elicit charitable giving for this obscure, unknown place from other Jews far away from here. Maybe my voice—the articles I would wind up writing, the people I would wind up connecting, the grants I would help communities apply for—could be like blowing a shofar on a mountaintop, an announcement, a mark of ceremony, a call to action.

Leaving Natchitoches for Felsenthal, Arkansas—named for four Jewish brothers who founded the town for their land and timber business in 1904—we pass a church sign that reads "God is an all-consuming fire." I realize then that for all this interest in Jewish history, I am simply not motivated to religion or deeds by God. God is not an all-consuming fire for me; nor am I seeking it to be one. I am driven by people, humans who walk or once walked the earth.

When I get home from this round of travels seeking lost Jewish stories in the Deep South, I will be inspired to research possible synagogues to join back at home. I'll look up options online, make calls, send emails; I will find out how many thousands of dollars it costs to become a member—since synagogues are private entities not funded by a central source—and pay into the building fund, or even the price to attend the High Holy Day services at several congregations near me in northern Virginia. And I will feel that familiar welling up of dread and a sense of obligation, the please-don't-make-me frightful feeling of my childhood. And I will wind up rejecting the idea of joining a large, traditional congregation in a metropolitan area once again, for its foreignness to my life and earthly needs. I am not seeking a building to pray in communally, nor dictated rituals and prayers, nor certain days of the week to be committed, nor order or answers or assurance, nor even spiritual awakenings. But I will keep visiting and supporting the temples of the lost places, where I don't feel any expectations, only welcoming, open arms.

Here, on these roads, in these towns, with the individuals I've been meeting, walking in the footsteps of history, this is what I value most, this is the spirit and life force that sustains me—connection to culture and people and the past, opening my eyes to new truths about humanity and the world, expanding my own little world. Being among southern Jews on their home soil has immersed me more in the world of Judaism than I've ever been, and I value that cultural connection, the kindness and generosity of others, the divine spirit and light that is within all of us under the sun. I bow to that. While I'm on this journey of discovery, I don't feel lost. In fact, more than ever before, I feel found.

TRUE SOUTH

The Delta, according to sociologist Rupert Vance in the 1930s, is "the deepest South." It is "the South's South," in the words of writer Richard Ford, or "Mississippi's Mississippi," as history professor John C. Willis puts it. Historian James Cobb referred to it as "the most southern place on earth." Because of these superlatives, I had to come to the Delta. It is, in fact, to be my culminating destination of the deepest Deep South.

We know right away there's something different about the Delta. The weather is weird.

We're in a place called Shaw, Mississippi, in a one-room, 324-square foot cottage on the edge of a corn and soybean farm, and all we see around us are tassel-top crops and sky. There is a small kitchen in the place, but cooking warms up the tiny room too much, so Neil makes our dinner on our camp stove on the screened-in porch under the shade of magnolias. He cooks up a dish new to us, rice grits, which we purchased at the gift shop of the world-class, history-of-American-music B. B. King Museum in nearby Indianola, an experience that from its humble speck-on-a-map location enlarged my world a hundredfold. These grits are small bits of white rice known as shorts, brokens, or middlins that are a byproduct of milling rice—once relegated to slaves—that become creamy and buttery like risotto when cooked. Despite the drenching humidity, Neil also makes a stew from bags of dehydrated backpacking vegetables and beans we've been carting around in our Subaru, fancifully envisioning we'd be able to save money sometimes by cooking our own food outdoors in the inferno. After snarfing

111

down our grub and in direct defiance of mothers' warnings everywhere, we head out to this Airbnb cabin's unexpected amenity: a swimming pool with an old, cracked-brick surround, to temper dinner's heat.

We hop in and wade around doing mini-laps in the leaf-covered water, giddy and splashing around like kids. But after about five minutes, a wind emerges, and the trees and bushes that form a fence around us begin to bend sideways and sway. The sky—just a moment ago a luscious sapphire—turns dishwater gray and then pea green, which back home would mean tornadoes. The waxy oval leaves of the magnolias start blowing off the trees into the pool, and then we see sparks of lightning in the distance and hear the low grumblings of thunder. We get out of the pool and wrap ourselves in towels and sit on lounge chairs and watch the sky get darker. We then move over to the back porch of the cottage overlooking a small field with hay bales in the distance, and we watch the sky become an abnormal, electrified hot pink. The crickets and katydids scream their chirps, louder than at our verdant Virginia home.

Neil points out that the clouds are hardly moving, whereas at home they'd be swift, with what seems like a thunderstorm coming in. He surmises that the wind blows lower to the ground here in Mississippi, on account of there being no elevation whatsoever—the great "horizontalness" of the Delta. He looks online at the radar imagery, and the storm is coming from the East and the South, from the Gulf of Mexico. I'm used to weather usually coming from the West. We watch and wait, spellbound by the unusual happenings, but the precipitation never does fall out of the sky here in Mississippi; it's all just winds from odd directions, nothing panning out as we expect, making us feel like we are truly in another world.

Like the travel writer Paul Theroux, I had always thought the term *the Delta* meant the river delta at the mouth of the Mississippi, where it pours into the Gulf of Mexico . . . which, once I got thinking about it I realized, would be in Louisiana, not Mississippi. That area may be the official Mississippi River delta in geologic terms (also called the "recent delta" because the river's moved so many times in the last two million years that there are other deltaic areas), but the Mississippi Delta, or Mississippi Delta Region, the storied mashup of music and history and poverty, is an entirely different place.

The Delta in this sense is the northwest section of Mississippi, between the Mississippi and Yazoo Rivers and between Vicksburg and the northern border of the state, a seven-thousand-square-mile alluvial floodplain of the Yazoo River that's said to be some of the most fertile soil in the world. At one time, the region commanded a higher price for the "long silky fiber" of its cotton than anywhere else—"nothing less than the answer to a cotton planter's prayers, [with] self-replenishing soil [that] could never be worn out," as one writer explained it. The Mississippi River generally marks the western border of the Delta, and the eastern edge is the clearly defined line where flatlands meet bluffs so that the whole area is about the size of New Jersey. It's an area designated by Congress as the Mississippi Delta National Heritage Area, with almost one hundred historically and musically significant locations that are part of the Mississippi Blues Trail. Highway 61 runs through the center of it, often called "The Blues Highway" because it travels from New Orleans through the Mississippi Delta to Memphis and St. Louis, the central geography of all American music. In between the river and bluffs, it's flat and low, close to sea level, with the Mississippi River dropping only seven inches per mile from Memphis to Vicksburg, so that when the river floods, it actually backs up into the Yazoo River and then into every bayou and creek in the Delta.

The Delta is different from much of the Deep South because, while being possibly the most southern place on earth, it was still nearly completely forested with thick leafy trees and canebrakes at the start of the Civil War. Only a small portion of land near the banks of the Mississippi and its tributaries had been cleared and drained for white plantations by their slaves even by the end of the war, with many of those plantations abandoned and growing back into forest. It's been said that in the 1880s, "the Yazoo Delta's millions of undrained acres were mainly a hardwood forest swamp ruled by snakes and black bears" and also wolves, panthers, and alligators.

We have come to the Mississippi Delta because it seems to be the most faraway, unexplored Deep South place we've encountered, and we have come for the Delta Blues experience Neil has added to our southern itinerary. I had added the landscape of the Civil Rights Movement to our trip on the way through the Alabama Black Belt, and the history of and intersections with African American history have wound up being the element I latch onto most in each of my journeys, what seems to be the most relevant and the most underdiscussed today. And so I agree that making a trip to the Delta is an essential part of the undertaking to experience some of the southern African American landscape, as the Delta is where the blues was born: the "one-of-a-kind, they-broke-the-mold, real-deal Delta blues," according to Roger Stolle, a Clarksdale blues lover and promoter.

It's a musical genre I knew nothing about and had never before been interested in. "Blues, as almost any Mississippian will tell you, came 'from the cotton patch,'" I learn from a historian of the area. This kernel of musical brilliance emerged after the Civil War, "created not just by black people but by the poorest, most marginal black people . . . [who] owned almost nothing and lived in virtual serfdom . . . [who were] not considered respectable enough to work as house servants for the whites or to hold responsible positions within their own communities." The genre would morph eventually into acid blues, African blues, boogie-woogie, Chicago blues, Detroit blues, dirty blues, electric blues, gospel blues, hill country blues, jump blues, Kansas City blues, Memphis blues, New Orleans blues, Piedmont blues, soul blues, St. Louis blues, swamp blues, Texas blues, West Coast blues, and so much more.

This quintessential American music, birthed from the hardship of slavery, started primarily as "an elaboration on work chants, 'sorrow' slave songs, and the lyrical and haunting 'field hollers,'" from spirituals sung with the rhythm of hand tools working plantations under the blazing sun, and it would become a powerful influence on—if not the root of—so much other made-in-America music: R & B, rock and roll, funk, jazz, zydeco, country, and hip-hop, all of which B. B. King's museum examines as it takes visitors on a state-of-the-art multimedia journey.

We have come to the Delta for a third reason too; as always, I've come to learn about the Jews. Having decidedly passed up large metropolitan areas during our southern excursions in favor of the small towns and rural places that seem more interesting, I've experienced in many ways only one part of the spectrum of southern Jewish life—the end of the story. These small, rural towns, I now realize, are the lost places, once brimming with Jewish infusion but now depleted. Although today there are 1.4 million Jews in the South (granted, a lot of northerners move to Florida), their locations have changed; 85 percent of all US Jews live in twenty metropolitan areas, including the southern cities of Atlanta, New Orleans, Memphis, Dallas, Charleston, and even Birmingham. And so what I have really wound up doing by keeping my itinerary rural and small-town has been exploring the places the Jews abandoned.

Because I have a penchant for life and times that are gone or nearly gone—somehow the interest and importance of a people and a place is heightened when there is so much at stake—I decided to continue the pattern of visiting the small, lost Jewish communities as we move forward. The Delta, as it turns out, may be the most sparsely Jewishly populated, formerly most Jewishly populated collection of small towns in the South. Luckily, it's easy to travel through the history of blues and Jews at the same time, though there is little indication that their histories ever crossed. The Jews and the blues are both so integral to each little Delta town, however, that they are inescapable—if you know where to look.

I don't need too much convincing to spend the next day reading and doing yoga at the little cabin by myself while Neil goes birding. Previously, at St. Catherine's Creek National Wildlife Refuge near Natchez, Neil was chased by an alligator—or, as he puts it, "felt compelled to run away quickly from a fast-moving alligator." This day, he'll hit up the Yazoo National Wildlife Refuge, where on a previous evening's reconnaissance there, we parked on a bridge over a bayou and were surrounded by a flock of about seventy cliff swallows, reeling and chirping and catching insects. Today, he sees thirty other species in five hours, including anhingas, white ibises, purple gallinules, and summer tanagers. He's satisfied with his birding foray, so we check out of our cottage and head to Greenwood, Mississippi, to begin our on-the-ground blues tour.

Our main purpose in Greenwood is to meet a stranger in town whom we again have just called at the last minute. This time, Neil makes the phone call to a number given in our blues guidebook. The man who answers, nameless, agrees to take us somewhere. He tells us to look for a 1980s Ford pickup coming into town. He will escort us to a piece of private land.

We want to see the home of Mississippi John Hurt (1892–1966), a country-blues singer and guitarist, a favorite of Neil's, and someone whose music I actually know and like, not too far afield from the folk music I grew up with. He's folky and acoustic, with delicate vocals and guitar fingerpicking. A sharecropper who began singing and fingerpicking and who recorded a couple of albums that were commercial failures in the 1920s, he wasn't famous for much of his life. But in the 1960s he was rediscovered. He played at the Newport Folk Festival and on the Johnny Carson show, becoming the "darling of the burgeoning folk music movement that had overtaken colleges and coffeehouses around the nation," as the Mississippi John Hurt Foundation describes him.

While we wait for our appointed meeting time, we spend about half an hour ambling around historic downtown Greenwood (population 14,000; 72 percent black, 26 percent white, 2 percent other). It's a town named for Greenwood LeFlore, a Choctaw chief who negotiated ceding Choctaw lands in Mississippi to the US government and was later elected Mississippi representative and senator. He became a planter and owned four hundred slaves, was friends with Jefferson Davis, and sided with the Union during the war. Altogether, he is the epitome of the South's complicated, can't-assume-anything-ness.

Greenwood is a small town with a bigger past, with low buildings, many of which are empty or abandoned, just like most other Delta towns we'll see. The town was once considered the "Cotton Capital of the World" when its shipping ports sent cotton to all the major markets of the time, and it was one of the cotton kingdoms that spurred the state to secede in January 1861 and proclaim: "Our position is thoroughly identified with the institution of slavery—the greatest material interest in the world. Its labor supplies the produce which constitutes by far the largest and most important portions of commerce in the world . . . a blow at slavery is a blow at commerce and civilization."

Greenwood is also where the White Citizens' Council was founded (though some argue Indianola), and it was the epicenter of civil rights protests and activity in the early to mid-1960s—where one black woman said, "There ain't nowhere in this whole world where a Negro has got it as bad," and a special report to the US Commission on Civil Rights wrote, "Blacks live in a 'reign of terror.'" Now the town might be making its way to a partial comeback—people are present on the sidewalk on a weekday at noon. New stores, like a gift shop selling Mississippi souvenirs, are evident, and it's got a fancy hotel, a spa, and a cooking school for tourists.

At the corner of Main and Market Streets where we park, I look up at the top of an old brick building and see "Klein & Blumenthal Department Store." Ah, Jews, I think to myself. Of course. When this type of store first opened here, a 1905 local newspaper article noted, "Greenwood is growing rapidly and substantially and will soon be the largest and prettiest city in Mississippi." We walk past the formerly Orthodox synagogue, which was built in 1923 and is still in use today. According to the Institute of Southern Jewish Life, the temple fills to capacity during High Holy Days, as people flock to Greenwood from other small towns throughout the Delta, which is a mostly empty agricultural area punctuated by clusters of life.

When we see the white truck barreling onto Main Street, we hop in our car and follow our mysterious guide through town and into the country, passing Goldberg's Shoes, "the Delta's premier shoe store" now and "one of the . . . highest class shoe stores" back in 1929, another example of a Jewish merchant.

The driver leads us on curvy dirt roads that have no name on our GPS, with blind turns that he takes so fast he practically comes up on two wheels. It's a wild ride, and both vehicles kick up red clay all the way. Neil says, "This guy drives like a redneck!" When I say that's insulting, he explains that the guy drives really fast on dirt roads, not worrying about oncoming traffic or us trying to follow him. We're going so fast trying to keep up with him that we pass the Greenwood Jewish Cemetery in the blink of an eye, the cemetery of the former Reform synagogue; all I see is the word "Jewish" on a metal sign, and we continue in this fashion until we come upon the bluffs marking the eastern edge of the Delta—the Carroll County hills, or Hill Country, with hilly forests that would not seem extraordinary except for the lack of elevation and mature trees anywhere else we've been in the Delta.

Mississippi John Hurt's shotgun shack sits three miles from its original location, in the backyard of his granddaughter's property. Our guide is connected with her somehow. He doesn't say much. When he gets out of his truck, we see that he is a tall, lanky, muscular, and handsome chestnut-skinned man in a white T-shirt and work pants, and we remark on his cool truck, which we learn is one of many he collects. He unlocks the front door of the tar-papered shack, hiked up on cinderblocks in the grass, turns on the lights, and then sets himself down on a lawn chair on the front porch with his long legs stretched out in front of him and a can of Raid in his hand. While inside, where it is lit by only a few bare bulbs dangling from the ceiling, we check out the letters, photos, old record albums, coffee cans, railroad spikes, and other memorabilia donated by fans, and he's on the porch nonchalantly spraying the air with hornet spray every thirty seconds, trying to hit the hornets encircling him and flying in and out of the house. We remark that city people (like me) usually freak out over wasps, but he says, "I just sit here. I just sit here," over and over, like a mantra, as he sprays them to death without concern. Inside, it's black and dingy and everything's yellowed and hot, so we don't stay long. We make small talk and say quick goodbyes amid the hornets, and then he takes off, and we're on our own for getting out of there.

We spend the next two nights in our own shotgun shack, about the size of Hurt's home, on the outskirts of Clarksdale at the Shack Up Inn. It's a collection of twenty-five former sharecropper shacks that have been reclaimed from other plantations in Mississippi and made into shabby-chic abodes. Ours is called Legend and was one of the compound's first structures, moved from the nearby town of Tutwiler. Structurally sound and refurbished, the shack's peeling and mismatched paint, yellowed newspaper hung as wallpaper, bead board paneling, and thrift-shop furniture make it much more palatable than the Hurt home. Blues radio comes in through the TV, the lobby building offers free moon pies, and the property is chock full of southern Americana like rusty old Fords and artsy bottle trees.

The land on which the buildings are located was once the Hopson Plantation—formerly about 3,500 acres owned by the Hopson Planting Company. It's a key site on the Mississippi Blues Trail. Here, in 1944, for the first time ever, a cotton crop was commercially produced entirely by machinery, from planting to baling. While Eli Whitney's cotton gin of 1793 had increased the speed of cotton processing by 4,900 percent, meaning slaves had to work harder and faster to pick as much cotton as the gins could handle, the complete mechanization of the cotton process also provided only good news for planters and only bad news for tenant farmers and sharecroppers. The tenant farmers and sharecroppers, mostly all black, now faced reduced demand for their labor, backbreaking work that they hated but needed.

Tenant farming and sharecropping weren't great for them, but the work was often all freed slaves had. After the Civil War, many white farmers and former planters were in debt and too poor to pay workers; former slaves didn't own any land, still lived in slave quarters, and needed work. The two groups worked out an arrangement: on small plots of whites' land that owners mortgaged for supplies, black farmers did the work of the land. Tenant farmers, allowed to farm the land however they wished with their own mules and equipment, paid the landowner rent for the land and house from the sales of their crops. Sharecroppers rented the land and house but also all the animals, equipment, and everything else they needed to farm crops of the landowner's choosing and were paid with a share of the crop. Tenant farmers and sharecroppers ran 87 percent of farms in the Delta by 1910.

Both systems often required the black field laborers to buy personal supplies from commissary stores, using the plantation's own printed money in which farmers were paid instead of real cash. Prices in these stores, even in real money, were often much higher than those at nearby town stores. Sometimes crops failed. No matter how hard they worked, farmers often ended up in constant debt to landowners. "It was never enough," wrote John Lewis, civil rights activist and Georgia congressman, in his memoir, a man who worked the fields with his family as a child. "I could see that from the beginning. Even a six-year-old could tell that this sharecropper's life was nothing but a bottomless pit." He describes working eight to ten hours a day, stooping over to pick cotton. "Your back would be on fire," and "fingertips [would be] chewed ragged and bloody."

These factors, as well as machinery that reduced the need for labor, contributed to the Great Migration between 1910 and 1970, when six million southern black people moved north, where labor was needed, to find a better life.

Of course, they also left because of legally and societally sanctioned segregation. And because of continued lynchings, extrajudicial killings—sometimes made into public spectacles

like carnivals "to excite a festive atmosphere"—usually of innocent people who had merely crossed or were perceived to have
crossed some racial boundary. There were around four thousand
lynchings officially recorded throughout the South between
1877 and 1968, with the highest number (581) in Mississippi.
There were likely many more lynchings that went unrecorded,
including instances of burning people alive, dismemberment,
and other forms of torture and killing.

While providing blacks more protection from the law, the
North wasn't all milk and honey either, as many middle-class
whites "believed they had fulfilled their obligation to former
slaves by fighting for the Union" and "only grudgingly endorsed
black voting rights," as one scholar wrote. Many northerners
were just as prejudiced as any southerner could be. It was dangerous to be a black person in the North in many places, and
rights were limited either through federal, state, or local law
or policy, societal "custom," and intimidation. For example,
between 1890 (after Reconstruction had elevated blacks, which
thoroughly rattled whites) and 1940, the majority of all incor-
porated areas, such as towns and suburbs outside the heart of
the South, excluded African Americans; these were known as
"sundown towns," often with signs saying "Nigger, don't let the
sun go down on you here." You didn't want to find out what
would happen if you violated that code.

Also from the 1930s to the 1960s, the home-mortgage
market and the Federal Housing Administration largely made
black people and the neighborhoods where they wanted to
buy homes ineligible for mortgages in a racial policy known as
"redlining." As Ta-Nehisi Coats puts it in his landmark article
in The Atlantic, "The Case for Reparations," "In the North,
legislatures, mayors, civic associations, banks, and citizens all
colluded to pin black people into ghettos, where they were over-
crowded, overcharged, and undereducated. Businesses discriminated against them, awarding them the worst jobs and the worst
wages. Police brutalized them in the streets. And the notion
that black lives, black bodies, and black wealth were rightful
targets remained deeply rooted in the broader society." In other

words, in contrast to so many white people's ignorant blaming
of blacks for their own condition of living in poor inner-city
areas, a comment I've heard numerous times but never had the
words or facts to counter, white people engineered these places
and pushed them there in the first place.

Clarksdale is in the heart of so much staggering racial and
political history of the South, but the music is what most people
come here for now, and they stay at the shacks for the proximity to the blues. Clarksdale is where, the story goes, Robert
Johnson, "the most potent legend in the blues," sold his soul
to the devil to learn how to play his brilliant guitar at "the
crossroads." This famous crossroads really could be any major
crossroads in any Delta town but is said to be the intersection
of two highways, Route 61 and Route 49, where Abe's Bar-B-Q
now stands.

So to pass the daytime hours waiting for nighttime blues, we
continue the Jewish tour. I arranged in advance to have lunch
with Arnold Himelstein and Louis Rhoden, two of fewer than
ten Jews of Clarksdale (population 17,000; 81 percent black,
17 percent white, 2 percent other) and to spend the day exploring with Neil what has, I realize now, become the same story
of small-town southern Jewish history nearly everywhere: the
Jews were here; they were merchants and civic leaders; opportunities moved elsewhere, and so did they. Himelstein, a quiet
man with thin lips who's nearing retirement, is one of five
or so Clarksdale-born Jews who remain, down from about
four hundred Jewish people at the end of the 1930s. When the
Torah for the first synagogue here arrived by train in 1910,
he says, the whole community—Jews and non-Jews—came
out for a welcoming parade, each paying a few dollars to carry
it a few steps as a form of honor and assistance. The Jews of the
community were established enough to start a fraternal organization, a Ladies' Aid Society, a Temple Sisterhood organization, a Jewish girls' club, and a youth group, and to throw
an annual New Year's ball. Now, according to these men and a
town historian, hardly anyone in town knows anything about
the history of the Jews here.

To honor this history, Neil and I walk past the still-operating Shankerman's Men's Ware Store on Yazoo Avenue and the empty storefront of Okuns, Rhoden's family's shoe store, now defunct. As in many other towns, Okuns sold to both black and white customers. Unlike other white-owned stores, many of the Jewish stores were full of black customers. In fact, 98 percent of Okuns's customers, Rhoden says, were black. "If you're going to be in business, you need to be in business for whoever comes into your stores," he tells me plainly. Unlike white storeowners, "The Jew was the merchant who said 'mister' to blacks," according to one scholar. Jews allowed blacks to try on ready-to-wear clothes without being required to buy them. Following the highest level of rabbi-philosopher Maimonides's eight levels of charity—anticipating a person's needs and assisting the person in need by strengthening his hand until he need no longer depend on others—Jews also were the only ones who employed blacks in their stores "to teach them the skills that they would need to open their own businesses."

We also walk past the first synagogue in Clarksdale, a small stucco house, now a private home, built with free prison labor from the community. Then we drive to the Jewish cemetery, which is across from a Sonic burger joint. The cemetery is mowed often and well-kept, thanks to Rhoden's attention and a perpetual fund, and then we see the larger 1929 Moorish-style synagogue in a quaint residential neighborhood that held both Reform and Orthodox services when the community demanded both; it closed in 2003 and was sold to a black church, according to Rhoden. Then, having established with the two gentlemen over lunch that the only connection they know of between the Jews and the blues of the Delta is that Jewish blues saxophonist and poet Dick Lourie plays in blues festivals in Clarksdale each year, our first night of blues starts that evening at Ground Zero, a blues club in Clarksdale.

The place I had really wanted to visit was Po' Monkey's, a "patched-up sharecropper shack," as one reporter described it, that was the last of the true, rural house-party-type juke (or jook) joints in the area. Juke joint, which means a makeshift social

club, is a term coined from the African-influenced Gullah dialect word for "a Negro pleasure house," where black workers "dance, drink and gamble," in the words of Zora Neale
Hurston, and have been welcoming to tourists. But just a few
months before we arrived, owner Willie "Po' Monkey" Seaberry
died of a heart attack. So instead, we find ourselves at Ground
Zero, co-owned by the actor Morgan Freeman, a warehouse-
like restaurant with plastic tablecloths, all the fried food you
could ever imagine, and a stage. The band is made up of white
folks playing halfway-decent, blues-inspired rock and roll, but
after about an hour and a half, I feel disappointed that the band
and audience are nearly entirely white and touristy, and a group
of white college students has descended on the place, jostling
together near the stage like it's the 1980s. Though I understand that white Americans (including me and Neil)—and
visitors from all over the globe—come to Clarksdale for blues
and have adopted blues as their own and help keep the live-
music scene alive for working musicians, this place has an
inauthentic feel about it. After we finish our beers, fried pickles, and fried green tomato sandwiches, we decide to head out.

Turns out our car is parked in front of what we learn is the
new Crossroads Cultural Arts Center, and music is emanating
from the open front door. We walk over to the unmarked building where people, black and white, are beckoning us in. There's
no cover charge, they say, and there's free beer and water set
up in neat buckets. We see a small, lit-up stage and a cavernous
room, nearly empty, with large round banquet tables, like someone was throwing a party but nobody came. Neil immediately
recognizes the face, voice, and harmonica playing of Watermelon Slim, a light-skinned musician whose band received seventeen Blues Music Award nominations. We actually have his
CDs at home. I am drawn immediately to his sound, and he's
playing along with a blond-haired, chubby-faced local guitar
player and singer whose drum set says "Lightnin Malcom."

So, yes, it appears to be two local white dudes playing some
killer blues. Then a man of color comes out from the sparse
audience and decides to play drums, and a heavily bearded

man who people say is from Spain gets called out from the audience to play steel guitar, and all of a sudden, we have what seems like the most awesome and authentic pickup blues band my tiny world of mostly never-listened-to-blues-before has ever heard, and I'm entranced. Within a half hour of listening to the rhythmic, chanting melodies, an "ingeniously systematic musical language," "a fusion of music and poetry accomplished at a very high emotional temperature," according to music critic Robert Palmer, I feel like I am high on drugs. I am blissed out and peaceful, the way I imagine a Dead Head feels grooving to a Grateful Dead jam. I close my eyes in the blue light, and I am floating.

All I knew of the Mississippi Delta before visiting there was from an article I read in the *Washington Post*. It's about Tunica, a community at the northern part of the Delta, and its great poverty; about how the whites' idea of bringing casinos to the area in the 1990s would benefit everybody, but really it only benefited the whites. "Instead of funding skills training and providing programs for the vulnerable, they poured money into a riverfront wedding hall, an Olympic-size indoor swimming pool and a golf course designed by a former PGA Tour pro," according to the article. African Americans, who when enslaved made up 79.8 percent of the population in 1860 and now constitute 75 percent of the community, still live in shacks; one woman the article profiled worried that her rotted, mildewed house was literally sinking into the mud.

The article cites Tunica's poverty rate of 30 percent, twice the national average; the public high school's 97 percent black student population and 57 percent graduation rate, compared with 79 percent nationally; the fact that one in four people does not have a bank account; and that the average life span in Tunica is sixty-seven for men and seventy-three for women, which is shorter than nearly anywhere else in the United States. Christopher Masingill, a co-leader of the Delta Regional Authority, an economic development agency that works on infrastructure, workforce, small business, and family issues in an eight-state region (which, a year and a half later, the new US president will propose defunding), says matter-of-factly: "You can't out-poor the Delta."

But we never see the true Tunica on our travels in the Delta. For the most part, we never see the real, behind-the-curtain life of any Delta town, the non-touristy places, the down-and-out places. What we see from the highway one summer in the Delta are the sweeping waves of agricultural plantations, vegetation swaying in the sun. In the winter, we find rows of fallow soil like wavy cornrows of abstract art, lands of "some of the nation's richest white farmers." We also see entrances to casinos, which, as one scholar says, "distracts visitors from the prevailing hopelessness of the rural poor." In towns, we see the city centers, where there are restaurants, museums, and clubs advertised in guidebooks and where money is invested for tourism. To reach some of our destinations, we've driven through unfrequented neighborhoods, as the GPS sends us on back roads we would not normally travel on, but we haven't spent substantial time in any black or white neighborhood. In the Delta, the closest we get to a real, non-touristy area where people live is when we walk, literally, to the other side of the train tracks for a couple of deserted blocks to get to Red's.

Red's is the other authentic juke joint, and here at least one local African American person—an elderly lady in a pink polyester dress—taps her feet to the music of African American musician Robert "Bilbo" Walker, who is celebrating his eightieth birthday this night in a shiny suit and shoes with gold heels amid a mostly white crowd of hard-core blues lovers. Even here, I recognize that what I'm really doing in the South is having a whitewashed experience.

It's in Greenville (population 32,000; 80 percent black, 17 percent white, 3 percent other), about seventy miles southwest of Clarksdale, where we get more of a taste of the real deal. Greenville (pronounced "green-vul") is where the rising waters of the Great Flood of 1927 broke through one of two levees and inundated the town up to its rooftops and where a "sea of water in the commercial and residential areas of down-town Greenville . . . [made] the town resemble . . . Venice, Italy, with its canals." In that emergency, while steamboats took white women safely away to other cities, community leaders would not allow black families to evacuate, making them stay on the levee to work without pay in flood-control recovery efforts and even threatening to withhold the food that the Red Cross was bringing in if they didn't participate.

Amid this backdrop we find ourselves again the only white guests at our hotel for the night; the place is full of families in town for a family reunion. I pull one of my last-minute phone calls, and Benjy Nelken immediately invites us, on a Sunday morning, to meet him at the Greenville History Museum down-town, which is also his real estate office.

Nelken, a tall, confident, and outspoken gray-haired man who seems to be of retirement age, is part of one of fifty Jew-ish families left in Greenville, down from a high of seven hun-dred individuals in 1968, and calls himself a "curious curator." He founded and operates this collection of photos, signage, machines, equipment, artifacts, and memorabilia dating from 1838 to the present. The museum draws more than 1,500 visi-tors per year. Its purpose is to "bring back to life the city of Greenville during a period of history that has been described as 'the golden years'" (golden years if you're white, I think to myself), from the end of the nineteenth century to the 1970s, when it was known as the "Queen City of the Mississippi Delta."

Black-and-white photographs from those days show the town crowded with people, wearing dresses and blazers and shopping at dozens of busy stores with awnings and signs of all shapes and sizes that extend for blocks. Greenville looked like a happening place back when it served as a commercial center for the Delta and the large cotton farms that supported the area's economy. A creative display of letterhead envelopes in the museum showcases the handful of mom-and-pop busi-nesses that once existed in this town. An antique "hot tamale" machine is on display, used for making the Delta's long-standing elemental food: a simmered, cornmeal wrapped, meat-filled bundle, which food writer Calvin Trillin describes as "a third cousin once removed of the Mexican tamale." (I insisted that Neil taste one in Indianola, despite his heartburn, and even this vegetarian took a bite; neither of us foodies was that impressed.)

Today Greenville's main drag looks like nearly any other small "once-was" main street in the South—no foot traffic. But it's Sunday, so I imagine the town's 135 churches are full. It's not quite seedy in broad daylight but has enough run-down or empty storefronts for us to know it once had a heyday and now's not it. Nelken says that most crime in the community is black-on-black and related to gangs. (One black resident, a retired bus driver we meet in a park later in the day, echoes this assessment, as he was once knifed during a gang initiation rite on his bus.) Nelken says that the public schools, 99.9 percent black, are awful and that the 0.01 percent of other blacks and all the whites send their kids to private schools instead, furthering the segregation that has always existed in this state. (Nearly a year after our visit, a federal court will order the nearby and similarly situated town of Cleveland, Mississippi, to combine its "naturally" separate all-white and all-black middle and high schools, ending a five-decade legal battle about integration.) Despite the poverty in Greenville, the city calls itself "the heart and soul of the Delta."

This white–black education dichotomy is an issue throughout Mississippi and other areas of the country: when the Supreme Court handed down *Brown v. the Board of Education* in 1954, public schools were ordered to integrate, so whites found a workaround by starting private schools for themselves and either left the poorly funded, generally ignored public schools to the black population or, in the case of Prince Edward County in Virginia in 1959, they just closed the public school system altogether. (Some people believe that echoes of this white-created problem of underfunded, poor-performing public schools, ongoing since the '50s, is being exacerbated by US Department of Education secretary Betsy DeVos's 2017 promotion of school choice, or vouchers; taxpayer funds are siphoned away from public schools, thus undermining them, and can be used to send children to private, charter, or parochial schools.) In 1973 the Supreme Court decided that education is not a fundamental right and that the Constitution does not require equal education expenditures within a state, a decision that had "the effect of locking minority and poor children who live in low-income areas into inferior schools." Also, in 1974, the court blocked citywide plans for busing to desegregate urban schools with high-minority populations, leaving many racially isolated urban districts.

Though some notable black authors like Richard Wright and Natasha Trethewey have come from Mississippi, the decades of lost potential in its neglected black citizens is evident in its (black) public schools in Mississippi, which have been listed among the lowest performing in the nation. The state, meanwhile, proudly boasts of producing more notable (white) authors than any other state: William Faulkner, John Grisham, Eudora Welty, Tennessee Williams, Richard Ford, and Rick Bass. Greenville is the birthplace of Shelby Foote (who is half Jewish), author of a trilogy on the Civil War, made famous by Ken Burns's PBS miniseries on the Civil War, as well as William Percy, son of influential former senator LeRoy Percy—the guy who used his standing and leadership among the white community to run the Klan out of Greenville in 1922. Nelken describes that moment in history as: "He fought all the shit-ass governors and racists to protect our black friends."

Even with its low points, "Greenville has always been an oasis of tolerance," according to Nelken. In fact, he says, it has a reputation of being the most open-minded city in the state. (Oxford, Mississippi, might disagree, however. On one trip, when I visited there with two friends in 2017 immediately after the new presidential administration tried to issue its first executive order banning immigrants from seven Muslim nations, the Oxford Mosque, the Oxford Muslim Society, the Ole Miss Muslim Student Association, and a nonprofit called Change Mississippi hosted a "Meet Your Neighbors" day. It featured Middle Eastern food, and women in head scarves, veils, and burkas answered questions about the Muslim faith, culture, food, and language to educate the community, which came out in force.)

But Greenville is considered to have always had an international population—that is, Italians and Chinese and the largest population of Jews in the state. The first mayor here was a Wilszensky, and Stein Mart, the chain of department stores founded by Sam Stein, a Russian Jewish immigrant, started here. Alexander and Goldstein Streets were named after prominent Jews. Wherever there was cotton, there was business, and wherever there was business to be had, there were Jews willing to sell and broker goods. By 1920 the Delta was "a plantation empire." As writer and Delta native David L. Cohn wrote in the 1960s, "Cotton is more than a crop in the Delta. It is a form of mysticism. It is a religion and a way of life. Cotton is omnipresent here as a god is omnipresent. It is omnipotent as a god is omnipotent, giving life and taking life away."

After perusing Nelken's history museum, we follow him across the street to the Hebrew Union Temple, once the state's largest synagogue, built in 1880 on land donated by a non-Jewish female plantation owner. Inside, Nelken and two others have organized a museum of memorabilia from the Jewish community, the Goldstein, Nelken, & Solomon Century of History Museum, recording the history of Jewish residents in Greenville since 1867. The Jewish community was so respected and integrated in Greenville in 1887 that a non-Jew recorded in his diary that a full-dress ball at the local Jewish club was "the largest public ball we have ever had."

We peruse the museum quickly and then take ourselves to the Jewish cemetery on the way out of town, large and full of Cohns, Goldbergs, Isenbergs, Pohls, and other Jewish names. As in many cemeteries in the South, there were three sections: one for blacks, one for whites, and a third for Jews. But Greenville had Chinese people too, who made their mark on the Delta with grocery stores. Although they reportedly had their own cemetery nearby, with stones carved in Chinese characters, at some point they had to be buried somewhere else and, apparently, no one knew how to racially classify Chinese people. Jews were the only other "nonwhite" whites, so in great humorous irony to me—because Jews have a special relationship with the Chinese in the Northeast, both being non-Christian minorities and Jews commonly eating out at Chinese restaurants on Christmas and year-round too—it is said that some Chinese people are buried in the Jewish section as well. The two groups share the same philosophy for their families' trajectory here: "Work hard, send your kids to college, watch them move away."

As it turns out, Jewish people in the Delta love Chinese food too; some even hold a Seder on the second night of Passover at a Chinese restaurant. This place is so unlike the places I've lived, and yet—with all the hundreds of Jewish family meals at Chinese restaurants over the course of my life under my belt, the way my dad and stepmom and their Jewish friends have become such weekly year-after-year regulars at their favorite Chinese restaurants that they get invited to the owners' weddings and are given gifts of free spicy lobsters and desserts brought to the table on a regular basis—I relate to the Jewish way here; I feel the Jewish forces connecting us no matter where I go.

The term *the Delta*, I learned, generally refers to the Mississippi side of the river, but the Delta exists on the Arkansas side as well—culturally, musically, and geologically. In fact, by 1930 the Arkansas Delta town of Helena "was the Delta's liveliest blues center"—"a little Chicago," as one resident said. Arkansas, too, was settled by a variety of enterprising European Jews, beginning in 1825. The Arkansas Delta gets its share of superlatives as well; author Willard B. Gatewood Jr. calls that area "the deepest of the Deep South." Helena is also now the poorest town in the second-poorest state in the country. No one I know has ever visited Mississippi or the Mississippi Delta, but at least they might have heard of it. Most people

I know probably have never heard of or uttered the words *Arkansas Delta*. Clearly, I had to go there.

A few months prior to this trip, I had read an article about a hundred-year-old man named David Solomon who was the last Jewish person in Helena (population 11,000; 75 percent black, 24 percent white, 1 percent other). I wanted to meet him, of course. He was born in Helena, and the town threw him a hundredth birthday party, attended by hundreds of people. By the time I tried to contact him, however, he was no longer using email, and a phone number I tried calling never got answered. So I searched his sons online and found out one of them worked in Washington, DC—with a good friend of mine—and that's how I wound up giving Lafe Solomon a ring.

I could tell that Lafe, a high-up public servant in the federal government for forty years and now retired, was a true southerner, not only from his warm demeanor and quick laugh but because he told me he'd fly out from DC to meet me when I planned to be in Helena and give me a tour of Jewish Helena himself. So, when the time came, Neil and I headed over the Mississippi River from Clarksdale to the place where the elder Solomon spent his life as a local attorney.

We meet Lafe at the former train station, now the Delta Cultural Center, and get into his car. Lafe's a straight shooter, and when he shares what life was like growing up in Helena in the 1950s and '60s, he says it without remorse, without irony, and without interpretation; this was just the way things were. He seems to shrug his shoulders, atop his tall frame, at the unbelievability at some of what he experienced. The first thing Lafe points out is Cherry Street, which he says was the "main white street" where all the Jewish people had their stores, like Meyer's department store, and the Danzinger store, and his own family's Ware & Solomon department store. One block away, parallel, was "the main black street," which he says is where all the blacks had their stores and nightclubs. While blacks and whites shopped together and went to the same movie theaters together (through different doors and with different seating areas in the days of Jim Crow), they never ate together in the

same restaurants, never spent time in each other's neighborhoods (the blacks' being on the other side of the levee), and,
"They had their Christmas parade down their street each year,
and we had our Christmas parade down our street, and neither
of us went to each other's," he says with amazement. "I never
even knew that world existed."

The main business district is mostly dead, with dilapidated
brick buildings still painted with old-time ads like a black
mammy character saying "Home Cooking Served Daily" and a
newly collapsed building with bricks in a heap in the middle of
the street; the only open storefronts appear to be a pizza restaurant and an upscale gift shop where I wind up dropping nineteen dollars for a made-in-Helena leather-scented candle as a
gift for a friend.

After scanning the remains of this town, Lafe drives us past
Temple Beth El. Built in 1880, closed in 2006, it's now owned
by the state and used for lectures and events. Back when he was
a kid, he tells us, the Jewish people of Helena were so reformed
that services and prayers were spoken entirely in English, with
no Hebrew whatsoever, and children could receive a confirma-
tion at the temple but not a bar or bat mitzvah. This level of
relaxed or accommodating rules, or traditions, of Judaism was
beyond any Reform-ness I'd ever heard of.

Passovers were held as community Seders at the Jewish
social club rather than in individual homes, and Jews from
a wide Delta region came to Helena for services for the High
Holy Days. While Rosh Hashanah typically involves a large
family meal to celebrate the new year, Yom Kippur, the day
of atonement, is a day of fasting. Here in Helena, however—
even topping the Jewish vice in Natchez—Mrs. Solomon, Lafe's
mother, would hold a Yom Kippur luncheon, the complete
antithesis of the day. Even the rabbi attended. "People who
traveled from out of town had to eat!" Lafe explained on behalf
of his late mother.

As we stroll over to the Mississippi River on a boardwalk,
twenty-five feet above the floodplain, Lafe smiles widely and
laughs when he describes growing up here as "idyllic," telling

us how he and his brothers and friends would leave the house in the morning on bikes, spend the day building forts in the kudzu vine, and not return home until dark. He says he never experienced any anti-Semitism until he moved to Washington, DC. But his parents always told him and his brothers to leave the town when they could, as other Jewish parents told their children. The local high school had no sciences or foreign languages, he says, so his parents sent them away to boarding school at age thirteen. In an earlier interview with writer Rex Nelson, David Solomon indicated, before his decline, that he did not—unlike so many other Jews in other towns—bemoan the closing of the synagogue and the dwindling Jewish population. "He simply views it as things having come full circle," Nelson reported. "The Delta Jews, after all, met in private homes in the 1800s [before there were any temples]. By the 21st century, they were meeting in private homes once again."

It seems to be part of the circle of life of Jews in the South. They're like matter; they don't necessarily disappear, they just move. Like Lafe and his brothers: far away from the Delta.

I miss the Delta after I leave, heading north to Memphis and then back to Virginia. I miss the vast sunsets across fields unobstructed by buildings or telecommunications or transportation, the silhouettes of farm equipment against the light. I miss the quiet.

I wonder often whether the Delta is or was or was not "the most southern place on earth." How do I define "most southern"? Should I define it by how I perceive the heat, though locals don't necessarily agree? In Archery, Georgia, where we walked the grounds of Jimmy Carter's boyhood farm in the early days of our very first trip, in sweltering ninety-one-degree heat, with inappropriate wicking polypropylene shirts matted against our bodies like plastic bags, a National Park Service ranger wearing dark long sleeves, denim overalls, and boots did not feel our pain. "It's not even a hot day," he quipped. Andersonville prison was even hotter. Neil and I—hikers who can usually cover ten miles in a day—could not get a quarter way around the mile-long perimeter of the prison yard before I thought I was going to die of heatstroke. When we spent a few days in and around Jackson, Mississippi, the news reported more than 37 consecutive days reached higher than 90 degrees, and 30 days had been above 95; when we arrived, it was 103. Men were wearing featherlight seersucker suits, and I understood why. But both of my trips to the Delta were cool and pleasant. Perfect, really.

Perhaps I could define what's "most southern" by the food. The stereotype about the South is that everything is fried, and by the time we reached the Delta, I'd eaten nearly every fried vegetable known to man: fried peanuts and fried green beans in Plains, Georgia; fried pickles and fried eggplant in Americus, Georgia; fried artichoke hearts at Selma's Tally Ho restaurant (a log cabin, fox-hunt-themed, seemingly all-white establishment with polite bow-tied black waiters that made me feel uncomfortably like I had been transplanted back into the 1950s); "okra croutons" (fried okra) on a salad, yam fries, and turnip fries in Natchez; and of course French fries, available everywhere. Neil convinced me not to order fried avocado at a Mexican restaurant in Vicksburg, saying that was just wrong. In Clarksdale, however, one restaurant, Yazoo Pass, offered a fresh salad bar and garlic-sautéed fresh spinach as a side, which were so invigorating because I was starved for fresh, nonfried vegetables that we returned three times.

The novelty of fresh food notwithstanding, does the Delta offer a food specialty worthy of being "most southern"? To me, the hot tamales didn't cut it. In Natchez, conversely, I discovered the life-changing lemon icebox pie, a relative of key lime pie that makes your mouth pucker, made with sweetened condensed milk, fresh lemon juice, lemon zest, and whipped topping. Then there's "comeback dressing," a central Mississippi dipping sauce or salad dressing that's so good you'll want to "come back" for more. Neil ate crayfish tail salad for the first time, as well as crawfish bread, French bread baked with a thick crawfish-tail sauce and cheesy roux. We both had our first po'boys there, sandwiches originating in New Orleans and characterized by special bread you can't buy at home (as I would come to discover later), spread with comeback dressing, shredded lettuce, tomato, and some fried meaty thing in the center—eggplant in my case and seafood for Neil. Do the rice grits, which I now order online from the Delta and have become a regular part of my diet, count as opening doors to a new culinary world?

Or, do I define "most southern" by the landscape? From my inexperienced northern perspective, the southern landscape in general seems not much changed from how I imagine it in the 1890s, and the Delta appears to be equally agricultural and vast as anywhere else in the South.

Maybe I'm supposed to define "most southern" by the level of poverty (although conversely, perhaps "most southern" is meant for a place most "New South" or most appropriate for a southern belle). The Delta was so impenetrable with forest that its ideal cotton-growing capacity was only recognized and harnessed late in the game, compared with most other southern places, and even then, that rich soil was only available to anyone willing to tame the thick and wild land—or rather, get someone to do so. Even land speculators hoping to make money by buying up a bunch of cheap land after the war went broke because there were no takers. The state of Mississippi had to take over large tracts but couldn't attract any of the new immigrants, who seemed to be settling everywhere else in the South, nor farmers from other states. Railroad companies purchasing land and completing a railroad line for cotton commerce from Memphis to New Orleans in 1884 didn't even make any money until the 1920s when they could finally find some white planters willing to buy, clear, and farm the land—with the poor, black labor that made up the majority of the population. So, yeah, maybe the Delta is and always has been the poorest place in the South. Is that how to define most southern?

Perhaps it's the level of hospitality or the attitude toward Yankees that should determine how southern a place is. Natchez, which, aside from my chastening at the African American museum, seemed warm and welcoming to me as a tourist.

But after ordering an "iced tea, unsweet" at a restaurant—which I had learned over my many Mississippi visits is the proper way to order unsweetened iced tea (as opposed to the South's national drink, "sweet tea")—I noticed that my bill called it something a bit off-putting: "Yankee tea." It was as if I had a big red *Y* on my chest while I thought I was fitting in. On the other hand, in Clarksdale, on our first visit to the restaurant with a salad bar, an older white man with a bushy white beard came over to Neil and me in our booth to ask where we were from and to welcome us to town. I guess he could recognize strangers in his small community, and he just wanted us to feel at home. In Natchitoches, Louisiana, we were treated even more hospitably by a complete stranger; after speaking with one of my Jewish contacts by phone before I'd even met him in person and mentioning we wanted to visit a nature preserve, this man called ahead to tell the preserve we were on our way so that the director could greet us in the driveway when we arrived to personally welcome us. Hospitality seems to be endemic to all of the South, not just the Delta.

I give up. How would I really know what's most southern? I'm a city gal from Philadelphia.

This I can say about the Delta: it has been the most surprising part of the South. It's been surprising in terms of how much beauty I have found in the clean lines of the landscape, like watercolors brushed lightly onto textured paper. I've been surprised how at home I started to feel in a place so unlike my own roots, how much I want to return and know it even more. How even when I brought my city friends from Philadelphia here, they loved it as much as I did.

I want to go back. The Delta as a concept and as a landscape and as a seat of history seems adrift from the consciousness of most of America, and it seems only those who have been there could get a glimpse of its richness, history, and draw—this place one writer called a "strange and detached fragment thrown off by the whirling comet that is America."

This year, in 2017, I take my memories of the injustices of the South and the post-presidential-election reeling angst of an entire astounded nation and dive a little more into political action: putting my senators, representative, and governor on speed dial on my phone and calling and emailing them on a regular basis on issues related to civil rights; getting trained in nonviolent bystander intervention in the tradition of Martin Luther King Jr. and John Lewis; attending the Women's March in Washington, DC; becoming a charitable giver to social justice and civil rights causes; hosting a fund-raising concert at my home to support science and education; and serving as a poll greeter, door-to-door canvasser, and postcard writer for the Virginia primaries and the first-ever-governor and house of delegates election in the new presidential era, where resisters showed the nation what broad civil engagement looks like.

Before we leave the Delta, we stop at Shiloh National Military Park in Tennessee, where in April 1862, the Federals prevailed over the Confederates in a battle that led to more casualties on both sides than in all other previous US wars combined. And before that, while we're still in the Delta, wanting to take all my southern lessons back home, I break an old dried clump of cotton off a stalk, full of entangled seeds. Here, sharecroppers once planted, picked, chopped, and fertilized this cotton, row after row, on their hands and knees, with the blazing sun "beating down so hard you'd give everything you owned for a little piece of shade and something to drink." I carry these cotton bolls with me and bring them back home. I want to always remember where my nation comes from and where I've been.

PART 3

INVESTIGATION

WHERE IT BEGINS AND WHERE IT ENDS

Last time I met Anita Moïse Rosefield Rosenberg at the Coming Street Cemetery in Charleston, South Carolina—the oldest surviving Jewish burial ground in the South and one of the oldest Jewish sites in the New World—I had time only for a quick "prove it to me" tour of the place, a kind of reality check that the city's (and country's) long history of Jews was real. I had no idea who she was or what her family line really signified to the history of Jews in Charleston and South Carolina and America.

Luckily, I get a second chance on a week-long trip to the small southern city, the heart of the Civil War, the heart of Reform Judaism in America, and the oldest Jewish community in the South, for an examination of the older and more troubling past of Jews in the South. This time, Rosenberg, seventy-eight, a petite woman with dark, curly hair and a friendly face, sits me down in the social hall of Kahal Kadosh Beth Elohim (KKBE). It's the second-oldest synagogue building in the country and the oldest in continuous use. Although I'll turn down an offer to attend Friday night services there this week, it's where Rosenberg wants to review the history of South Carolina, to remind me that this was the place where religious liberty really began in America, the cause that Jews have fought for in America more than anything else.

King Charles of England owned large tracts of land here, she says, and he needed people to defend it, make something of it. Lord Anthony Ashley Cooper became the lead lord proprietor of "Carolina" and the man believed to have collaborated with philosopher John Locke to write the initial constitution for the

141

colony around 1669. In terms of rights, it said colonists had no right to expel or negatively use the Native Americans, and the colonists should not scare or take away the religious liberty of "Jews, heathens, and other dissenters from the purity of Christian religion." In fact, if there were seven or more people of any religion, they could have a church.

So the Jews started coming over. Many had been expelled from Spain during the Spanish Inquisition and fled to Portugal, only to find forced conversions and deportations there and finally the Portuguese Inquisition. They fled again, often to islands in the Caribbean such as Curaçao, Barbados, Saint Thomas, Jamaica, and Trinidad, and from there they came to the southern United States.

"We came here for economic and religious freedom," she tells me of those first Jews—and she should know. She descends from at least six of the old Jewish families, many with names that to my ear don't sound very Jewish: Harby, Moïse (pronounced "mo-ize"), Moses, Lopez, Lazarus, and DeLeon. When she takes me to the temple library, she pulls out a giant book, *First American Jewish Families, 1654–1988,* and shows me larger-than-legal-size sheets of small-font family trees that she's a recent leaf on. One page, for example, traces her lineage to Edwin Warren Moïse, a man who formed a cavalry company in the Civil War called the Moïse Rangers, one of the few Confederate companies named for a Jewish Confederate. Many other pages track her bloodline back to Isaac Harby and Abraham Moïse, two of twelve reformers who broke away from their temple where they sought change in their worship services and engaged in a "religious revolution," thus founding Reform Judaism in America right here in Charleston. These young, American-born, innovative Jews did not want to do things like their parents and grandparents and ancestors in the Old Country, and so they established the Reformed Society of Israelites and struck out on their own to "transform and revitalize" their faith, "to make Judaism more suitable to its new American setting," as one scholar described it, and to encourage new members at synagogue. She tells me that her ancestors also include a descendant of Luis de Torres, the Jewish interpreter on Christopher Columbus's first voyage to America—a forced convert to Catholicism during the Spanish Inquisition, though he died in 1493 and the book doesn't go back far enough to show their connection.

With my mind already partially blown by her long history— she is possibly the 'first person (Jewish or non-Jewish alike) I've ever met who goes so far back in this country—she leads me into the sanctuary of the temple, which is quiet, light-filled, and airy. I know from reading about the Reform movement that started here in 1824 that in the early days, when essentially all Jews who came to America were strictly observant in ancient customs, the synagogues' *bimah,* or stage, from which services are led, was set in the center of the sanctuary. Women sat in balconies separate from the men and played no role in the service; there was no music or singing and thus no organ. "Most rabbis believed that the destruction of the First Temple warranted the removal of joy from religious services," one writer explains; the services could be six hours long, in Hebrew and in some Spanish or German, depending on the congregation.

The second- and third-generation Jews didn't buy into these traditions. Like many children and grandchildren of immigrants in America, they didn't think the old ways fit into their lives in America. "Under the influence of the spirit of the age"—sparked by the Declaration of Independence, Thomas Jefferson, Andrew Jackson, Romanticism, and more—the immigrants fought for something new, assimilative to the culture of America and the practice of religion here, more akin to the church services of their Christian neighbors, but still true to their own faith. Now, here, like all Reform temples nationwide, the bimah is at the front of the sanctuary, the way Jews had seen churches set up. There is no balcony, and men and women sit together. The congregation delights in and celebrates God with organ music or other instruments as well as song, much like Christian services that early Jews had witnessed. And services are truncated and conducted in English as well as Hebrew, among many other significant changes.

Walking through the building, with its geometric and fanciful splashes of color emanating from floor-to-ceiling stained-
glass windows, Rosenberg leads me up onto the bimah and the
ark that contains several Torahs and tells me the provenance
of each one. Our conversation over the last hour has spanned
various events in Charleston history that had ruined buildings
and wreaked havoc on the city: the 1838 fire that destroyed the
first synagogue and leveled a fourth of the center of the city;
the great fire of 1861, which burned through the historic area;
and the 1886 earthquake that caused widespread damage.
When she asks me what event destroyed the original Torahs
from this temple, I wrack my brain to think of something in the
past hundred years. I can't.

"The War Between the States!" she exclaims. During Union
Major General William Tecumseh Sherman's "March to the
Sea" in 1864, when he intended to break the South with his
swath of destruction from Atlanta to Savannah, Charlestonians
got word of his march north through South Carolina in early
1865 and assumed they would be affected. Congregants then
rushed the Torahs, minute books, and organ to Columbia for
safekeeping. But Sherman didn't hit Charleston, and, instead,
Columbia burned to the ground.

"Oh, I thought you meant an event that happened recently,"
I explained, trying to justify why I couldn't answer her question.
"Well, it seems like just yesterday," she says, with a chuckle, but
in all seriousness.

To continue our lessons, we bundle up in the January cold,
and she takes me in her car to the Coming Street Cemetery,
about a mile away. The oyster-shell entry path is new, and she
tells me it's historically accurate: it's made of sand and finely
crushed oyster shells, a reminder of the city's "inheritance"
from Barbados, where many of its slaveholding founders were
from. But what's familiar to me is the memory of a ghost story
she told last time we were there.

"Didn't something happen with a ghost here?" I ask. She
reminds me that a workman, forty feet high in a tree that he
was taking down, took a photo of the cemetery. The print

showed a white image of a human form near a Confederate's box tomb. Based on a photo displayed in the temple museum, Rosenberg and another volunteer thought the figure looked like Theodore Belitzer, a congregant of KKBE who was a Confederate soldier and prisoner of war on a Yankee steamer that caught fire off the coast of Wilmington, North Carolina. They don't know if Belitzer died in the fire or jumped overboard and drowned, but apparently he never had a proper burial. After Rosenberg told that story to any visitors who would listen, one tourist said she got goose bumps and felt his presence, and she wanted him to be at rest. This tourist and her companion donated money for a plaque to be installed in his memory, which Rosenberg shows me. The ghost hasn't been seen since.

The cemetery's tall brick and stucco walls, some of which are held up by bolsters, hide the oldest grave, dating to 1754. We see a collection of stones, some repaired and others dilapidated. They include upright tablet gravestones, box tombs, table-top tombs, columns, and obelisks, with names I would not typically associate with Jews, including DaCosta, Lopez, Cardozo, Seixas, Massias, and De LaMotta.

Rosenberg shows me the same graves I visited last time, but they have more meaning to me now—like Marks Lazarus, her Revolutionary War relative, for example. Being a Philadelphian and a Virginian, I had always thought these two places and other northern locations were the Revolutionary War hot spots of the nation. I don't remember my northern schools ever teaching that after the Patriots whooped the British up North, the Brits went down South to embark on their Southern Strategy. After capturing Savannah (what a city—it's also known for surrendering to the Union in the Civil War as a way to save that gorgeous place), they headed to Charleston, the center of commerce in the South at that time, where they attacked three different times over a period of years. Lazarus, there through all of it, was eventually imprisoned from May 1780 until the end of the war in 1783, along with five thousand other Patriots, when Charleston surrendered to the British in what some call the "worst defeat of the revolution."

Rosenberg then shows me the grave of Gustavus Poznan-ski Jr., the son of an early religious leader at the temple who had sermonized about how sons would fight for this land as their fathers had done. Poznanski the elder was right; Jr. was killed at age nineteen on the side of the Confederacy at the Battle of Secessionville. Rosenberg also takes me to visit the grave of her ancestor Penina Moïse, a poet whose 1833 book, *Fancy's Sketch Book,* was the first poetry volume by a Jewish American woman. Moïse's hymns became the first ever used in Jewish Reform services, sung across the country for more than a century.

And then we walk the grounds, which, in all, hold one vet-eran of the Cherokee War of 1760 (the first Jewish military officer in the American colonies); 9 veterans of the American Revolution; 6 soldiers of the War of 1812; 2 soldiers of the Sem-inole Wars of Florida; 23 Civil War soldiers; 4 of the 11 found-ers of the Supreme Council of the Scottish Rite Masonry; and 14 members of the Reformed Society of Israelites, demonstrat-ing the broadest interpretation of the saying I had been told years ago: "Jews were the mortar in the bricks" of much of the new nation.

More literally, the cemetery also holds David Lopez Jr., one of America's first-known Jewish builders, who built many of Charleston's historic buildings, such as Institute Hall, where South Carolina set off on a new revolutionary course when it signed its Ordinance of Secession here on December 20, 1860—the first southern state to do so. There, it announced its withdrawal from a union that had shown, in the words of South Carolina's declaration of secession, "increasing hostility on the part of the non-slaveholding States to the institution of slavery," a union whose northern states "have denounced as sinful the institution of slavery."

Taking assessment of many of the men buried here whose service benefited Charleston and beyond, Rosenberg gives me her own wisdom: "There'd be no developed South in the early days without Jews."

She also explains a sculptural element we see on many graves: a pair of hands, each with the first two fingers separated from the next two fingers, a kind of V configuration that we tend to associate with Spock's Vulcan symbol for "live long and prosper" from *Star Trek* and that appears on a sheet of *Star Trek* postage stamps. Turns out, it is part of a rabbinic blessing ritual, and Leonard Nimoy, who was Jewish and first saw it at an Orthodox synagogue as a child, appropriated this symbol for use in the show. His character was going to the planet Vulcan for a betrothal ceremony. "It was the first time we were seeing other Vulcans, other people of my race, so I was hoping to find some touches that could develop the story of the Vulcan sociology, history, ritual," Nimoy said. He suggested to the director that they create some special greeting among Vulcans, and this symbol stuck. "Most people don't know what it's all about," he says. "People don't realize they're blessing each other with this."

On this return visit with Rosenberg, I wanted to learn more about the old Jewish families and the history of Reform Judaism, but I also traveled to Charleston (population 131,000; 22 percent black, 74 percent white, 4 percent other) to inhabit some of the dark side of southern Jewish history—the lives of Jewish plantation owners and slave owners. After all, while South Carolina may have been progressive in terms of religious liberty, Charleston seems to have been founded in essence "to exist as a slave-society: a society whose economy could not exist without the practice of slavery"; the "most thoroughly Africanized urban center in the United States . . . governed as a miniature police state," as described by historians. And it wasn't only Christians who participated in this institution; Jews adopted it as they did all other customs in their new southern home, in about the same percentage as any other white people.

According to the 1860 census, about 8 percent of the entire US population owned slaves, as did 25 percent of the population in the South. In the state of South Carolina, however, overall slave ownership was much higher—46 percent; in the

Lowcountry region, the South Carolina coast where rice and indigo plantations abounded, slave ownership was at more than 74 percent in 1850. On a smaller scale, in urban Charleston— the central port of entry for most slaves in the state and for nearly half of those transported to the United States, and a predominantly black city because house slaves were common—the numbers of urban slave owners were even higher: 87 percent of whites owned slaves. As in other places, Jews in the state were accountants, tailors, clerks, owners of clothing stores, grocers, and merchants of various sorts; although very few owned plantations, Jews in Charleston were slave owners at a rate of 83 percent.

Although generally not much involved with the Atlantic slave trade from abroad, which was abolished in 1808 after whites brought over nine million to thirteen million people from Africa (Jews were involved in less than 1 percent of the African trade to America), as merchants and auctioneers who sold all kinds of goods, some Jews participated in the sale of people once they arrived on American soil. So at the cemetery, I ask Rosenberg's help to look for some of these typical urban slave owners and rare plantation owners—who are all Rosenberg's relations as well. If I want to know more about the intersection of Jews and the South, I can't overlook this issue.

Mordecai Cohen is the main person I'm focused on: a plantation owner, a slave owner, and one of the richest men in Charleston and all of South Carolina. He was also a benefactor to the town and the Jews of Charleston. Originally from Poland, he served as commissioner of the Charleston Poor House, commissioner of markets for the city, director of a railroad, and commissioner and long-time donor to the Charleston Orphan House, the first public orphanage in the United States, whose cornerstone was laid by George Washington. He was also at one time the president of the congregation. Cohen started as a peddler and shopkeeper like most other Jews from Europe and eventually became a plantation owner, keeping his shop and adding real estate speculation and "the auctioning, mortgaging, and leasing of [slave] babies, parents, and families" to his occupations, as one scholar explains it, which increased his fortunes. He owned twenty-seven plantation slaves, which meant he belonged to the group of people who owned most of the South's agricultural wealth, based on historian Bruce Levine's scale. He is buried with a well-preserved tabletop tomb, given no more or less attention at this cemetery than anyone else.

We also visit plantation owner Isiah Moses, remembered on his box tomb in small cursive writing. Moses also increased his wealth by moving from grocer to shopkeeper to planter and eventually owner of 794 acres of land and 19 to 50 slaves in Goose Creek, a rice plantation called The Oaks, now a golf club, about 20 miles from Charleston. He had always wanted to become a planter because in his native Hanover, Germany, Jews were not allowed to own land. But his plantation may have only been for show, as it was never profitable. I bite my tongue at each grave, holding in my outraged commentary and questions that most likely have disappointing answers.

For someone who's not looking, it's easy to say that amid Charleston's Fort Sumter appeal—its bustling College of Charleston student life; its charming, old-moneyed, pastel-colored, architecturally significant collection of homes and buildings; its lovely waterfront park, Eden-like gardens, intricate hand-wrought iron gates, cobblestone streets, and secret alleyways—all this early Jewish history is unfindable, unknowable, hidden. But when you clear away the typical tourist destinations and the eye candy of the city and delve beyond the assumed Christian slant on history, as I've been doing, the Jews are everywhere.

It's also easy to say that most people don't know the Jewish history here and that these early leaders are forgotten by all but the die-hard genealogists and relatives. But then Rosenberg tells me there's a mural that includes Isaac Harby at the Footlight Players Theater in town. She had already shown me a mural in the synagogue social hall depicting congregant Judah P. Benjamin, born on Saint Croix but schooled in Charleston; his father, Philip Benjamin, was one of the original twelve dissenters who organized the Reformed Society of Israelites. A cousin of Rosenberg's will later tell me that he personally commissioned a plaque to memorialize Benjamin at the fountain of the Dock Street Theater, because Benjamin has no national memorial; some consider him "the first Jew to break through the barriers of bigotry into the councils of national power," according to Benjamin's biographer.

Notably, the city of Charleston chose to honor Mordecai Cohen as a great benefactor to the city, with a marble tablet usually displayed at the temple, and the city erected a bronze plaque on the wall of quaint Washington Square Park to memorialize Francis Salvador, a Sephardic Jewish Briton (via Netherlands and Portugal) whose family bought land in South Carolina in an area known then as 96, or "Jews Land," and now known as Ninety-Six, where he planned to become an indigo planter. He was the first identified Jew to be elected to public office in America when he was chosen for the Provisional Congress, and the first Jew killed in the Revolutionary War, at age twenty-nine—one of about a hundred Jews who fought for the Revolution. His memorial, which reads "An Englishman, he cast his lot with America; True to his ancient faith, he gave his life for new hopes of human liberty and understanding," is a bit weather-beaten, tucked away behind some bushes, and overshadowed by the statue of George Washington and the memorial to the South Carolina Confederates, but still, it's there.

I ask how Rosenberg, as a ninth-generation Jewish Charlestonian, feels about being part of these long histories. "It feels normal," she says. "We just grow up in it." And then I steel myself for asking my next question. I know historically even rabbis have defended slavery—Rabbi Morris J. Raphall of New York was the most prominent one, defending the institution in concept as biblically acceptable; in a famous speech in 1861, he said:

> How dare you denounce slaveholding as a sin? When you remember that Abraham, Isaac, Jacob, Job—the men with whom the Almighty conversed, with whose

names he emphatically connects his own most holy name, and to whom He vouchsafed to give the character of "perfect, upright, fearing G-d and eschewing evil" (Job 1:8)—that all these men were slaveholders, does it not strike you that you are guilty of something very little short of blasphemy? And if you answer me, "Oh, in their time slaveholding was lawful, but now it has become a sin," I in my turn ask you, "When and by what authority you draw the line?" Tell us the precise time when slaveholding ceased to be permitted, and became sinful?

In his next breath, though, he concedes: "I am no friend to slavery in the abstract, and still less friendly to the practical working of slavery."

So I ask: how does Rosenberg feel about her ancestors and other Coming Street Cemetery residents once owning slaves? Isaac Harby once attacked abolitionists, saying that South Carolina abolishing slavery "might not only jeopardize the well-being of the Planting States but . . . shake the 'married calm' of the whole Union."

"Well, it was the mode of the day," is all she says on the matter, a factual non-answer that silences me in my wish to hear some representative of my religion somehow atone, to quell the discomfort it makes me feel in knowing some of my own kind were involved with such an institution.

One of the last burial sites we look at is her own. A large modern granite gravestone in the center of the cemetery memorializes her husband, who passed away one year ago, and her—with the year of her death missing. One gravesite next to hers is spoken for, and there are four more open spots available. Then, the cemetery will be full. The final resting place for eight hundred souls that "tells the history of what was once America's largest and most prosperous Jewish settlement" has no endowment and no continuous source of funding, and Rosenberg has devoted her life helping to protect and restore one of the greatest treasures of Jewish history in America. But a new generation—the tenth or eleventh generation, or outsiders, even newcomer

Yankees who take an interest in this significant southern place—
will be responsible for ushering it into the future.

Visiting someone in their death is a powerful reminder that the
person was real, but I wanted to know more about the Cohens
than the Coming Street Cemetery could tell me. I wanted to
know more about them in life, to see what it was like to be
them in an age of wealth and slavery. Like nearly all Jewish-
owned plantation homes throughout the South, however—
with the exception of Leon Godchaux's in Reserve, Louisiana,
which has been moved and is under renovation—neither
Mordecai Cohen's nor the plantation houses of his two sons,
David D. and Marx E. Cohen, still stand. These plantations
of more than a thousand acres are now either middle-class
suburban subdivisions or trailer parks in North Charleston,
with some undeveloped marshland riverfront that is part of a
protected viewshed.

But they were all located in what is now the Ashley River
Historic Corridor, across the Ashley River from the grand Mid-
dleton Place, Magnolia Plantation and Gardens, and Drayton
Hall, the three popular plantation homes currently open for
tourism. All these estates once operated as rice and indigo plantations, two of the most common crops of Lowcountry South
Carolina, and, aside from sugarcane plantations, presented
grueling working conditions for the enslaved. On a clear, brisk
afternoon, I set out to Drayton Hall, about forty-five minutes
from Charleston up Ashley River Road, which will serve as
a representation for the places I can't get to, a perch from
which to look across the narrow waterway to the land where
Jews once owned property and people.

Drayton Hall is the oldest preserved plantation house in
America still open to the public; its austere, unadorned brick
Palladian architecture was common in the 1700s and so differ-
ent from the ornate plantations of Mississippi and Louisiana.
From the river walk on the Drayton shore, I can see a low
reedy area of what was once Soldier's Retreat, a plantation of

more than a thousand acres purchased by Mordecai Cohen in 1825 and transferred in 1830 to his son David, who owned it for twenty-five years. An original yellowed 1784 map reveals this spot to be an old rice field and salt marsh, as the Ashley River is tidal. Beyond that, all I can witness is a low horizon of young trees, an area that was once pastureland with a settlement in the center, surrounded by oaks and hickories, low pineland, and swamps in the far reaches.

A bit upstream was Clear Springs, a rice plantation that Cohen bought in 1830 and transferred to son Marx (who was married to Armida Harby, daughter of the famous religious reformer Isaac Harby). With 673 acres of forested highlands, 484 acres of rice fields, 28 acres of salt marsh, 26 acres of freshwater swamp, and between 20 and 42 slaves who cleared land, dug potatoes, ground corn, cut hay, and burned brush, Marx ran the estate mostly as a rural family retreat, not as a working plantation. He had the slaves cultivate rice mostly for the Cohens' and slaves' domestic needs.

Primarily, he had his slaves cut and haul wood—oak, loblolly and yellow pine—and make bricks, which turned out brown, gray, and red, and then sell these products downriver in Charleston. In fact, Marx's best customer for this material was Jewish builder-architect and slave owner David Lopez Jr., who supplied building materials to other contractors, built and repaired numerous structures in Charleston after the fire of 1838, and, most notably, built the second iteration of the KKBE Greek Revival Reform temple of 1840 that still stands today. The uncomfortable fact is that the first Jewish builder of a synagogue in America built that structure with slave labor; and, most likely, the synagogue that's the symbol and genesis of Reform Judaism in America was built with some of Jewish slave owner Marx E. Cohen's slave-made bricks.

The bricks, "Carolina Grey Bricks" used in the walls and the arches, are stuccoed over and painted white, literally whitewashed, to look like stone. But this trompe l'oeil cannot mask or undo the darker truth underneath: the home of the largest denomination of Jews in America—the religion of my family,

most of my Jewish friends, and all of Reform Jewish America—
was built by the labor of slaves. The proof of their labor, like
in other bricks across South Carolina and the South, is in the
fingerprints stamped in the clay, hidden.

When I come to this realization, it's a pivotal moment for
me. I think it's the moment when I finally understand what
"white privilege" means. It's how Jews—who have always
been, and still are, discriminated against—could get ahead
in America. It is the moment I see how small and dangerous,
as civil rights activist Joan Mulholland's son Loki puts it, the
"I-never-owned-any-slaves-syndrome" is. This pass-the-hat
attitude, which my family or I or other white people may have
thought or said one or more times in our lives as the reason for
not being responsible for racial injustice or involved in rectifying it, just doesn't hold up. That condition doesn't negate the
benefits white people have knowingly or unknowingly received
over one or more generations. The lack of personal or famil-
ial involvement doesn't mean that white people don't have an
obligation to seek out information about this issue and listen
to others speak uncomfortable truths, to try to understand and
recognize and to attempt to do something about the inherent,
racial inequality at the core of the founding and building of
our nation, which has contributed to white people's overall
success at the expense of others and which continues to exist.

Meanwhile, the historic situation I'm discovering on the
grounds of the Ashley River just keeps getting worse. Lee
Cohen Harby, Marx's daughter (who went on to become a
writer, including composing the "Flag Song of Texas"), recalls
in a series of newspaper articles titled "In the Days When We
Were Young," the "splendid days of [her] childhood" at Clear
Springs. She says she and her family "passed the days in outdoor
exercise and sports, and indoors in merry chatting, reading, and
fancy work," sitting "long around the table, sipping their wine,
eating their nuts and fruits, jesting, laughing, and talking, at
ease with the world, satisfied with themselves and happy in this
'incomparable' life." At night, she says, "there were games of all
kinds, singing and dancing, either to the piano or to the fiddle

of some negroes" and "old folks . . . played cribbage or inter-changed reminiscence of the days of their early life."

During those evenings, she writes, "a circle of dusky faces, with gleaming eyes and teeth . . . listened to the laughter and the merry voices of their owners, taking an inexpressible delight in the scene," as "so naturally joyous and pleasure loving [was] the whole negro race." The rosy picture she paints completely discounts the views of an entire group of people living at Clear Springs.

Over at her uncle David Cohen's place, Soldier's Retreat, within my view from my position on the grounds of Ashley River, an enslaved man named Jim—likely James Matthews who worked as a hostler and in the field and who eventually escaped to freedom in Boston—had written his recollection of what life was like under Cohen, likely not much different from life on his brother's plantation: "I have often wished that I was a dog; they seemed so much better off than we."

In Lee Harby's telling of Sundays at her father's Clear Springs plantation, when the enslaved people got their supplies for the week, they

> assembled at "the bank" and received their sweet pota-toes; next they went to the barn and got their rations of corn, peas, and rice; to the smoke house and drew their allowance of bacon or pork and fish; from their master's store-room they were given their salt, syrup, and tobacco, and the gardener gave out to them the cabbages or turnips. . . . In summer they had plenty of bonny-clabber from the dairy. . . . The fruits of the woods, berries, and nuts, were free to them; they caught terrapin in the swamps and ponds, fish from the rivers, snared rabbits and birds—and so lived better and easier than any other working class on the face of the earth.

But Jim relates this experience much differently. He explained that the slaves' weekly allotment of food lasted only four or five days; sustenance—fuel for their sunup to sundown work—for the rest of the week depended on stealing. "I did not think it was wrong to steal enough to eat," Jim wrote. "I have sometimes been so faint from hard work, and from eating green and raw food, that I had to go over the fence and sleep." Although David Cohen raised hogs, he didn't eat them—possibly due to keeping kosher—and he wouldn't let his slaves eat them either. "When I came back the [slave]driver would say, 'what you gone so long over the fence for? you're lazy.'"

If slaves were caught stealing, they'd be punished, whipped until they bled and until they fainted. Then they'd get "a dose of salts" or be "washed down with brine" and put "in the stocks" in the pitch black, Jim reported, chained and fastened and made to lie on their backs for two or three weeks, with frequent whippings. Then, the slaves had to go back into the fields "when their skin is so cut up they have to keep all the time pulling their clothes away from the raw flesh."

He said that often slaves would run away after a whipping to try to heal their bodies before working again or just to escape for good. Jim ran away from Cohen after being whipped, and the person who caught him brought him to the infamous Sugar House in Charleston, a workhouse for runaway slaves that was part of the Charleston City Jail. Because Jim would not go back voluntarily to Cohen's plantation, Cohen left him there, with orders to give him fifty lashes—with paddles, whips, cow skins, cat-o'-nine-tails, and blue jays, the latter of which Jim said were "the worst thing to whip with of anything they have"—it "has two lashes, very heavy and full of knots" and "it makes a hole where it strikes, and when they have done it will be all bloody." Then he was to be put on the prison treadmill for three days, a wide paddle wheel that slaves climbed to power a gristmill, grinding corn, which was "like walking upstairs for hours on end." The routine was continued for three months.

"The truth was," Jim wrote, "the sugar house was worse than the plantation. . . . I have heard a great deal said about hell, and wicked places, but I don't think there is any worse hell than that sugar house."

Peg Senturia, seventy-eight, a direct descendant of David Cohen, grew up in Washington, DC, where she remembers people singing "Dixie" with enthusiasm. On the issue of slavery in her family history, she says, "It's very complicated. Times were different. But that doesn't take care of the issue. It makes me feel awful." She also reports she is the only one in the family who is interested in the history and has traveled to South Carolina to research it. While information about David Cohen and his family is available, she questions why no one has ever tried to trace the slaves her family once owned. But she doesn't know if she has it in her at her age to do the research on her own.

Now, all that's left of these Jewish men are the diaries, maps, oil paintings in museums, wills, a plantation journal, and a few typical city homes in Charleston known as "Charleston single houses," with the short end facing the street with a faux front door and the long side with two-story porches turned sideways and facing the house next door, fitting neatly into narrow lots. Mordecai Cohen's three-and-a-half story home at 119 Broad Street served for many years as the offices of the Roman Catholic Diocese of Charleston; his more modest 97 Broad Street home, considered a tenement then, purchased in 1811, is now a law firm. Marx's town property, the 1844 half-house at 85 King Street that's now a 3,600-square-foot, two-million-dollar private residence, was a summertime abode. There is no physical legacy of life on the plantations remaining—but this way of life has made an everlasting mark on the country and culture, on attitudes and assumptions, on opportunities and benefits—a hard-to-swallow reckoning I never expected to make about the early Jews of the nation. Eventually, those expansive riverside lands were sold to mining companies that tore them apart for phosphate, strip-mined for use in making fertilizer. In fact, what was once Soldier's Retreat became the largest phosphate processing facility in the world.

Aside from what I've seen in Charleston, at Coming Street, and on the river, there's one more place nearby to trace this family: Sumter.

* * *

I had been sick for several days since arriving in Charleston, cold, fatigued, head stuffed full, and coughing, holed up in a townhouse near Colonial Lake, but I urge myself onward and get in the car for the trip two hours north and inland. I take off from Charleston on Septima Clark Parkway, which I had recently learned was named for an African American civil rights activist and educator who founded citizenship schools for blacks throughout the Deep South to help increase literacy and voting rates. Civil rights activist and Georgia congressman John Lewis had said of Clark in his memoir in the 1990s that "Her name might be generally unknown today," and so I am glad that Charleston has honored her. I already feel the trip is off to a promising start.

Sumter (population 40,000; 49 percent black, 45 percent white, 6 percent other), named for a Revolutionary War general and once known as a plantation settlement that held the greatest per-capita wealth in all of South Carolina, is where Moseses and Harbys started moving from Charleston in the 1820s, and Cohens and Moïses came after the Civil War. "We all have cousins there, ancestors," Rosenberg told me. "Families intermingled." In fact, the Reform temple in Charleston considers itself the "parent temple" of Sumter. Marx E. Cohen and his family sold Clear Springs and moved to Sumter in November 1868 "because of the drastic change in conditions," which could mean his bereavement over losing his son in the war, the emancipation of his slaves, and/or the loss of money. He bought several properties on South Washington Street, which someone tells me is where the poor people live now, where there's a small subdivision of ranch homes, a nondescript old farmhouse, and an empty lot.

I had other reasons for going to Sumter as well: unlike Charleston—which has five Jewish congregations, including Reform, Conservative, and Modern Orthodox, some with hundreds of families as members, and whose greater metropolitan area boasts approximately 9,500 Jews—Sumter is one of the "lost" Jewish communities. Once a community of 390 Jewish people, now the one temple has only forty members, and only about five to seven people show up on the two Friday night services offered by a lay leader each month. I decided to go visit one of them.

I meet Elizabeth Moses at the Sumter County Museum— an 1848 house that once belonged to her relative Octavia Harby Moses, another daughter of reformer Isaac Harby, and Octavia's husband—where Elizabeth works as the educational and outreach coordinator. When I heard that Elizabeth was an eighth-generation southern Jew, for some reason I expected her to be intimidating and aristocratic. I guess I feel out of my league in the Charleston area because of my family's short history in this country and our general lack of observant Jewishness or anything of great historic value to protect. Instead, I find her warm, friendly—like Rosenberg, whom she's related to—down to earth, and only a few years older than me, in her fifties. We bond immediately over our love of history and cats— there's a friendly orange one strutting about the old house— as well as our way of thinking; she says she is "profoundly liberal and progressive." Also, she's wearing jeans, and one of the first things she tells me is that she was raised Catholic and officially converted to Judaism as an adult and that "whether vegetarians or nudists, all converts are nuts." As a vegetarian myself, she puts me at ease right away.

I am surprised to hear that she had converted to Judaism, though, because I had heard people mention that her father is Jewish—Robert Moses, ninety-six—and because many different Charleston Jews had suggested I talk with her about the Jewish history here. Turns out, her mother was a Protestant who converted to Catholicism, and part of the agreement in marriage was that the kids had to be raised Catholic, which, her father says in an interview, was "a bitter pill to try to swallow." I had heard that many of the old Sephardic Jewish family names, like Moses, were no longer held by practicing Jews, that over the years so many of them had assimilated, intermarried, and converted that many of the non-Jews in Sumter have Jewish ancestors, and mostly the only Jews left are from the second and third waves of Jews to this country. "The Jews in Sumter were loved to death by the non-Jewish people" is how Robert Moses put it.

So Elizabeth Moses grew up going to Catholic school, while also attending temple with her father—though he also made sure they always had a Christmas tree so she and her siblings didn't feel left out; Ashley River's Lee Harby also remembers her Jewish family's "Southern Christmas" where they "made merry . . . for weeks." Elizabeth Moses converted to Judaism at age thirty. Moses now calls herself a nonbeliever, though she's a devoted lay leader for Shabbat services at the temple. Her father's second wife is also Catholic, but in a twist I have not seen anywhere else in the South—this place where nothing is as it seems or as I'd expect—she holds the position of secretary of Sumter's Temple Sinai as well as president of the temple sisterhood organization.

After showing me around the high-ceilinged house with walls covered in fancy framed portraits of the family and other historic displays, we get in my car and I follow Moses's directions to the Jewish cemetery a few minutes away on tidy suburban streets in an area that seems so neat, flat, and low that we could be in the Midwest. It's my fifth day in South Carolina and the first one that's finally somewhat warm. I've been traipsing around interviewing people, doing walking tours, and visiting plantations in the freezing cold—thirty degrees and windy, so stepping outside into the sun and strolling slowly for an hour at the burial ground feels nice. This cemetery is much larger than the one at Coming Street, is not in a city, and has no high fences; the sky is wide. The name Moses appears frequently on gravestones and in addition to the Sephardic names I've seen before, I also notice a Suares, yet another in the hard-to-believe-they're-Jewish collection. (Another fun fact I learned about Sephardic names is that, while the Ashkenazi, or Eastern European, Jews name their children after the first letter of deceased relatives—so the angel of death would not get confused and take the wrong person with the same full name—Sephardic Jews name babies after living relatives, leading to many people being called the same name within families.) Familiar German and Eastern European last names appear in this cemetery as well; those names belong to the people who came later and who turned the downtown into a bustling business community with groceries, dry goods, department stores, saloons, iron works, insurance companies, and law practices.

Marx E. Cohen, the brickmaker of Clear Springs, rests here—Elizabeth Moses's great-great-grandfather—as well as his wife, Armida. In an oral history interview, Elizabeth's father says his family and forefathers lived in Marx's home in Sumter for about a hundred years, which Robert Moses remembers as having pecan trees and a lot of cats in the back-yard. But despite the close family connection, it doesn't seem that the elder Moses's fortune trickled down much, as Robert doesn't remember his father having two dimes to rub together. We also visit Elizabeth Moses's mother, who is buried there despite not being Jewish. According to Robert, "There were Murphys buried in the Jewish cemetery and Weinbergs buried in the Catholic cemetery" as a result of so much intermarriage and a general feeling of relaxedness about religion.

Then Moses directs me a few blocks away to Temple Sinai, a 1912 building that's the second iteration of the synagogue, a Reform temple that welcomed any Jewish denominations since it was the only one around; it never faced the strife among Judaic approaches to worship or the breakups of congregations that happened in Charleston. It's a squat, square Moorish Revival-style red-brick building on Church Street, famous for its eleven stained-glass windows, each about five feet wide and twenty feet tall, with Biblical scenes from the Old Testament. It's the only temple whose windows I can remember with images of people, as opposed to just decorative symmetrical designs, as strict Jewish rules prohibit the creation of images that could be considered idolatry; here, the windows depict Abraham, Isaac, Jacob, Moses, David, and others, who are portrayed with brown skin.

162 · WANDERING DIXIE

Due to the dwindling number of people coming to services, the Sumter County Museum is taking over the building, which Robert Moses calls "the light at the end of the tunnel," in the face of "utter sadness" over the decline of the Sumter Jewish community. The Temple Sinai Jewish History Center will inhabit the adjoining social hall to provide information about Jewish history in South Carolina, and the museum will keep the temple open for Friday night and holiday services as long as people will come. In the best news I've heard on all my travels through these lost places, Elizabeth Moses says, "This place is taken care of for a long time." They've had fund-raisers, big donors have stepped up, and the museum has won several grants. How did they manage it, I wondered, given the hopelessness I saw in so many places, and even the struggle for the Coming Street Cemetery to raise funds? "This place has a lot of meaning for people who grew up here and moved away," she says.

On the way back to the museum, we stop in the relatively bustling, rejuvenated, quaint old town of Sumter, a main street out of the 1950s with low buildings that look like mom-and-pops, where Moses suggests we pick up Chinese food takeout for lunch (thus proving to me that she's truly Jewish). Then we sit down to eat in the old house's office kitchen, where I assume all my enlightenment of Sumter Jewish history will come to a close. Instead, she mentions offhandedly that on her mother's side, she's related to the wife and children of William Tecumseh Sherman, the man known in the South as a "villain, war criminal, [and] devil," and on her dad's side she's related to the half-Jewish "robber governor" Franklin J. Moses Jr., a man two other Charleston Jews had mentioned to me as the "scalawag governor"—the only time my sheltered northern ears have heard the word *scalawag* spoken (definition: a southern white who supported Reconstruction; a "carpetbagger," by contrast, was a northerner who moved South [with a carpet bag suitcase that was a popular style at the time] after the Civil War, whom southerners hated as well).

I'll learn eventually that Franklin J. Moses "Jewnier," as he was sometimes called, though it was said he was a practicing

Christian, was a controversial Reconstruction-era governor of South Carolina, that generations of southerners still revile, though in his earlier life he was a devoted Confederate who raised the Confederate flag over Fort Sumter at the start of the war. According to historian Benjamin Ginsberg of Johns Hopkins University, Franklin Moses Jr.—in complete defiance of southern white norms—supported the federal government's Freedmen's Bureau, which assisted newly freed blacks. He also launched social programs for blacks, integrated state institutions, built a black militia to protect freedmen's rights, helped blacks attend state universities, visited the homes and churches of his black constituents, invited black people to his home to socialize, and insisted that blacks be treated with respect. Although no one denies that he did some small-time thieving and engaged in corruption while in office, according to Ginsberg, "If Moses was a robber, what he stole was not so much white South Carolinians' money as their sense of racial exclusivity." Apparently, many of his relatives in Sumter felt so disgraced by the man that they changed their last name to DeLeon or Harby. Now Elizabeth Moses and I are eating in the kitchen of his first cousins, people who owned sixteen slaves and were a divided family in terms of whether they believed in secession.

When I asked her how she feels about her slave-owning family's past, she says, "To me, it's all history. We can't do anything about history." But, she adds, "I've spent my life apologizing for slavery, feeling guilty for slavery. Enormous guilt. It's a heavy burden to live with."

She gained some of that empathy from her father. "I was completely empathetic with the plight of the blacks and faced a stone wall of inbred discrimination to overcome," he said. He remembers seeing signs that said, "No blacks, dogs, or Jews allowed," and he said he wanted to "protect the children from what we were brought up in . . . I was very, very anxious never to pass on any of the ingrained discrimination that I suffered."

It pains me and warms my heart to hear these sentiments, but the thought of my two-hour drive back and the growing sneezy cold that prevented me from visiting Robert Moses in person weighs on me as well, so I bid goodbye to Elizabeth after a lovely day. She's still eating, slowly, so I feel awkward and a bit rude to leave, but she urges me to go and take care of myself.

On my way back to Charleston I think about the people and places of Jewish and non-Jewish Charleston's and Sumter's past and present. In fact, I think about it for weeks, so foreign is it all from my own life and background. More than a month after my Sumter visit, the idea of the deep-seated hatred among any South Carolinians I came across toward Governor Moses continues to gnaw on and befuddle me. According to Ginsberg's book, Moses's crimes weren't any worse than those of anyone else in power. It was more like everyone thought Moses must be out of his mind to behave and believe as he did; he was a Jew, so that was a mark against him. And one person I met said he was a cad and a womanizer, as evidence of his poor character—though being either has rarely mattered in white-male American history. Whites would eventually overthrow all the gains blacks had won during Reconstruction and reinitiate a segregated society. None of my contacts seemed to think his achievements overrode his corrupt ways, which stunned and confused my northern, liberal mind.

I decide to pay a visit to Ginsberg at Johns Hopkins to probe the psychology of this conundrum.

"Politics and criminality were inextricably linked, by our standards," Ginsberg explains of the US South in the late 1800s. "There was almost no such thing as an honest politician; Moses didn't steal that much." His criminality, Ginsberg repeats, "was that he broke the one law—the first commandment—of southern society: socializing with blacks." Ginsberg isn't the only researcher coming to this conclusion. A 1950 paper by a Sumter resident concludes, "It can with safety be said that Moses's associations with the negro on a basis of equality is the grounds for most of the enduring odium that surrounds his name in South Carolina." In fact, "White supremacy has been their most effective weapon, politically, and with it they have stamped into the minds of South Carolinians, permanently and indelibly, hatred of everything connected with Franklin Moses and Reconstruction." Exactly what I had been witnessing.

Southern whites just could not handle being equal to blacks. Reconstruction, a time of revolutionary changes, was perhaps more dramatically felt in Charleston than anywhere else in the South due to its loss of such concentrated white wealth and the freed and emboldened black majority. Despite Sherman's apparent dislike of black people and his belief that blacks and whites were not equal, he ordered troops to confiscate abandoned plantations and redistribute the land to freedmen, but the plan never came to fruition due to the pushback of southern whites. And while blacks voted and held political office for the first time in history, white Charlestonians considered those who supported these abrupt changeovers of societal power to be radical and loathsome—like "an American Taliban," according to Ginsburg, referring to the Sunni Islamic fundamentalist political movement that held power in Afghanistan and forced a strict and violent interpretation of Islamic law there. During this time, when armed militias and violent conflicts were common, Moses was "peddling phony securities to buy weapons to arm Republican and black militias to fight it out with the KKK, the militia of the Democratic party, who got to keep their Confederate weapons after the war"—not the kind of southern hero, I guess, that South Carolina educators teach in schools.

"Some people simply can't let go," Elizabeth Moses says. And when I think about the scary rise in uncivil discourse, partisanship, white supremacy, anti-Semitism, racism, and hate in the forty-fifth president's "America First" campaign and white nationalist agenda, a divide that seems reminiscent of the prelude to the Civil War, I realize how right she is.

THE LONGEST MEMORY

Michael Kogan, a retired religious studies professor and a New York City transplant living in Charleston, described himself recently as "a wandering nineteenth-century Confederate Jew."

"I'm a man without a country," he says of his affiliation with the Confederacy, which stems from descending from about half a dozen Confederate soldiers and being a distant cousin to Robert E. Lee. He is a proud member of the Sons of Confederate Veterans, for which he served as commander while living in New York City, and which he says he joined at fifteen years old, after aging out of the Children of the Confederacy, where he learned about Confederate heroes and sang Confederate songs. At the same time, his mother was an officer of the Daughters of the Confederacy for forty years in New York City, a place Kogan, seventy-five, says was a haven for Confederates after the war. When he tells me these things, I have another seizure of cross-cultural disharmony, which he tries to heal by saying, "We were southern, Jewish, and New Yorkers. If you're raised this way, nothing seems strange."

Charleston was my portal to the old Jewish past and the Jewish slave owners, and it was also to be my portal to the Jewish Confederates, that unexpected demographic that had shattered my understanding of America and sparked this whole journey in the first place. Kogan is my guide into this world. So in January, while the Jews of Charleston involved with the Jewish Federation march in a Martin Luther King Jr. Day parade "just as Rabbi Heschel marched with Dr. King" in Selma, as the federation describes it, I walk the lovely narrow streets of Charleston in the opposite direction to visit Kogan on King Street instead.

Years ago, someone in Charleston told me I must talk with Kogan, calling him a great intellectual and an "unreconstructed Confederate," but I needed time to work my way through a lot of experiences in and lessons about the South before meeting him. I knew his views might be startling to me and I'd need context to understand them. I wanted to be better educated and learn from other people on my travels first. After visiting Alabama, Mississippi, Louisiana, and Arkansas, with stints in Tennessee, Georgia, and South Carolina, now I'm ready.

Before my journey to Charleston, he and I had already engaged in several phone conversations about his rah-rah Confederate beliefs and the controversy surrounding Confederate monuments, as the nation was right in the middle of it in 2017. He was thoroughly dismayed by an article I had written about Moses Ezekiel, the first Jewish Virginia Military Institute cadet, who fought as a teenage student in the Civil War at the Battle of New Market, Virginia, and later became the first nationally and internationally renowned Jewish American sculptor. Ezekiel's living relatives had recently expressed their wishes to remove the Confederate monument he designed at Arlington National Cemetery because of the revisionist history they feel it exemplifies, glorifying the Confederacy. I wanted to explore whether we'd lose anything as a society in terms of art history, American history, or Jewish history if the monument were taken down. The magazine had edited the article so that it only presented the experts' views, not my own; experts generally said that the monument had some value but had no place on public lands. The editor had omitted my own view, which is that this particular monument should stay for the educational opportunities it provides but be contextualized with information to incite discussions and put it in perspective.

"This issue hits me with great power," Kogan had said, as I had only presented "a demonized view" of the Confederacy. "The assumption is that somehow there is something evil about the Confederate cause—that's the mythos we're dealing with now, and it's unfortunate. Any balanced presentation has to show our cause and what our boys fought for—to defend their homes against invasion of the federal government's troops." He tells me often that there were many reasons for secession, slavery among them; but there was only one reason for the war: the federal government would not let the South secede.

Many of these monuments, he had said, are not monuments to the Confederacy at large but are "monuments to our dead heroes, human beings. Whether they believed in slavery or not, we don't know." The situation today, he said, is "like ISIS in the Middle East—we tear down monuments to prior points of view that we now disagree with." The idea of revisionist history, he says, is "outrageous slander." That way of thinking, he says, makes out the men who fought in the Confederacy to be people who wanted to support slavery, oppression, and racism. "It's so unjust and so unfair. This anti-statue madness is sweeping the country—*that's* the revisionist history, and it should be resisted."

In short, on a message left on my voicemail, he called my article "a propaganda piece."

When I arrive at his perfectly appointed apartment of art and history collections, he seems much more genteel. He's dressed in a wool suit and bowtie with a matching pocket-handkerchief and cuff links. Kogan lives, conveniently for him, across the street from the Battery, which faces the Charleston Harbor and, more importantly, Fort Sumter. Depending on how you look at it, this island is either where the War of Northern Aggression commenced with Lincoln's naval resupply of food for a federal fort located in a state that had seceded from the Union, a violation of a sort-of promise not to do so without adequate notice to South Carolina—or it is the place where the Civil War began when southerners fired the first shots, after the US fort refused to evacuate and surrender.

Charleston is a peninsula sandwiched between the Ashley and Cooper Rivers, similar to how Manhattan is sandwiched between the Hudson and East Rivers. The two cities are also similar in the sense that the older section of the jut of land is the lower, or southern, part. In New York we call it Lower Manhattan; here, it is simply "south of Broad." In this aristocratic town, the only large city south of Philadelphia in the eighteenth century and the wealthiest one in the original thirteen colonies—"A more hedonistic, pleasure-oriented society never lived on the North American continent," one historian wrote—Broad Street marks "the line between longing and belonging," as historian Harlan Greene tells me on a walk around the town, with the southern end of Charleston most coveted. Kogan lives at the southernmost point.

Kogan's apartment houses his enormous collection of miniature Civil War soldiers, which he began acquiring when he was six years old, some of which are custom made. There are at least two framed photographs of Robert E. Lee and a nearly life-sized black bust of the general, so detailed I could see the stubble and pores on his face. A separate den, in brown tones, with leather furniture, is nearly entirely devoted to the Confederacy, with framed original newspapers from the 1860s (*Harper's Weekly*), portraits and signatures of Robert E. Lee and Jefferson Davis, old Lost Cause posters, and a large "stars and bars" Confederate flag in the corner. He points out that this was the first official Confederate flag. The one neo-Confederates have aligned themselves with came from the first battle flag, he says, used only because the stars and bars were too similar to the US flag to be recognized during battle. Kogan does not display the battle flag (the one removed from the South Carolina statehouse in 2015), though I see a battle-flag pillow resting on a comfortable-looking leather chair, because, he says, it "has been fatally compromised" by hate groups, with which he does not affiliate. He calls those groups "some of the worst people in our country, who have an evil agenda of their own." He also does not display it because it offends his (black) "house man," whose opinion he values and whom he does not wish to disrespect. He says he does not want to offend black people at all. This perplexes me because his main mission at the moment seems to be preventing the city's John C. Calhoun monument from having a descriptive plaque installed to interpret it in context.

I wasn't well-schooled in Calhoun before coming to Charleston, but I am in the big league now in this historically pivotal city, the intersection of so many pasts and presents, so I bone up on my history. Charleston has been awash in Calhoun fever, not only because of the charged nature of who the man was but because of his statue's location as well. It's in Marion Square, down the street from the Emanuel African Methodist Episcopal Church, or "Mother Emanuel," as it is known, where the Charleston shooting of nine black church-goers occurred in 2015.

Calhoun was a US secretary of war, the seventh vice president of the United States, a US secretary of state, and one of the five greatest US senators of all time, according to a senate committee in 1959 headed by Senator John F. Kennedy. Calhoun belonged to the Great Triumvirate, or the Immortal Trio, of powerful congressional leaders, along with congressmen Daniel Webster and Henry Clay. Known for calling slavery "a positive good," he owned two plantations and more than a hundred slaves. In fact, one book calls him "slavery's greatest champion." Most people who lived in South Carolina during his lifetime, however, were slaves, and, according to College of Charleston history professor Bernard Powers, slaves considered Calhoun evil. When Calhoun died in Charleston in 1850, it is said that white Charlestonians draped public buildings and private homes in black and wore black armbands, whereas black people rejoiced in the streets.

Back in 1838, when southern disagreements with the federal government about tariffs, expansion of slavery to new states, and return of slave property and talk of secession were already simmering issues, Calhoun had said, "It is the most difficult process in the world to make two people of one," and he was long dead before South Carolina—led by Charlestonians, said to be "single-mindedly fixated on secession"—took the step of being the first state to secede. But many people credit him with helping to build the South's position on secession—

in particular, Charlestonians', who many report "had for years been agitating for war and discord"; most notably, for promoting the idea of "nullification." Yet another term uncommon in my daily life, nullification is the concept that a state could invalidate any federal laws it felt were unconstitutional and detrimental to its sovereign interests. Calhoun also espoused "interposition," the idea that a state can interpose itself between the federal government and its residents by taking action to prevent the federal government from enforcing laws that the state considers unconstitutional.

In Jefferson Davis's farewell address to the US Senate, announcing his resignation as senator from the seceding state of Mississippi, however, he holds a different view of Calhoun's intentions: "Nullification and secession, so often confounded, are indeed antagonistic principles. Nullification is a remedy which it is sought to apply *within* the Union" (emphasis added). Davis explained that Calhoun "advocated the doctrine of nullification because it preserved the Union. It was because of his deep-seated attachment to the Union, his determination to find some remedy for existing ills short of a severance of the ties which bound South Carolina to the other States, that . . . Calhoun advocated the doctrine of nullification, which he proclaimed to be peaceful, to be within the limits of State power, not to disturb the Union."

These subtleties about Calhoun's promotion of nullification aside, after the Calhoun statue was vandalized in the weeks after the Charleston shooting, with more recent calls for its removal, the mayor of Charleston asked the Charleston History Commission to develop language for a plaque to put the man and his values in the context of those times; the city was barred by a South Carolina statute from removing the statue. Kogan was not asked to be on this commission, much to his chagrin, but he has been attending all relevant public meetings, fighting any attempts to put up the "defamatory" context. He claims to have brought as many as sixty men to city meetings to pressure the commission and the city council to abandon the plaque. In an email to me, he says, "What fun! We will fight them on the beaches, we will fight them in the streets, we will fight them in the hills, we will especially fight them in the Council chamber. . . . We will never surrender!," appropriating, possibly in jest, Winston Churchill's famous words in regard to fighting Nazis, but leaving me a bit stunned, given the context. Then, he signs off, "Deo Vindice" ("With God as our defender," the motto of the Confederate states). "We will win one for the 'Lost Cause' yet."

Commission member Robert Rosen drafted the wording of the plaque. Rosen, a Jewish Charlestonian, divorce lawyer, historian, and the author of *The Jewish Confederates*—one of the books that rocked my world when I discovered that these folks existed—had penned for the plaque, among many other words recounting and praising Calhoun's achievements, the following: "This statue is a relic and a powerful reminder of the *crime against humanity* which was slavery" (emphasis added). Apparently Kogan objected to the use of those Nuremberg Trial words—not only because he feels Calhoun was a respectable statesman but also because he doesn't believe Calhoun should be compared to Hitler.

Professor Powers, whom the mayor has consulted on the statue issue, counters this argument: "If slavery was not a crime against humanity, what is an example of a crime against humanity, aside from the Holocaust? Is there any other example?" I talk to him a few weeks after the city tabled the discussion of the plaque for a year, given the controversy over the wording. "If kidnapping people from across the ocean, consigning them to death in the process of transportation, forcing them to work, separating them from members of their families, taking sexual advantage of the women, preventing them from being able to read and write, if all of those things taken together don't represent a crime against humanity, then what has to happen to qualify?"

He surmises that "folks who object to this language are really saying, 'well, it wasn't that bad.'" He also believes that part of the problem with the idea of contextualizing this and other monuments on the mayor's agenda is that "when we tell the truth about these people, I wonder if the public can stand the truth." He says that for many of the individuals involved with the monument's controversy—and I think about Kogan, who seems to have grown up with all the opportunities that educated white people are generally afforded—their lives haven't been impacted by these issues, which are "purely academic and theoretical."

Later in the day over lunch atop a rooftop restaurant, Kogan explains that what he thinks is so interesting about the current controversy is that within one year of the beginning of the forty-fifth president's term, "they are unraveling federal protections for the environment, for consumers, and our whole future," he says, and "the states are rising up again" to protect people. Issues about whether the federal government or the states are sovereign and to which of these entities residents will have more allegiance are becoming more relevant today, as they were in the years before and during the Civil War. Indeed, within two months of this chat with Kogan, in March 2018, the forty-fifth president's then-appointed attorney general, Jeff Sessions of Alabama, will slam California for passing laws to protect immigrants by creating sanctuary cities—ignoring the fact that everyone in the administration is descended from immigrants, refugees, or slaves. "There is no nullification. There is no secession. Federal law is the supreme law of the land," he'll say, ironically. "I would invite any doubters to go to Gettysburg, or to the tombstones of John C. Calhoun and Abraham Lincoln. This matter has been settled." *The Atlantic* will call the *United States v. California* case "not quite firing on Fort Sumter, but . . . [an] all-out legal war." Here, in Charleston, in January, after imbibing a vodka with lemon or two, Kogan shouts in excitement to make his grand point: "Calhoun lives!"

Robert Rosen's law office is located along Broad Street, a main thoroughfare in Charleston, and I walk past some of the iconic landmarks of the old city to get there: First, Berlin's men's clothing store, at Broad and King, the oldest Jewish store still standing in the city, opened in 1883, after Henry Berlin moved up from peddling. Then, the "Four Corners of Law," as the locals call the intersection of Broad and Meeting Streets, home to the city hall, county courthouse, federal courthouse, and St. Michaels Episcopal Church. While there, I barely catch a glimpse of the dark statue of Judge J. Waties Waring in the garden of the federal courthouse, a civil rights judge who opposed segregation and whose opinion in a Charleston case about school desegregation became the legal foundation of the US Supreme Court's decision against segregation in *Brown v. Board of Education*. The statue was erected at the behest of Judge Richard Gergel, a Jewish judicial civil rights historian— once an unknown US district judge, now known as the man who presided over the trial of the Charleston shooter, Dylann Roof, whose jury sentenced Roof to death.

I meet with Rosen in his light-filled office. He's got wavy, salt-and-pepper hair and a bowtie, which seems to be de rigueur in Charleston, and we chat for a couple of hours, by which I mean I listened.

Rosen is as enlivened as Kogan, though I'm struck by how, in many ways, he is the complete opposite. Kogan comes from the old Sephardic Jews, many of the same relatives as his cousin Anita Rosenberg; Rosen's a relative newcomer, with Polish ancestors who came to Charleston after 1900. Rosen's a working lawyer, and Kogan's a retired professor, and Rosen generally disdains academics. And while Kogan was not invited to be on the Charleston History Commission—perhaps because he does not have adequate history credentials—Rosen, having written several books on American history, is a member, giving him more power over the monument issue. Most notably, during my back-to-back visits with these two men, Kogan emerges as the traditional southern gentleman, speaking eloquently and delicately, apologizing for potentially offending me for even bringing up the idea of prostitution during the course of a conversation about a historic figure. Rosen's got a sailor's mouth and is charmingly irreverent, referring to "stupid shit" and "fucking idiots" frequently during our conversation. It seems Kogan tries to sound like he's from Charleston, softening any remnant of his New York roots as he can, whereas when listening to Rosen's rough talk, I could be convinced he fits the stereotype of a born-and-bred New Yorker.

Unlike Kogan, who delights in the *New York Times* for its unparalleled coverage of the arts, Rosen calls that paper "an unspeakable publication" due to what he believes is a distinctly anti-South perspective. "I'm sick and tired of everyone saying the South is anti-Semitic," he says. In fact, the reason he wrote his book, *The Jewish Confederates,* was to "defend the South." Most northern and northeastern academics, he says, are "full of bullshit" and believe that "the Northeast is the center of goodness, and the South is the center of all benightedness," and that "the South is the stepchild of the country." The Union didn't go to war to end slavery, he says. It went to war to save the Union— no doubt referring to Lincoln's own words about the matter ("If I could save the union without freeing any slave, I would do it, and if I could save it by freeing all the slaves, I would do it"). He rails, too, against the racist behavior toward blacks of many northerners, local and state governments and policies, employers, and even abolitionists before and after the Civil War. He says southerners "resent that snide, condescending attitude."

Rosen admits, "The South has its issues. We can't cover up racism and slavery. We have to pay for that. But the South— and particularly South Carolina—was good for the Jews."

He stops a moment in his semi-tirade. Maybe he noticed a change of expression on my face. "You know that saying, right?" he asks me, about being "good for the Jews." This is good for the Jews, or that is good for the Jews. . . .

"Not really," I tell him. "I didn't grow up hearing that."

"You're not very Jewish, are you?" he says. And thus here in Charleston, the heart of Reform Judaism, despite our shared Jewish understanding—history, culture, language, attitude—he calls me out as an outsider.

But Rosen quickly moves on. He says Kogan "used to be an arch enemy, but now is a good friend," which is funny because Kogan had independently referred to Rosen as "an old friend and adversary." This similarity is not that surprising because also completely independently, Rosen echoes Kogan's statement that "I love to confront people," by saying about himself, "I'm a contrarian." They both seem to delight in debate, which even I recognize as being very Jewish—what some might call the "Jewish national sport," derived from the traditional study of Jewish texts and discussion of different interpretations. And while Kogan complained to me about not being invited to speak at a conference on monuments, Rosen complains about not being invited to speak about Jews and slavery. Both seemed to feel unrecognized and stifled in their ability to make a contribution or to argue a point in a public setting.

On the Calhoun issue, though, Rosen says, "I hate Calhoun. Even the founding fathers didn't defend slavery like Calhoun. We could excuse Washington and Jefferson because they knew slavery was wrong and were in a quandary. But Calhoun brought out the worst in the South."

Nevertheless, Rosen—like Kogan, and even like Powers—does not believe in tearing down monuments. Rosen says that "crazy white liberals" and a few people in the black community want to tear down the monument. But he doesn't see the logic in their argument; he doesn't seem to see the power in symbols. "It's stupid to say that monuments were put up during Jim Crow as a symbol of white supremacy and to further it. . . . Monuments weren't put up to intimidate black people. They didn't need any friggin' monuments to do that. They had guns and intimidation and the Klan!"

The truth, he thinks, is that "white people wouldn't let black people govern them—even if the Union army had stayed here [during Reconstruction] for fifty years!"

The frequent talk of Reconstruction here is also different from any other southern place I've visited. Nowhere else has anyone mentioned it as a force for good or evil; no one mentions it in Virginia at all. But in my first talks with Kogan over the phone and in many other conversations with him, Rosen, and others, Reconstruction still lingers in the air here like old cigarette smoke. What I learn in cramming on my Civil War history in Charleston is that under military districts established by Congress throughout the South, US Army troops were stationed in (some might say "occupied") Charleston for eleven years during Reconstruction, justified because the region "remained so chaotic and because some white southerners remained so hostile to the US government," according to a recent government explanation. After Reconstruction, considered by some to be one of "the most dynamic, inspiring, heart-rending, and transformative periods in American history" but whose leadership Rosen calls "the most corrupt government in American history," whites took back all political control.

This post-Reconstruction period, after 1877, is what historian C. Vann Woodward calls the "abandonment of the Negro as a ward of the nation, the giving up of the attempt to guarantee the freedman his civil and political equality, and the acquiescence of the rest of the country in the South's demand that the whole problem be left to the disposition of the dominant Southern white people."

Rosen's other issue with the monuments is determining "what is the rule for what stays and goes?" Without that standard, "we'd have to take down ninety-eight percent of all monuments." He says he understands taking down monuments of KKK leader and Confederate General Nathan Bedford Forrest, and he can see renaming black schools that are currently named for Lee, Calhoun, or the like, saying "Black people are entitled to their feelings, and we should change things that are offensive to them." He doesn't want the history of Charleston to be erased; yet, inherently, much of Charleston's history is offensive.

In any case, he tells me conspiratorially, he plans to put back the "crimes against humanity" language that had been taken out due to Kogan's objections because some people on the commission of four black and nine white members think the language is too soft now, and the black members and the community don't like it. Meanwhile, Kogan had told me secretly that he plans to suggest dropping the whole plaque idea entirely and work on convincing people to put up a monument to the Emanuel 9, referring to those murdered in Mother Emanuel church. "I'll even put up the first thousand dollars myself," he said.

After visiting Kogan and Rosen, I decide to see the Calhoun statue for myself. It's the end of the day, cold and gray. I walk through the campus of the College of Charleston, past clusters of college students on Calhoun Street, to the ten-acre, one-block, worn-down grassy park of Marion Square, formerly known as Citadel Green. It's where the old Citadel is located (now a hotel), which was established originally as a training school for white militia, including teenage boys, to contain slave rebellions and quell the city's fear after the squelched rebellion planned by Denmark Vesey in 1822. Vesey, formerly enslaved in the islands and then free in Charleston, worked as a carpenter, cofounded Mother Emanuel church, and wanted to help his enslaved brethren break free from oppression. As one scholarly paper ironically described it, he was "convicted for his crimes against humanity" and hanged, highlighting the absurdity of the fight against the proposed wording for the Calhoun statue. Marion Square is also where, years later after Charleston fell to the Union after a 545-day siege, "hundreds of newly emancipated men, women and children rejoiced when a company from the [African American] Massachusetts 54th marched . . . 'old men wept. The young women danced and jumped, and cried, and laughed' in an outpouring of emotion that brought even the soldiers to tears." A month after that, ten thousand people gathered for a parade of black Union soldiers: "a jubilee of freedom, a hosanna to their deliverers."

It's also where the owners of the green space, the Washington Light Infantry and Sumter Guards, recently denied a permit to place a statue of Denmark Vesey. Later, in 2014, the city sited the statue at Hampton Park, which is named for Confederate General Wade Hampton III, who was one of the largest slaveholders in the Southeast, a fact that kills me with its irony. But that park is also land that Vesey may have once walked, and it was where the more than ten thousand members of the black population of Charleston initiated the first Memorial Day, when they visited in May 1865 to fix up and leave flowers at what the Confederates had operated as a prison and then shallow-grave cemetery for captured Union men.

According to Professor Powers, the Charleston shooting brought Calhoun to the attention of many people who hadn't known who he was. "People were looking at the landscape to take a measure of the lay of the land and figure out how someone could become so deranged and deeply committed to white supremacy as the murderer was." The answer, he says, lies in the landscape: "Look at the people we honor in the landscape. When you inscribe these things in the landscape, you're sending a message." One black Charleston resident named Mamie Garvin Fields, born in 1888, said the same thing, writing in her memoir, "As you passed by, here was Calhoun looking you in the face and telling you, 'Nigger, you may not be a slave, but I am back to see you stay in your place.'"

Amid the bright young students' faces and what could be a couple of homeless people, I walk the square and look at the Calhoun monument from all sides. What impresses me about this monument, erected in 1896, is its height. The statue stands atop a plinth that's ninety feet tall "so black people would stop throwing objects at him," according to Powers, referring to the first iteration of the monument, unveiled in 1887 by the Ladies' Calhoun Monument Association, that was much shorter. Now it's so high that viewers can't see Calhoun very well.

But what stuns me more is the proximity of the Calhoun monument to the town's Holocaust memorial, a large, metal configuration of rectangular space that one expert likens to a synagogue, a prison, or even a gas chamber. The two are situated side by side. It is there that I find the lesson at the heart of the Calhoun issue, at the heart of the Charleston shooting, perhaps at the heart of my whole journey of discovering the South. Just a few feet from the Calhoun monument is a large engraved stone that's part of the Holocaust memorial. Within sight of the Mother Emanuel church where Dylann Roof carried out his hateful massacre, the simple, smooth, gray stone offers wisdom to absorb. The line that strikes me is this: "We remember the Holocaust to alert ourselves to the dangers of prejudice, to express our outrage at the scourge of racism, and to warn the world that racism can lead to genocide."

If I have learned anything in the South, it is that we are not finished with this business. I must take this outrage and warning with me.

My trip to Charleston had begun its first day with my visit and lunch with Kogan, and a week later, after my cemetery visits and trip to Drayton Hall and to Sumter and other immersion in this place, it is bookended by spending the evening of my last night at Kogan's apartment. I had been alternately anticipating, denying, dreading, and looking forward to attending a soiree at his place for which I received a much-coveted invitation: his Robert E. Lee birthday party, held annually in some fashion since 1970. It's January 21, which is actually Confederate General Stonewall Jackson's birthday, but having a party on Lee's date of birth, January 19, would have meant a party on Friday night, the start of the Sabbath, and Kogan spends his Friday nights at temple. In many southern states—particularly, Virginia—Lee-Jackson Day (or sometimes the mind-bending Lee-Jackson-King Day) is observed on the second Friday in January, but when I called the Daughters of the Confederacy in Charleston to ask what was happening in the city for the occasion, a representative responded, "Not much of anything is done these days, unfortunately." So, Kogan's party is the place to be for people who care about that sort of thing. When the night approaches and I don a black blouse and a long gold-and-black lamé leopard-print skirt—what does one wear to such an occasion?—I am buoyed to attend, despite my dragging cold, out of an insatiable curiosity: What will others there be like? And, even more so, what will be the party's effect on me?

Of the Jewish people I met in Charleston, with short and long histories in the city, one told me the party was controversial but worth going to, and another told me to "prepare to be horrified." And surprisingly, while Kogan says he has normally feted a hundred people in his apartment for the occasion, the total in attendance this time seems closer to fifty. Although he had told me in advance that most people would not be Jewish, as he's the only member of the Sons who is, I count at least eight fellow Jews.

Kogan appears again in a bowtie, with a Confederate flag handkerchief in his breast pocket and Confederate flag cuff links. My fellow urban northeasterners and I are all wearing black—not out of mourning, but because, well, that's just what we wear. I mingle, but mostly only talk to Kogan and the friends I met during my week in Charleston. My head is clogged. I don't even drink; I stick with club soda, keeping alert to any signals I might observe around me; of what, I don't even know, but I am in untrod territory here.

None of us Yankees sings during the musical program. A quartet of musicians and a soloist lead the group in six southern songs, including "Carolina," the state anthem adopted in 1911; "Lorena," an 1856 love song popular on both sides of the war; and the more controversial "The Bonnie Blue Flag," an 1861 marching song that refers to the unofficial first flag of the Confederacy. Its eight verses, which count out the seceding states one by one, begin with: "We are a band of brothers, and native to the soil / Fighting for the property we gained by honest toil. / And when our rights were threatened, the cry rose near and far / Hurrah for the Bonnie Blue Flag that bears a single star! / Hurrah! Hurrah! / For Southern rights, hurrah! / Hurrah for the Bonnie Blue Flag that bears a single star!" Some of the guests sing with smiling gusto; others with serious faces, perhaps wondering which part of enslaving others to do your work counted as honest toil. The soloist casts a sideways smirk and wink to some audience members—perhaps a secret signal—even amidst her great vocal enthusiasm.

The concert concludes with "Dixie's Land," known colloquially as "Dixie" or "I Wish I Was in Dixie," composed by a northern man in the 1850s; Kogan introduces the piece as a blackface minstrel song "that makes no sense" and also "the national anthem." Looking around, I am amazed at how many people know this five-stanza song by heart. "I wish I was in de land ob cotton / Old timers dar am not forgotten / Look a-way! Look a-way! Look a-way! / Dixie Land." The concert is meant to be festive, and people are smiling, and I sit there on Kogan's fine upholstered furniture pondering, trying to eke out the meaning of this night, with my shifting views on the Confederacy and the South. I also muse on the inscription Kogan had written in a book he authored and gave me as a gift earlier in the week in which he called me an "honorary Daughter of the Confederacy." Does he see some streak in me that sympathizes with Confederates? Is he trying to convert me? (Even Abraham Lincoln knew "Dixie" by heart, I ponder—it was his favorite song. He asked for it to be played after the fall of Richmond in 1865.) Or does he recognize I'm open-minded and willing to acknowledge multiple truths?— that many white descendants of Confederates do truly and innocently believe what they've been taught about the Civil War: that it was fought for states' rights and in defense of a northern invader, not to defend slavery. That the history of the war and the Confederacy has been purposefully and dramatically rewritten in the decades after the war by the Daughters of the Confederacy and other southerners to euphemize the causes of war and the blood on their hands. That also, frankly, northerners can't understand the South's fixation on the war because most of the battles didn't happen on northern ground; the devastation happened down here, on these fields, in these cities, in these homes. I ask myself whether I have moved from ignorance to tolerance to acceptance over the years in the South's version of the war. Have I been willing to concede too much to the white South during all these years of indoctrination in Virginia and beyond? Or do the two separate stories that exist within the minds of northerners and southerners both warrant some measure of consideration? And what do I do now when I am confronted with what I perceive as ignorance—especially willful denial?

If I lived here, Kogan, I'm sure, would be a friend. But the aura I'm surrounded by here—attention, time, and energy spent on the Confederacy, defense of the Confederacy, glorification of the Confederacy—is not my world. Here, in the cradle of secession—or as Sherman called it, "the Hellhole of Secession"—I've come face-to-face with the heart of the beast.

Meanwhile, in a speech he gives about the glory of Lee, whom many Jewish Confederates idolized, calling him "our father," whom Kogan says looks "Christ-like" in one of the portraits in the room, Kogan remarks that, in his opinion, the most important Jewish commandment is "Do not forget." This is his guiding mantra. He points out that "Jews have the longest memory of any people in the world," citing the example of still being angry at the Pharaoh for our enslavement in Egypt after several thousand years. But "the American people have the shortest memory in history," he says as well. And so, combining his Jewishness and his Confederateness, he has no plans to forget or stop fighting for the memory of any of the Confederate dead: like the ten Jewish Confederates killed at Shiloh, five at Second Manassas, seven in Antietam, six at Vicksburg, six at Gettysburg, and all the others who fought in every major campaign.

His talk then takes its inevitable turn. He criticizes the Calhoun statue work of the Charleston History Commission, of which Harlan Greene, a guest at the party, is the commission's chair. Kogan thereby breaks the one cardinal rule that he and at least three other people have taught me is the single true religion of Charleston: politeness. Greene texts me from across the room to point out the weirdness in this situation involving Jewish Kogan vs. Jewish Rosen and Jewish Greene, engaged in a battle about whether the words are too Hitler-esque. Greene also lets me know that earlier at the party, he took the liberty of flipping the Confederate flag pillow in the den so that it wasn't a back cushion of the chair but a seat cushion instead. Kogan eventually saw this, looked aghast, and righted it so it could not possibly receive anyone's rear end. Greene, a Charlestonian by birth, was tickled by this little trickery he pulled—this little resistance. Meanwhile, another guest tells me Kogan's bar has run out of bourbon, a distinctly unsouthern act.

In the end, the party did not win me over to the Lost Cause, but I admit it won my heart by the food; the southern feast is the highlight of the evening. All the food is kosher, and what this means for me is that for the first time in my travels through the South—several years of vegetarian food struggles—I do not have to abstain from the greens for their ham hocks or the rice and beans for their pork sausage or the sweet potato biscuits for their lard. The collard greens are wilted and spiced and vegetarian. I can pile my plate with all these items, as well as peppery potato-pancake-cum-hush-puppies; crisp, colorful coleslaw; and whole, pickled (not fried!) okra. I bypass the beef barbeque and lemon chicken, the latter a favorite of General Lee, according to Kogan. When I ask why he does not serve Robert E. Lee cake for dessert, Kogan knows what I mean. "The general favored a white cake with lemon curd," he says, but his usual caterer is out of town and this one could not produce a kosher white cake that would be moist. "I do not want to give my guests dry cake," he says more than once. The cake, therefore—a replica of Stratford Hall in Virginia, Lee's birthplace and the original Lee family home, where Neil and I visited recently—is chocolate. Kogan commences the slicing of it with a Civil War era sword that belonged to one of his ancestors.

As a Confederate, Kogan could come off sounding shocking to someone with virgin northern ears; when talking about social issues, he sounds like a liberal—calling the Civil Rights Movement "a righteous mission." And when he talks about religion, he is boyishly excited, eloquent, and truly lovely to listen to, and that is what I will remember most about him. While eating this delicious kosher southern feast, I can't help but return again to something he said when we met earlier this week, a thing that's at his core.

We were some of the only people in the cavernous restaurant, and Kogan had taken to imitating past conversations he'd had with people, singing bits of song in a raised voice, and otherwise replaying parts of the reel of his life history—from a happenstance meeting of civil rights activist James Farmer on a train to Chicago to his volunteerism and philanthropy, including helping disadvantaged African Americans in Charleston. "I want to be a good citizen," he had said. When he got to describing how he had surveyed world religions and decided to take up Judaism more seriously and become kosher at age twenty, he explained why he did it, coming from a family that celebrated Christmas in earnest, loved Jesus, and "thought having a relationship with God was like having a relationship with Mars."

"Jewish rituals are occasions of God consciousness," he had said, explaining he wanted to bring more occasions of God consciousness into his life. First he started attending synagogue twice a week—Reform on Friday night and Conservative on Saturday morning, drawing on his basic childhood schooling in Hebrew to teach himself prayer book Hebrew—pronunciation, reading, meaning. Then he started keeping *kashrut,* or kosher.

Keeping kosher, he explains, requires one to think about God when shopping and looking at ingredients. It requires one to think about God while cooking the food. And it requires one to think about God when eating the food, including snacks. "Even walking into kitchen, I am thinking about God," he says, and he has modified his kitchen to be completely kosher, with two distinct halves, two sinks, two sets of dishes and utensils, to separate meat and dairy. He also points out that Jews can think about God while walking through doorways, by touching a mezuzah. "There is even a prayer for going to the bathroom!" he says giddily. "Prayer is silent, but it permeates. Judaism is in everything I do."

He says keeping kosher is tremendously important to his Jewish practice "because it asks me to really sacrifice things I love: snails, spareribs, fried chicken properly cooked in buttermilk. It's a way of getting close to God and reminding me constantly of God."

"When I walk through the streets of Charleston, I feel God," he says. "The air is thick with meaning. I feel embraced. I feel a personal experience with God, within me and all around me." God and human beings interpenetrate each other, he explains, and they're part of each other—the finite and the infinite breathing life into one another. He says this interpenetration is what leads people to perform mitzvot, or good deeds.

Kogan thinks the streets of Charleston are beautiful for another reason, too. He told me that he could just as easily be a member of the Sons of the American Revolution as Sons of the Confederacy, due to his ancestry. But "if you win, you move on," he explained; "If you lose the war, you're stuck." Though he says, "the war came out as it should have," saving the Union, he believes the Confederacy "is glorious because we lost."

"Charleston," he says wistfully—the city that was essentially destroyed by the war, "more terribly punished" than any other city; reduced to rubble by fire and bombardment "like the rubble of ancient Rome or Athens"; full of starving, small-poxed, and homeless people with "ruin, ruin, ruin, everywhere and always," a status its once-wealthy white residents preferred over leaving it "prey for Yankee spoils"; the city that is perhaps the one true love of his life—"is beautiful because we lost."

As for me, the next day I leave the boundaries of this lovely, old "Holy City," as it is known, locked in time as if still walled in by its own colonial boundaries, and I struggle to recall if I ever felt more like a stranger in a foreign land in my own country as I have felt here.

ROAD TO JERUSALEM

I have returned to Virginia.

Neil and I are sweating through our shirts on a hot tour bus. The giant bus is lumbering down narrow backcountry dirt roads that bisect flat, fallow peanut fields and chopped-down cotton stalks. We are touring murder sites.

Rick Francis, sixty-two, is at the front of the bus, speaking to our group of about fifteen tourists—black, white, and brown. Francis is a large white man, well over six feet tall, with substantial girth, and he's kind and jovial, a "recovering lawyer," as he calls himself, and former mayor of a nearby small town. For the past ten years he has been clerk of the circuit court where he oversees all the records of the county. He is dressed this Saturday morning in a shirt and tie. With a true historian's enthusiasm, he's narrating the story of the only truly notable historical event this county has known: a humid August night and day in 1831 when fifty-five men, women, and children were slaughtered. He's a descendant of one couple who survived, and yet he speaks only of the facts of the matter—dates, times, names, places, and actions— detached from any emotion. He tells me he leaves it up to visitors to decide if the man at the helm of the bloodbath is a sinner or a saint.

We are on a Nat Turner tour in Southampton County.

It was Easter Sunday when I realized that Nat Turner's famous slave insurrection happened not in a faraway, somewhere-else place, but here in Virginia, my own state. Two days earlier I had been in Central Florida with Neil, my dad, stepmom, and sister, celebrating Passover. Traditionally, each Passover, Jews recount the story of when they were slaves in Egypt, forced into back-breaking labor; when Moses implored the pharaoh to let them go but was repeatedly denied; when God sent a series of ten plagues down upon the Egyptians, culminating when the angel of death came for each first-born child, except the Jews, whom it passed over when they marked the doorposts of their homes with the blood of a lamb; and when Moses eventually led the Jews out of bondage into the desert wilderness, where they wandered for forty years until they reached the promised land.

The common refrain at the end of the Seder is "Next year in Jerusalem"—a wish that next year, the temple destroyed there two thousand years ago might be rebuilt with the coming of the messiah; a metaphor that next year will see peace in the land of Israel and peace in the world; and the traditional assumption that the Jews of the diaspora still long to return to their traditional homeland.

I've never had such a longing, but I found myself in Jerusalem anyway three weeks later—Jerusalem, Virginia, that is. Named in 1791, Jerusalem is what the hamlet was called back in Nat Turner's time; now it's known as Courtland (population 2,000; 48 percent black, 46 percent white, 6 percent other). It's the epicenter of the Nat Turner slave revolt. This "Old Jerusalem" tour is my long-overdue purposeful and necessary plunge into the African American history I feel I have only come across sideways in my travels through the Deep South.

Nat Turner was born into slavery in 1800 on a farm owned by Benjamin Turner, a man who didn't protest that Nat, a slave, was learning how to read and write. Nat was born with certain unusual marks on his body, and his mother told him from an early age that those marks were God's way of saying he was "intended for some great purpose," as he reported in his "confessions." He became a preacher because even his master "remarked that I had too much sense to be raised . . . as a slave," and he devoted his time to "fasting and prayer." He even baptized a white man, which was unusual for the time. At one point, he ran away from the plantation, from a new overseer, spending thirty days in the woods, but then he returned when "the Spirit appeared to me and said I had my wishes directed to the things of this world, and not to the kingdom of Heaven."

Then, he had a vision that signaled him to act:

> White spirits and black spirits engaged in battle, and the sun was darkened—the thunder rolled in the Heavens, and blood flowed in streams. . . . I discovered drops of blood on the corn as though it were dew from heaven . . . and then I found on the leaves in the woods hieroglyphic characters, and numbers . . . and the Spirit instantly appeared to me and said the Serpent was loosened, and Christ had laid down the yoke he had borne for the sins of men, and that I should take it on and fight against the Serpent, for the time was fast approaching when the first should be last and the last should be first.

One of the signs he said he had received was the solar eclipse of February 12, 1831, which cut a swath across southern Virginia. When that happened, Turner decided "I should arise and prepare myself, and slay my enemies with their own weapons." He gathered a few trusted compatriots—enslaved and free—to lay out a plan.

Back in 1831, this area was considered "thinly settled" with a "large expanse of forest." Described in 1861 as "rural, lethargic, slipshod," it had its "due allotment of mansion-houses and log-huts, tobacco fields and 'old-fields,' horses, dogs, [and] negroes," one of which was the famous Dred Scott. In the Dred Scott case of 1857, the US Supreme Court ruled against Scott, saying that African Americans were not US citizens and therefore had no standing to sue in federal court for their freedom.

Francis says that although in the early 1800s, this county was one of the top five wealthiest counties in Virginia, by 1831 it had fallen to the forty-sixth. While whites were still outnumbered by blacks (6,500 whites to 9,500 blacks), only about one-third of the whites owned slaves, usually no more than ten, and the enslaved people and owners sometimes lived in the same room and shared fieldwork. There were plenty of "poor white folks," and one of the relatively less wealthy was Sallie Travis, Francis's great-great-great-aunt, along with her husband, Joseph Travis, the man who owned Nat Turner. Francis is embroiled in this history in more ways than one.

The Turners' was the first house the posse hit on August 21, 1831, after assembling at Cabin Pond for what Francis called "the last supper." We, too, begin our travels through time at Cabin Pond, a small, shallow woodland pool off the side of a dirt road, not too far into a forest of bedraggled small trees, where nearby on the bus Francis is setting the scene of the revolt. I get out of the bus to walk in the mud, litter at my feet, to be in the uncomfortable place where Turner readied himself for becoming a heroic freedom fighter or a terrorist, depending on how you consider the context in weighing his actions.

Then we head out to what's left of the Turners' place, what was once a long clapboard house with a tin roof where Nat tried to kill his master but could not strike a deadly blow and instead allowed another man, known as "Will, the executioner" to finish the job; Will also killed his master's wife, Sallie; their two boys; and a child in a crib. Now all that's left is a sandy-colored dirt road going off into the distance of wide blue sky and a pile of rocks.

The second site we come to is the home of Salathial Francis, where Rick Francis's bachelor great-great-great-uncle was killed. After the crew knocked on the front door, Francis answered, and they gave him a blow to the head. Now Salathial Francis's land is a field of geometrically pleasing green farm rows; back then he grew corn. It was there that a ten-year-old slave named Red Nelson ran from the house to warn Nathaniel and Luvenia Francis, Rick Francis's great-great-grandparents, of the impending danger. In addition to recounting conversations from his friendship with some of Nat Turner's descendants, Francis tells us more than once during the day that he owes his life to Red Nelson, who helped pregnant Luvenia crawl into a hidey hole and then escape to the woods, thus preserving the Francis line. As noted in the family bible, the child that would eventually lead to Rick Francis was born "1 m. 7 days after insurrection."

The tour goes on like this for hours, with murder sites and empty house lots: Piety Reece's plantation, where Francis says the woman was known to be living in a "state of fornication" (having sex without being married), which is still illegal in Virginia today; the home of the widow Mrs. Elizabeth Turner where again Nat Turner's axe was too dull to strike a deadly blow on Mrs. Sarah Newsom, who was visiting, and again Will the executioner did the job; the Catherine Whitehead house, where seven family members were killed and Francis says there were still bloodstains on the floorboards seventy years later before the house moldered away.

We also visited the place where a rumor started that the British were invading, the only way some people could make sense of what was happening. Another place on our route was where a slave demanded his master hide in the woods, and when the master wouldn't go, the slave carried him there over his shoulder to save him. Another spot was where a white man overheard the insurrectionists call Nat "General." At William Williams's house, the posse allowed the man and his wife to lie down together to die.

The 1790 home of Mrs. Rebecca Vaughn—where she and three others were the last white people killed in the revolt—is the only home of murder victims that's still standing. It's a simple one-and-a-half story house that's been moved from its original location and restored by the Southampton Historical Society. Mrs. Vaughn's niece was murdered in the yard, Mrs. Vaughn was murdered in the house while praying on her knees, and her sons were killed while approaching the house from the lane nearby.

All the while, the men in Turner's group had been stealing "Southampton brandy," getting drunk, and disobeying orders. Turner had been trying to lead them on the road back to Jerusalem where he was expecting reinforcements, arms, and ammunition, but plans went awry. Some of his men were killed and captured. At least one was decapitated, likely a man named Alfred, a blacksmith owned by Levi Waller, whose wife and children were murdered in the revolt. His head was placed on a pike as a warning to other blacks, somewhere along a road that to this day is still called, disturbingly, Blackhead Signpost Road.

Turner wound up hiding in a hole in the ground for two months on a large parcel of farmland now owned by a couple dozen of Turner's descendants. On this day when our bus sidles up next to a farm gate on that property, which Francis says is roughly four hundred acres, the sign the family posted at the edge of the road—"Nathaniel 'Nat' Turner, a literate minister, slave, and leader of the Southampton Slave Insurrection of August 21, 1831, hid in caves near this site until his capture on October 30, 1831"—has been defaced with three blasts of buckshot. Francis shakes his head in dismay when he sees this, takes a photo, and texts it on his flip phone to his good friend, Bruce Turner, one of Nat's descendants.

There were sixty insurrectionists in all, who had acquired horses, guns, axes, swords, clubs, and ammunition along the way, the largest group of people that had been assembled in Southampton County (population 18,000; 33 percent black, 62 percent white, 5 percent other) since the War of 1812, according to Francis. As they traveled from house to house in a twenty-mile stretch, he said they used "a full gallop approach to instill paralyzing fear in those they were attacking." Nat Turner had said "neither age nor sex was to be spared" in "the work of death and pillage," and he said "'twas my object to carry terror and devastation wherever we went." When the day and a half of killing was done, they had murdered more women and children than men, at least twenty women and at least twenty children, several at school, because, as he put it, "nits turn into lice."

But they did pass over the homes of the poor whites, the non-slave owners, and the white people who had been Nat

Turner's childhood friends. The killings, kind of like the slay-
ings of the Egyptians' first-born three thousand years ago,
were selective.

It is evening by the time Neil and I get to the Great Dismal
Swamp after an exhausting day on the Nat Turner bus. We
had told a few people on the tour where we were going next,
and the bus driver had told us to watch out for snakes and
alligators (although there are no alligators in the swamp), and
others mentioned mosquitos and spiders. None of those crea-
tures concerned me. Neil and I had other things on our mind.

The Great Dismal Swamp National Wildlife Refuge, south
of Newport News and Norfolk, Virginia, is the largest intact
remnant of a vast habitat that once covered more than a million acres of southeastern Virginia and northeastern North
Carolina. It was a huge waterlogged natural area known in
1728 land records as the Great Dismal (dismal being a term
once used for a swamp or morass), where William Byrd II of
Virginia and his team, the first white discoverers of it, were
"almost devoured by yellow flies, chiggers and ticks." Byrd
called the place a "horrible desart [sic]."

Today, it is still one of the largest natural areas on the East
Coast, now more than 112,000 acres, or 170 square miles in
both states, and it is a draw for Neil and me due to its significant birding and history locations. It includes designations for
state and globally important bird areas, home to more than
two hundred species of birds, and it is a National Park Service
National Natural Landmark as well as a designated site on the
Underground Railroad Network to Freedom.

Driving east from Courtland to Suffolk and south to the
refuge, we begin our exploration on Railroad Ditch, one of few
dusty gravel roads that are built up next to ditches and canals.
Starting in 1763 with the Dismal Swamp Company, of which
George Washington was a shareholder, generations of enslaved
men had been put to work trying to drain the swamp with
150 miles of ditches and canals to try to make it into arable land.

As early as about 1680, escaped slaves fled to the Dismal Swamp, forming a hidden community of freedom seekers, known as maroons. Up to fifty thousand people may have lived in the thick swamp over time, on slightly raised islands, building cabins and engaging in small-scale farming, fishing, and hunting. Dan Sayers, an archaeologist at American University, who is studying the remains of these communities, said, "These people performed a critique of a brutal capitalistic enslavement system, and they rejected it completely. They risked everything to live in a more just and equitable way, and they were successful for ten generations."

We make a right at West Ditch and drive until we reach the intersection to Interior Ditch. All roads are straight with right angles, surrounded on both sides by great swaths of forested swamp—pine, Atlantic white cedar, maple, black gum, tupelo, bald cypress, sweet gum, oak, and poplar—and deforested swamp pocked with cypress stumps. Generations of men have also realized the futility of draining the swamp—in fact, in 1795, George Washington tried to sell his share in the company to Henry "Lighthorse Harry" Lee, Robert E. Lee's father, and by 1810 the company started harvesting cypress and cedar for shipbuilding.

Moses Grandy was one of the men involved, both as an enslaved man and later when he was freed. Born enslaved in approximately 1786, he began working in the swamp when he was owned by a child-master and hired out by other employers. First he was a "car-boy in the Dismal swamp; [he] had to drive lumber," as he describes his life in his 1843 memoirs, which he recorded eight to twelve years after the Nat Turner revolt. When his young master came of age, the master allowed Grandy to work for himself, giving the master part of the earnings. Referred to by his employers as "Captain Grandy," he provisioned and manned canal boats for excursions into the swamp and for delivering goods outside of the swamp. During the course of his work, he recorded that he "sold some cargoes" to Moses Myers, a Jewish merchant in Norfolk.

In the swamp, he saw many gangs of slaves cutting canals. "The labour there was very severe," he wrote. "The ground is often very boggy: the negroes are up to the middle or much deeper in mud and water, cutting away roots and bailing out mud: if they can keep their heads above water, they work on." Later, Grandy "undertook the lightening of the shingles or boards out of the Dismal Swamp," and by this time, logging had opened up access to some of the maroon communities, who began to trade with enslaved workers like Grandy; they would help the "shingle gatherers" meet their daily quotas from cedar trees in exchange for food, clothing, and other necessities.

After six miles of kicking up dust going 20 mph in my car, we come to Virginia's largest natural lake at 3,100 acres, Lake Drummond. It's the darkest, bluest body of water I have ever encountered. Not the deep muddy-brown or black of most natural lakes. Not the bright turquoise of Caribbean seas. Instead, a deep sapphire navy. The color is said to come from water percolating through organic soils and peat. The wind has chopped up the lake, with shark-fin waves but no whitecaps. I walk a wooden pier out into the lake to surround myself with this otherworldliness, but Neil, who hasn't seen any good birds and feels that the swamp is mostly devoid of wildlife, is too cold, even in the sun, to join me.

It was on the shore of this lake, "among snakes, bears, and panthers," that Moses Grandy built himself "a little hut" and had provisions brought to him, to recover from rheumatism and probably try to recover from the stress of his life. He had worked toward and paid for his freedom three different times after various owners reneged on their agreements. The merchant Moses Myers tried to tell one of these new buyers that he could not purchase Grandy because Grandy had already purchased himself, and, as Grandy reported it, "further said I was one of their old war captains, and had never lost a single thing of the property entrusted to me," but to no avail.

His life's tribulations also included having had one wife who was sold away and never heard from again; having to endure "the continued misery" of seeing his second wife abused, without being able to protect her, and later, of buying one of his sons' freedom but having to withstand three other boys and three girls being sold to New Orleans, with one of the daughters being sold three times after being taken from Virginia and made to work sugarcane and cotton fields; and of not knowing what ultimately happened to most of his children, whether they were dead or alive.

In learning Grandy's story of the lake and the swamp, this godforsaken place where Neil and I have chosen to spend our evening, I remember back a few Passovers ago to a conversation about slavery with some guests who had been invited to my parents' house. I knew there were people who, astonishingly to me, believed that slavery was not that bad and that most slaves loved their owners and were happy, but I had never actually heard anyone say the words out loud until one of the guests said them that night. I had been so flabbergasted by this remark, which was made in all seriousness, that I was nearly unable to speak.

But I did speak. I informed this person that this was wildly incorrect, that they had drunk the Kool-Aid from the wrong pitcher. I wasn't rude. I was sad at the ignorance, lack of inquiry, easy-way-out assumptions of America, which were represented here. I also knew that only my curiosity about history, nurtured from an early age, had saved me from being equally unaware, but I also knew there was still much I did not know and didn't even know that I didn't know, so I was not that much more enlightened.

I had learned that this denial had its roots in the decades after the Civil War. Even in the slave-trading center of Charleston, generations of post–Civil War white Charlestonians didn't believe that Ryan's Mart or the Old Slave Mart (now the Old Slave Mart Museum) on Chalmers Street was actually a slave auction complex, a place where slave brokers regularly sold people. Tourist information from 1911, a Charleston newspaper in 1930, and the Charleston Historical Society in 1936, claimed that there was no record that the Old Slave Mart was ever used for slave trading. Well into the 1970s, these entities made a point of promoting that Charleston never had a city-sponsored slave mart, omitting the fact that, according to historians, "the buying and selling of human chattel was actually an everyday feature of commercial life in the city." Obituaries of slave traders didn't mention their work, and records with biographies of those men left this information out as well. Scholars have deduced that "Few things troubled white southerners more than the notion that their ancestors had actively engaged in the sale of men, women, and children and facilitated the destruction of families. So they tried to distance their region from human trafficking whenever possible." In other cases, they said, those with ancestors involved began saying "unequivocally that the practice had been foisted upon them by outsiders."

While some people dealt with these troubling facts by denying them entirely, others rationalized their own, and eventually their ancestors', involvement in slavery by reasoning that slavery wasn't so bad. Apparently, while the original slave owners in the Americas "were at least forthright in their assumption that the slave population would murder its masters if given half a chance," in the words of one scholar, it seems that "by the fifth generation of masters and slaves . . . masters perceived themselves as benevolent but firm parents, ordained by God to direct the errant energies of a childish black race."

"By the time Lincoln was elected," one scholar says, "nearly every white man and woman in South Carolina was condemned to believe that slavery was positively good and, stranger yet, that the abolition of slavery was absolutely evil."

The "domestic charade," or "Magnolia Curtain" of denial and obfuscation flourished during the era of the Lost Cause, which is defined as the last decade of the 1800s through the first couple of decades of the 1900s. That was the period when white southern women in particular—mothers, grandmothers, sisters, daughters, and granddaughters, first as Ladies' Memorial Associations and later as the Daughters of the Confederacy—wanted to enshrine the culture of white supremacy from Virginia to Texas to "instill in white children a reverence for

the political, social, and cultural traditions of the former Confederacy" and to ensure that history would not be written in
such a way that would make their husbands and sons seem
like traitors who had died in vain, sullied by the suggestion
that they had fought to preserve slavery. The Daughters monitored, wrote, or rewrote textbooks to be pro-southern and
pro-Confederacy; renamed streets, highways, counties, and
towns for Confederate heroes; hung portraits of Lee throughout southern classrooms, often next to George Washington,
thus teaching southern students to equate the two men (as
evidenced at Washington-Lee High School in Arlington where
I live); and poxed the southern landscape with monuments to
the Confederate cause, despite the fact that even Confederate General James Longstreet remarked, "Why not talk about
witchcraft if slavery was not the cause of the war. I never heard
of any other cause of the quarrel than slavery."

Of the often-mistaken notion that slaves singing while they
were working in the fields was evidence of their happiness and
contentedness, Frederick Douglass, the abolitionist, writer, and
statesman who was formerly enslaved, wrote in 1845, "It is
impossible to conceive of a greater mistake. Slaves sing when
they are most unhappy. The songs of the slave represent the sor-
rows of his heart."

Grandy is explicit in his portrayal of his masters, and there
can be no doubt as to the slaves' unhappiness. He says that one
of his owners always kept a black man to whip the others in
the field. A slave forced into this position would attempt to
work in a field different from his wife, "for with his hardest
labour, he often cannot save her from being flogged, and he
is obliged to stand by and see it; he is always liable to see her
taken home at night, stripped naked and whipped before all the
men." Some of the nursing mothers, he says, could not keep up
with the other field hands because of their condition; "I seen
the overseer beat them with raw hide, so that blood and milk
flew mingled from their breasts."

He also witnessed enslaved mothers having to lay down
their children in the hedge-rows while they worked where the

infants were "in danger from snakes . . . I have seen a large snake found coiled round the neck and face of a child when its mother went to suckle it at dinner time." And he says pregnant women who "give offence" in the field were beaten, sometimes with a paddle with holes in it, where "at every hole comes a blister." He says, "One of my sisters was so severely punished in this way, that labour was brought on, and the child was born in the field." The overseer, he says, "killed in this manner a girl named Mary . . . he also killed a boy about twelve years old. He had no punishment, or even trial, for either."

Similar to other slave narratives that tell about being flogged then soaked in brine or rubbed with sand to increase the pain, Grandy adds that "the exposed and helpless" then attract flies and mosquitoes in great numbers . . . and "put the sufferer to extreme torture." He also says he saw an overseer flog slaves "till their entrails were visible: and I have seen the sufferers dead when they were taken down," and the white man is "never called to account in any way for it."

He also notes that after Nat Turner's insurrection, in some places slaves were only allowed to attend white people's churches; they were forbidden to meet on their own for worship as they had when Nat Turner was a preacher—look what happened then! If they were found singing or praying, they were flogged. "My wife's brother Isaac was a coloured preacher," Grandy wrote. "A number of slaves went privately into the wood to hold meetings; when they were found out, they were flogged, and each was forced to tell who else was there. Three were shot, two of whom were killed."

These are just a few examples of the brutality that white people intentionally and legally inflicted on the black people they enslaved, and that doesn't even include the ruthlessness experienced by the 1.5 million to 2 million Africans who died en route from their native countries to the United States in the slave ships, from sickness and starvation, some being thrown overboard as food for sharks. Roughly 3.2 million enslaved people lived in the United States in terror; and in 1831, Virginia was the state with the highest population of enslaved people.

Given these conditions, Nat Turner and his helpers can hardly be blamed for taking violent action. In comparison, few quibble over the reverence afforded the leaders and participants of the Civil War—which Lincoln once called an "inexcusable insurrection" that led to 620,000 to 850,000 dead on both sides, a massive and avoidable multistate, sanctioned slaughter.

Even more relevant, though, was Turner's status. Like most slaves, Turner had few options to break free of his captivity and live as a fully realized human being. While slaves protested in many ways—such as feigning sickness, stealing, destroying property, committing suicide to make the slave owner lose money, or running away—others took to insurrection, willing to risk captivity and even death in the fight against unjust laws for their freedom. There had been more than 150 slave revolts or attempted revolts in the United States from when the first slaves were brought to America in 1619 until the time Nat Turner got his chance. In all, putting an end to slavery and ratifying the thirteenth amendment to the Constitution in December 1865 took enslaved protestors and their allies 246 years.

Rick Francis won't come out and say that Nat Turner was a hero because, he says, none of the documentation proves explicitly that Turner revolted against an unjust system of slavery to free his fellow men from bondage; most records paint him as acting on directives of what he says God told him to do. But Francis admits, "I am not so 'keyed up' about the death of my ancestors ('ancestor worship') as perhaps I should [be]—being from the South. . . . If their, or my, life had to be forfeited to end slavery, then such a death would not have been in vain."

Nat Turner never made it to freedom, except in the afterlife. After the revolt, the Virginia General Assembly of 1831–32 considered a bill to abolish slavery in the commonwealth, and it came within seven votes of passing, which would have truly changed the course of history. Instead, on January 25, 1832, the General Assembly resolved it "inexpedient for the present to make any legislative enactments for the abolition of slavery."

* * *

Before there was Nat Turner, there was Denmark Vesey, a name I came to know while I was in Charleston. Vesey, originally named Telemaque, was born enslaved on Saint Thomas, a Danish island at the time, and was sold to work on the French colony of Saint Domingue on the island of Hispaniola, where he worked the sugarcane plantations, where slaves were branded and butchered—ears cut off, skin whipped into ribbons, hamstrings cut, and where more than two thousand enslaved people ended their lives in suicide each year. Through clever tactics, his general intelligence and comportment, and an ability to learn numerous languages, he managed to move up the slavery ladder, so to speak, and work for a captain of a slave ship instead of in the fields, eventually buying his freedom and coming to Charleston.

After working as a carpenter for twenty-two years in that port city and building up considerable wealth, Vesey became a "messianic leader," using his planning, recruiting, and organizational skills to ready perhaps nine thousand slaves, free blacks, and mixed-race people (known then as Mulattos, or "browns") in and outside of Charleston to participate in an insurrection. Perhaps he took his inspiration and guidance from what he could glean from the successes and failures of other attempted slave revolts in the United States as well as the most successful slave revolt ever: the 1791 antislavery and anti-colonial revolt and insurgency led by Toussaint L'Ouverture, which eventually led to the 1804 liberation of Saint Domingue to become the independent country renamed Hayti (now Haiti).

According to one Vesey scholar, Vesey encouraged his flock to see "themselves as God's chosen people, and Charleston as Jerusalem being ransacked for becoming ungodly," and he planned to lead a violent rejection of slavery and a mass exodus, assassinating the governor of South Carolina and other state officials in Charleston; then murdering all the whites of the city with axes, knives, and clubs; burning the city down entirely; and seizing

202 · WANDERING DIXIE

the US arsenal and all the ships in the harbor to escape back to Haiti or Africa. "Vesey believed that as God had delivered the Jews from Egypt so He would liberate the Negroes of Charleston," and he planned to do it July 14, 1822.

But some of the slaves leaked the plans on June 16. So instead of gaining liberation, blacks—slave and free—faced tighter restrictions, like no longer being able to worship at their church because whites had closed or burned down the black churches. In the end, Vesey and thirty-four others were hanged. White people with whom Vesey had conducted business could not believe "that a free black man treated kindly would revolt." In the 1970s, when the city of Charleston wanted to commission a painting of him for an auditorium, one angry white resident wrote a letter to the editor saying that if they were going to honor Vesey, "we should also hang portraits of Hitler, Attila the Hun, and Herod the murderer of babies."

And before there was Denmark Vesey, there was Gabriel Prosser. Born in 1776 at a plantation in Richmond, Virginia, Prosser was taught to read and write, was trained to become an artisan with skills in smithing and carpentry, and was allowed to hire himself out for work, much like Moses Grandy. In July 1800, he revealed his plan for liberty to enslaved field hands, who had gathered on their day off to socialize at a popular location for barbeques, fish fries, outdoor preaching, and gambling. It's an area known today as Young's Spring, part of Joseph Bryant Park in the city of Richmond, site of the former Rosewood plantation, built by a member of the Jewish Mordecai family in the late 1830s, whose farm was worked by enslaved labor.

It is said that there, his fellow enslaved men elected him "Gabriel the General of the Rebel Army." Prosser carried his ideas of freedom to enslaved dockworkers and boatmen, artisans, free men, religious supporters, and French sympathizers whom he visited and recruited during his travels around the area in Richmond and eleven counties beyond. The plan would involve hundreds of slaves. During the Revolutionary War, blacks and whites had caught revolution fever, with blacks embracing the white population's messages of freedom and liberty from tyranny. Prosser's plan was to write "Death or Liberty" on a flag made of white silk, borrowing Patrick Henry's 1775 declaration, and, like Nat Turner thirty-one years later, to kill his owner first. Then, his band of freedom fighters were to kill the other plantation owners of the area and make their way to Richmond to capture the Virginia State Armory and kidnap Governor (and future president) James Monroe and persuade him to free Virginia's slaves.

Thunderstorms and a washed-out bridge foiled the plan initially, and before it could be enacted the next day, a slave (ironically) named Pharaoh and another man gave the scheme away.

Like Denmark Vesey and Nat Turner, Gabriel Prosser and his co-conspirators were hanged. But unlike Vesey and Turner, Prosser has been effectively pardoned. In 2007 Virginia Governor Tim Kaine, who said Prosser was motivated by "his devotion to the ideals of the American Revolution . . . risking death to secure liberty," stated that "Gabriel's cause—the end of slavery and the furtherance of equality of all people—has prevailed in the light of history."

And then, after all of them, there was John Brown, a white abolitionist who—along with his sons and a band of free men, liberated slaves, and slaves—captured a musket factory, the US rifle works and US armory and arsenal, and two bridges in Harpers Ferry, Virginia (the state had not yet seceded to become West Virginia), where Neil and I have walked in town and hiked the nearby trails many times. Brown took two slave owners hostage and freed their slaves, and his overarching idea was to incite a slave rebellion.

Things didn't work out as planned. A mass of enslaved people did not join the revolt as he had hoped and expected. Instead, he was captured and quelled by the work of US Army Lieutenant Colonel Robert E. Lee, a military engineer, and Lieutenant J. E. B. Stuart, a US Army officer. On the last day of Brown's life, in 1859, he handed his jailer a prophetic note

204 · WANDERING DIXIE

that said, "The crimes of this guilty land will never be purged away but with blood."

Then Brown was hanged, with Lee among the witnesses, as well as Virginia Military Institute (VMI) professor Major Thomas J. Jackson—eventually knowns as "Stonewall" during the war—whom the governor of Virginia had sent, along with a contingent of the VMI Corps of Cadets, to provide additional military presence in case of another uprising. Maryland-born southern sympathizer and white supremacist John Wilkes Booth was there as well.

Lee, Stuart, and Jackson, known during and after the war for their strategy and leadership, reconnaissance skills and boldness, and tactical prowess, now have hundreds—maybe thousands—of buildings, monuments and markers, military facilities, ships, parks, roads, schools, universities and colleges, and US towns and counties named after them. Meanwhile, there are few memorials in the United States to the millions of enslaved people, as individuals or as a group, whose labor over hundreds of years contributed to the accumulation of wealth of white America, which has passed along wealth and opportunity over generations; slaves helped build the United States into an economic superpower, literally and figuratively exemplified by having built the US capitol building and the White House. Aside from a roadside historical marker to Nat Turner in Southampton County and a new antislavery monument planned in Richmond, the statue of Denmark Vesey in Charleston, and explanatory signage about Gabriel Prosser at Young's Spring in Richmond where he planned his revolt, and at the African Burial Ground, where he was hanged, it's hard to find other monuments or memorials, and certainly few, if any, schools, churches, roads, counties, parks, ships, or colleges, named for these leaders. These men might have appeared in textbooks as heroes if their revolt and revolution had been successful. Instead, Lee is considered a great general even though he took up arms against his countrymen.

It seems the population at large does not fully understand, appreciate, or even acknowledge the unpaid toil—literal blood, sweat, and tears—that millions of enslaved people provided for the benefit of the country. Aside from Harriet Tubman, Martin Luther King Jr., and a few other people or events often commemorated during Black History Month, very little official remembrance occurs for the unnamed, the unknown, and the unsung African Americans who were the backbone of our country—the ghosted heroes.

These folks were the leaders of a different America. It's this other portrait of America (or the absence of it)—the stories, successes, and the souls of the men, women, and children who were enslaved, and their descendants—that has captivated me over the course of my travels through the South. I am drawn to the hidden, the denied, the lost, the vulnerable, and the valuable. And I am drawn to the forgotten stories most of all because so much is at stake.

Despite my focus on some important African American history in Virginia, in the back of my mind I wonder where the Jews were in all this. After all, Southampton County, Virginia, the site of the Nat Turner tour, "may be the least Jewish place in America. . . . There has never been a single synagogue or temple," according to the *Washington Post.* "The Jewish population even today is virtually nonexistent [and] in Turner's time the closest Jews—no more than a handful—would probably have been . . . 50 miles away." In those other places—the Tidewater region, Fredericksburg, Richmond, Petersburg, and Albemarle County/Charlottesville—Jewish individuals, not communities, could be found as early as 1757, but religious freedom was not guaranteed in Virginia until 1786. Moses Myers, the man with whom Moses Grandy conducted business in the Dismal Swamp, along with his wife and children, were the first Jewish American residents in the Norfolk region in 1787, for example, and they made up that area's entire Jewish population for more than a decade.

But Jews were there, like they were nearly everywhere else in the South. If there's anything my travels have shown me

about the Jews from the South, it's not so much the surprise
of them having lived and still living in particular locations
(Jewish Confederates! Jews with southern accents! Jews eating shellfish!) but that they have assimilated so thoroughly.
They've belonged. In the beginning of my journey, I assumed
that being Jewish and being southern were mutually exclusive.
But in fact, we Eastern European Jews, the newcomers to the
United States, were really the outsiders for a long time. Now
we're the dominant Jewish culture in the nation, and we assume
this has always been so.

Here, in southern Virginia, wherever Jews could be found,
they were intersecting with the area's slave-owning culture, just
like everyone else. They held public positions such as turnkeys
of the jail, constables, city marshals, and city deputy sheriffs.
They were detectives on the police force, required to enact laws
that punished slaves, to manage the incarceration and disposition
of runaway slaves, and to supervise the sale of slaves to sat-
isfy creditors. Jewish members of the Richmond Light Infantry Blues were among those called out to handle the Gabriel
Prosser revolt.

Later, they were the observers and the recorders; for example, members of the Jewish Mordecai family in Richmond
wrote to one another to describe what they heard about
the Nat Turner insurrection. "An account of all the horrid transactions we have heard of would more than fill my
paper, but if the conduct of the blacks was outrageous, that
of the whites was most barbarous toward many of those who
were arrested," Emma Mordecai wrote in a letter to her half-
sister Rachel Mordecai Lazarus a month after the insurrection. "For instance they burnt off the foot of a negro whom
they had taken in on suspicion and found at last that he was
innocent."

She agreed with her fellow white citizens that the insurrectionists "deserved to be punished in the most severe manner
warranted by civilized society," but she was disgusted with the
barbaric treatment of the blacks at the hands of their white
captors.

Jews also reflected on their personal role on what was happening around them. In a letter from Rachel Mordecai Lazarus of Wilmington, North Carolina, to Ellen Mordecai in Mobile, Alabama, she states, "It is a sickening state of things, one to which we are always, in a more or less degree, liable, and it will require more than a herculean effort in ourselves to burst the fetters of our slave population."

Jews benefited from slavery, escaping some prejudice and discrimination by not being the lowest rung on society's ladder. But some Jews believed that safeguarding the rights of blacks would help ensure their own rights and safety. According to Rabbi Bertram Korn, who wrote *American Jewry and the Civil War,* no southern Jews considered themselves "abolitionists," however, in part because abolitionists "drew motivation and inspiration from their evangelic Protestant convictions" and "moved in circles that sought the conversion of Jews to Christianity through active missionizing." But some Jewish slave owners or beneficiaries of the slave-owning society looked for alternative solutions.

Isaiah Isaacs in Charlottesville, Virginia, freed his slaves in his will in 1806, for example, because it was then legal to do so; some left money, land, or homes to their slaves. Others, like Samuel Myers of Petersburg, Virginia, purchased a woman in 1796 with "the obvious intention of emancipating her," as did Solomon Raphael of Richmond in the same year.

Moses Myers of Norfolk, one of the most important people in the growth of the city and one of the richest men in Virginia, would wind up going bankrupt in 1816. When he was told he could avoid debtor's prison by trafficking in slaves, he refused to do so.

Then there was the stand taken by men like Richmond's Alfred Mordecai, who referred to slavery as "the greatest misfortune and curse that could have befallen us." He resigned his forty-year post as an officer with the US Army and refused to take up arms for the Confederacy.

In Micanopy, Florida, about an hour from where I spend Passover with my parents, a man named Moses Levy—slave owner, first cousin of the father of Judah P. Benjamin, and a man who purchased fifty thousand acres of land there as a refuge for persecuted European Jews—penned *A Plan for the Abolition of Slavery* anonymously in 1828. It is now considered "the earliest and most important antislavery document by an American Jew"; in it, he advocated for the humane treatment of enslaved people.

These were small but important actions, and they remind me that listening to the perspectives of others, paying attention, learning with an open mind, writing, speaking, and advocating are some of the many ways to protest.

As for me, I'm not sure what my own education, road to enlightenment, activism, or protest will look like going forward. But I know that my trips to the South, combined with my preceding and subsequent research, has unleashed something in me. I know more about the country now, not much, but enough to want to continue to peel back the layers, look beyond myself and the little world I've been inhabiting for so many years.

When I wonder why people didn't fight against slavery with more resolve, I have to wonder what I would have done, what I'm doing even now. Unjust arrests with mass incarceration of African Americans has become a new form of legal slavery. The made-up concern of voter fraud and a variety of state restrictions and race-based gerrymandering are preventing certain US citizens from being able to exercise their right to vote, affecting our entire democracy.

I don't know if donating money to voting rights and civil rights causes and campaigns, corresponding with my elected officials, and handwriting postcards to encourage citizens to vote is enough. I don't know if relinquishing visits to battlefields and reenactments, which glorify the white Confederacy, and instead focusing on events that celebrate African American history, like commemorations of Juneteenth and Emancipation Day, is enough. But step by step, I want to live with more awareness and intention.

I want to draw out my inner Andrew Goodman, that force of goodness working for change; to embody the words of the Talmud, that 600-year-old collection of rabbinic teachings, which suggests that helping a single person is equivalent to helping the entire world. Before my Deep South journeys, I had thought what I knew, believed, and did was enough. But now I know it is not.

At the lunch break during the Nat Turner tour, a catered affair provided by the African American Bryant Baptist Church in Capron, working toward racial justice was all very much on my mind as I held my plate full of mac and cheese and corn cakes, my glass of iced tea, unsweet, and walked out into the room. I had to decide where to sit among all the tables, with Neil following me. I didn't want to start my own table of the many empty ones left, as my normal introvert self would like to do; nor did I want to segregate myself among the other white people, which would have been easy. Instead, I decided to sit across from a young black man and woman, who were already eating at a large otherwise empty table. It seemed the natural, friendly thing to do and only slightly awkward, perhaps because sitting with anyone I didn't know required some extroversion on my part and because race was so much on my mind. Once Neil and I sat, others—black, brown, and white—sat and ate with us.

The four of us had an outstanding conversation about the food we were eating, often a great common denominator; about farmers markets and community-supported agriculture and organic food and vegetarianism. Once they heard the subject of my writing, they told me about Durham's Black Wall Street, a four-block span known as the Hayti District where more than a hundred African American businesses once thrived during the height of Jim Crow. The black-owned N. C. Mutual Life Insurance Company offered the only cafeteria in the city that would serve black people. The black-owned

Mechanics and Farmers Bank was the only bank that would offer mortgages to black people. The district was also home to furniture stores, five-and-dimes, grocery stores, and more. But starting in the 1960s, the bricks of these strong foundations began crumbling, literally. Urban renewal and the building of Highway 147 destroyed the community, forcing more than four thousand homes and five hundred business to relocate or shutter. Our lunchmates, who live in Durham, invited Neil and me to go out for vegan food if we ever visited the city.

Just as I am starting to evolve and recognize my shortcomings and blind spots, America is evolving, too. The lauded Virginia plantation homes of Mount Vernon, Monticello, and Montpelier have (finally) initiated permanent and highly publicized tours, exhibits, and multimedia experiences about the enslaved people who lived and worked in those places. J. E. B. Stuart High School, in Fairfax County, Virginia, changed its name to Justice High School; in Richmond, the school board voted six-to-one to change the name of J. E. B. Stuart Elementary School to Barack Obama Elementary School. Arlington County has decided to change Washington-Lee High School to Washington-Liberty. Two months after my Southampton trip, the nation witnessed a white woman in my childhood neighborhood of Rittenhouse Square in Philadelphia call out injustice when she shared her now-viral video of two black men getting arrested in Starbucks for simply wanting to use the restroom while waiting to meet someone for coffee. White people are starting to pay attention.

Every time I go back to Arlington National Cemetery, ten minutes from my house, I will walk through that microcosm of American history to honor people who have something to teach me. I will see again and again, always in new light, Jewish Confederate sculptor Moses Ezekiel's Confederate monument and the 482 Confederate dead of Jackson Circle; the Tomb of the Unknown Civil War Dead, containing 2,111 soldiers "gathered from the fields of Bull Run"; the 1,500 US Colored Troops, the first black combat soldiers of the Civil War; and nearby, the 3,800 citizens, or contrabands, former slaves who lived in government settlements in the DC area. There will always be Medgar Evers, the World War II veteran and civil rights activist, whose gravestone seems to be the most decorated by visitors of any I see regularly in the cemetery; and Thurgood Marshall, the first African American associate justice of the Supreme Court, who argued the 1954 *Brown v. Board of Education* desegregation of schools case.

I have visited the gravesites of Rabbi Bertram Korn, the author and historian and highest-ranking Jewish chaplain in US armed forces history; Nathan Bedford Forrest III, the great-grandson of the infamous Forrest, who died young in Germany in World War I; and Captain Humayun Kahn, a Pakistani American killed in a suicide attack in the Iraq War whose father admonished candidate Trump for not standing up to the ideals of the US Constitution.

Soon there will be a new addition. Arlington House, the hilltop home of Robert E. Lee and his wife, Mary Custis Fitzhugh Lee, built by enslaved people using bricks they made by hand from the red clay soil of the plantation as well as shells from the nearby Potomac River, will acquire a sculpture of James Parks, the only enslaved man to have been born at Arlington House (in 1843) and to be buried in Arlington Cemetery (in 1929) as well. I have already walked to the far end of the cemetery to visit his grave many times, but now, inside the house, visitors will be able to see a detailed bronze bust of his weathered face. Enslaved until he was nineteen, he worked as a gravedigger at Arlington Cemetery, digging its very first grave, and he provided information about the plantation house and grounds that was important in the site's restoration. His sculpture, even more so than the Lee bust I saw at Michael Kogan's, is something I will want to see up close, pores and all.

But before then, and before Norfolk and the visit to the Great Dismal Swamp and the Nat Turner tour, there was the Haggadah my sister and I prepared for when we sat at the head of a table of nine for our annual Passover Seder in Florida with my dad, stepmom, Neil, and other friends. A Haggadah ("telling" in Hebrew) is a written guidebook for the Seder and includes prayers, blessings, the story of Passover, songs, and other information. Because my stepmom, Marci, was a pre-school teacher before she retired, we had often used her child-friendly Haggadah, which was just my speed at the time. In other years, my sister, Sara, selected the Haggadah and led the service when planning Passover was not a priority to me.

This year, although I had again renounced the idea of increasing my religious practice, I did feel the call to make the Judaism I did engage in as meaningful as possible. I felt the spirits of all the lost Jewish communities of the South with me—Eufaula, Selma, Vicksburg, Port Gibson, Natchez, St. Francisville, Natchitoches, Greenwood, Clarksdale, Helena, Sumter, and more. I felt connected to the souls of the suffering masses of history in the United States and the world over. So I decided to find a new service and shape it into my own vision.

I borrowed a social justice Haggadah from the American Jewish World Service, an organization that works to end poverty and promote human rights in the developing world. With Sara's help, we pasted, printed, and created a customized Haggadah, and then Sara and I led our people in reading about rousing ourselves to injustice, recognizing our own capacity to make a difference, committing ourselves to building a better world, and speaking out against acts of hate—which, in this second year of the most divisive presidency of my lifetime, had grown significantly (later reports would indicate a 50 percent increase in documented hate crimes in 2017 in Virginia, motivated predominantly by bias against race and religion). In reading the traditional four questions of Passover, this Haggadah beseeched us, as descendants of slaves, not to succumb to compassion fatigue even if we cannot respond to every injustice; we must still uphold our responsibility to help others.

I thought back to the stories I'd heard of southern Jews allowing themselves to be served by slaves around the Seder table, but also of the Jews, blue and gray, coming together on Passover during the Civil War to welcome co-religionists who were strangers in a strange land. I thought of Passover 1865, that day on April 14 when Fort Sumter again raised the flag of the United States after four long years of war, when more than four thousand people gathered to sing "The Star-Spangled Banner," including freed slaves from the nearby plantations of Charleston—and Denmark Vesey's son. And the next day, when President Lincoln died from the wounds inflicted on Good Friday by his assassin, John Wilkes Booth, who said of the terms of the surrender, "That means nigger citizenship." Many Jews would learn of the tragedy while at synagogue, as it was the Sabbath, and rabbis wept at the news. So did former slaves, one of whom said, "We have lost our Moses."

I thought, too, of the people of color I know—classmates, colleagues, relatives, of my own age—who have been spit on, called names, rejected from people's homes, and refused service because of their race, and I thought of the four-hundred-year history of "the preferential treatment of white people" or what I have finally understood to be the inherent racism in so much of American life: the default, the assumed, the "norm," the unnoticed wallpaper of white America. All of this history washed over me and through me: America, with its fangs and its beauty. America, the simple and complex, the consistent and contradictory; the black, white, and gray.

My family's Passover table was full of wine, gefilte fish, matzo ball soup, tzimmes, potato kugel, brisket, and charoset—my favorite dish of chopped apples and nuts tossed with cinnamon and sweet red wine, a symbol of the mortar Jews used as slaves in Egypt to build Pharaoh's cities, a reminder of bondage and freedom. As we retold the story of Passover, I felt the past few years of traveling through history and exploring race, religion, the South, the Confederacy, and the nation's history coming together. I felt like I was in the process of cleaning house—cleansing my own house, my ignorance and assumptions about my heritage and my country, just like observant Jews clean their cupboards, closets, and cabinets before Passover of any crumbs of leavened bread, part of the Passover tradition to reenact the Jews fleeing Egypt in such a hurry that they didn't have time for bread to rise. Passover is, in a sense, a spring-cleaning of the heart and soul.

So at the end of our meal—"the world's oldest Emancipation ritual," as the gay, African American, Jewish chef, historian, and writer Michael Twitty calls the Seder—when our group of not-very-observant northern Jews eating dinner in the South concluded our little service by saying together, "Next year in a just world," I had completed a new revolution around my relationship to America. More than I had asked for when I started my journey, but more necessary than I ever could have imagined.

ACKNOWLEDGMENTS

I am beyond-words grateful to the following individuals who shared their personal stories with me: Sara Hamm and her family in Eufaula, Alabama; Felecia Chandler and Shirley Johnson in Notasulga, Alabama; Ronnie Leet, Hanna Berger, and Charles Pollack of Selma, Alabama; Benjy Nelken in Greenville, Mississippi; Elise Rushing and Amelia Salmon of Natchez, Mississippi; Ann Gerache of Vicksburg, Mississippi; Arnold Himelstein and Louis Rhoden in Clarksdale, Mississippi; Susan Good and Adrien Genet of New Orleans, Louisiana; Mark Sutton and the late Kerlin Sutton in Natchitoches, Louisiana; Lafe Solomon in Helena, Arkansas; Nat Finkelstein of Opp, Alabama; Michael Kogan, Anita Moïse Rosefield Rosenberg, and Robert Rosen in Charleston, South Carolina; Robert Moses and the late Elizabeth Moses in Sumter, South Carolina; Peg Senturia in Massachusetts; and Rick Francis in Southampton County, Virginia. I also give thanks to David Goodman of the Andrew Goodman Foundation.

Thanks also to the following people for sharing information and helping me make contacts and receive tours: Betsy Levasseur, Helen Williams, and Anne Butler in St. Francisville, Louisiana; Al and Anne Rotenberg from Baton Rouge, Louisiana; Leonard Nachman of Baton Rouge; Lisso Nachman of Alexandria, Louisiana; Art Williams in Natchitoches, Louisiana; Mickey Parker in Felsenthal, Arkansas; Harlan Greene in Charleston, South Carolina; and Ruth Hirshey Lincoln of the Jewish Community Legacy Project.

Writing this book would have been much harder without the help of the amazing Rachel Myers, who gave me contact names in various small and large communities throughout the South when she worked at the Institute of Southern Jewish Life. Likewise, some of the best experiences I had while conducting research were at the annual conferences of the Southern Jewish Historical Society (SJHS). I thank the leadership and members of the SJHS whom I met in Nashville and Natchez for helpful hints, small and large.

A huge special thanks to Dale Rosengarten in Charleston, South Carolina, for providing me with contacts, ideas, opportunities, and encouragement for several years. I am so grateful. I appreciate her suggestion to apply for, and appreciate Shari Rabin for awarding me, the Charleston Research Fellowship for 2017–18 through the College of Charleston Pearlstine/Lipov Center for Southern Jewish Culture. Thanks, too, to the College of Charleston's Yaschik/ Arnold Jewish Studies Program and Mark Swick for their hospitality and also to the Special Collections and the Jewish Heritage Collection at Addlestone Library for its resources.

I am also thankful for the Virginia Center for the Creative Arts (VCCA), Carole Weinstein, and the Dominion Foundation and Dominion Resources for financial support of several residencies at VCCA, during which I formulated ideas for and wrote part of this book. Thank you to Trudy Hale of The Porches, for providing such a beautiful and serene writing retreat space, where I wrote significant parts of the book.

I am indebted to David Everett, a masterful critical thinker and creative mind, for reviewing the manuscript twice and helping me crystallize what this book was about—and having faith. I am grateful to Rabbi Lance J. Sussman, a historian of American Jewish history, author, and senior rabbi at Reform Congregation Keneseth Israel in Elkins Park, Pennsylvania, for contributing to the research for several articles I wrote leading up to this book and for reading the manuscript. I would also like to thank again Harlan Greene of the College of Charleston for his time and wisdom in reviewing sections of the manuscript and again Dale Rosengarten of the College of Charleston for reviewing the manuscript. I appreciate Sari Boren for leads, and Nolizwe Mhlaba, a graduate student at University of Massachusetts Amherst, for research assistance. Thanks also to Rachel Unkefer for expertise on Jewish genealogy.

Thank you, my dear friends Laurie McClellan, Kim O'Connell, Karen Richardson, and Diana Friedman and her writing "hive," as well as my mom, Bonnie Eisenfeld, and my stepmom, Marcine Eisenfeld, for reading or listening to early drafts of the book and providing feedback. Special thanks to Marcine Eisenfeld, for coming with me to Jackson, Vicksburg, Port Gibson, and Natchez, Mississippi, for the 2016 SJHS conference. I'm also grateful for the wonderful trip to Clarksdale, Mississippi, with my good friends Sacha Adorno and Brian Biggs.

I am thankful for editor Clay Risen at the *New York Times* for publishing my story "Passover in the Confederacy" (April 17, 2014), during the sesquicentennial of the Civil War. Writing this article helped spawn the idea for this book. Thanks also to Adam Langer and the *Forward* for publishing "These Are America's Most Endangered Jewish Communities," and "Should We Remove Confederate Monuments, Even If They're Artistically Valuable?" in 2017, derived from research for this book. Much appreciation to Dana Shoaf, who in 2019 published "Moses Ezekiel: Hiding in Plain Sight" in *Civil War Times*, which stemmed from research for this book.

Huge thanks to Kristen Elias Rowley, my editor at Mad Creek Books/The Ohio State University Press, for taking me on again. I am grateful for the many people at the press who worked hard to make this book happen, including the anonymous reviewer whose comments were invaluable.

I want to acknowledge the contribution of all the sources I've quoted. I've pulled a lot of words and ideas from scholars, writers, and other thinkers to help me understand my own journey and explain it to others.

I want to acknowledge my appreciation for the National Park Service (NPS) for being a significant contributor to teaching me the history of civil rights in this nation and other American history. The role of the National Park Service in providing American history education to the public is understated, underappreciated, and often unknown. In this book, NPS sites were often my guide.

I am saddened to be writing this thanks after his sudden, untimely death, but I wish to give appreciation to Tony Horwitz, whose book

Confederates in the Attic was an inspiration, many years ago, and who was always kind and encouraging to me as a writer.

Love and appreciation to my family—Bernie, Marci, and Sara Eisenfeld, and Bonnie Eisenfeld—for all the encouragement and interest. And also to my late great-uncle Fred Brafman, who shared with me many times the stories of my great-grandfather. Only through Uncle Freddie have I been able to get a glimpse of what the immigrant experience and early days in America was like for my ancestors.

Above all, always and forever, I want to thank my husband, Neil Heinekamp, for finding my quirky interests interesting and supporting my work, for traveling with me to the South, for being a great reader and editor, and for always fulfilling the wedding vow we made of having great adventures together.

* * *

Please note that while this book generally follows the chronological and geographical order of my trips to the South and thus my journey of discovery and understanding, it is not presented in strict order.

As this book is not a comprehensive history of the Civil War, the Confederacy, the South, Southern Jews, American Jews, slavery, the Civil Rights Movement, African American history, or American history, I recommend the following works for those who wish to read more on these topics (see the complete source list as well):

Aron, Bill, and Vicki Reikes Fox with Alfred Uhry. *Shalom Y'all: Images of Jewish Life in the American South*. Chapel Hill, NC: Algonquin Books, 2002.

Coates, Ta-Nehisi. "The Case for Reparations." *The Atlantic,* June 2014. https://www.theatlantic.com/magazine/archive/2014/06/the-case-for-reparations/361631/.

Cox, Karen L. *Dixie's Daughters: The United Daughters of the Confederacy and the Preservation of Confederate Culture*. Gainesville: University Press of Florida, 2003.

Dyson, Michael Eric. *What Truth Sounds Like: RFK, James Baldwin, and Our Unfinished Conversation about Race in America*. New York: St. Martin's Press, 2018.

Evans, Eli N. *The Provincials: A Personal History of Jews in the South.* Chapel Hill: The University of North Carolina Press, 2005.

Korn, Bertram Wallace. *American Jewry and the Civil War.* Philadelphia Jewish Publication Society of America, 2018.

Kytle, Ethan J., and Blain Roberts. *Denmark Vesey's Garden: Slavery and Memory in the Cradle of the Confederacy.* New York: New Press, 2018.

Landrieu, Mitch. *In the Shadow of Statues: A White Southerner Confronts History.* New York: Viking, 2018.

Lewis, John, with Michael D'Orso. *Walking with the Wind: A Memoir of the Movement.* New York: Simon & Schuster, 1998.

Loewen, James W. *Sundown Towns: A Hidden Dimension of American Racism.* New York: New Press, 2005.

Sarna, Jonathan D., and Adam Mendelsohn, eds. *Jews and the Civil War: A Reader.* New York: New York University Press, 2010.

Suberman, Stella. *The Jew Store: A Family Memoir.* Chapel Hill, NC: Algonquin Books of Chapel Hill, 1998.

Weisman, Steven R. *The Chosen Wars: How Judaism Became an American Religion.* New York: Simon & Schuster, 2018.

NOTES

JEWS, THE CONFEDERACY, RACE, THE SOUTH, AND ME: A PROLOGUE

3 "the saddest day of my life" (National Park Service, 2015)

3 597,000 Federals who were killed, wounded, captured, or missing, but also for the 490,000 southerners who received the same fate (American Battlefield Trust, "The Cost of War," 2019)

3 "What are you fighting for anyhow?" (Foote, 1958)

4 the Nazis got their blueprint for what to do with Jews from what the southerners did to blacks (Whitman, 2017)

7 Jews had begun coming to America as early as 1654 (Sarna, 2004)

7 After establishing a community in 1655 in what is now New York City and in 1678 in Newport, Rhode Island (American Jewish Archives)

7 they started creating a settlement in Charleston in 1695 (Kahal Kadosh Beth Elohim, "History")

7 which became the largest Jewish community in North America through the 1830s (New York Historical Society, 2017)

7 with about five hundred Jewish people, compared to only about four hundred in New York (Ashton, "Slaves of Charleston," 2014)

7 "This synagogue is our *temple,* this city our *Jerusalem,* this happy land our *Palestine*" (Evans, 2002)

7 "Nowhere else in America—certainly not in the antebellum North— had Jews been accorded such an opportunity to be complete equals as in the old South" (Rosen, 2010)

8   "like the mortar in the bricks" (Congregation Kahal Kadosh Beth
    Elohim, 2015)

11 "all the great battlegrounds of the civil rights movement" (Lewis
    and D'Orso, 1998)

THE PEANUT LADY OF EUFAULA

17 "Sara Hamm . . . and her family . . . are now the last Jews left in
    Eufaula." (Institute of Southern Jewish Life, "Eufaula")

17 "gents' furnishing goods," "ladies underwear . . . ready-made suits"
    (Besson, 1875)

17 "town wore a rather lonesome look on the main business street"
    (Institute of Southern Jewish Life, "Eufaula")

18 "re-fashioned it . . . at considerable expense . . . [into] a beautiful
    synagogue," (Besson, 1875)

22 "who became known as the embodiment of resistance to the civil
    rights movement" (Pearson, 1998)

23 "campaign of racial oppression . . ." (Raines, 1998)

23 "white-hot segregationist" (Biography.com)

23 "Segregation now, segregation tomorrow, and segregation forever"
    (Freemark and Richman, 2013)

23 "Judge George Wallace was the most liberal judge that I had ever
    practiced law in front of," (McCabe and Stekler, 2000)

23 But since he was fourteen, his life's goal was to become Alabama's
    governor; and being interested in helping the poor, many of whom
    were black, became politically unpopular (McCabe and Stekler,
    2000)

23 "Faustian bargain" of selling his soul for power, as described by
    many who knew him—biographers, historians, civil rights lawyers,
    and even his children (McCabe and Stekler, 2000)

23 "out-segged" (Pearson, 1998)

24 Some believe his lack of enforcement of civil rights—lawlessness really—led to the bombing of the 16th Street Baptist Church (Biography.com)

24 "What we need are a couple of first-class funerals" (Biography.com)

24 Some say the true, original Wallace came out again by 1982 at age sixty-three (McCabe and Stekler, 2000)

24 "We thought [segregation] was in the best interests of all concerned. . . . We were mistaken" (Pearson, 1998)

24 white planters in Barbour County . . . owned twelve thousand slaves in the mid-1800s (Besson, 1875)

25 "There are over fifty brick stores in the city . . ." (Besson, 1875)

25 a circa 1865 one-and-a-half-story restored brick building (US Department of the Interior/National Park Service, 1986)

26 a brick building with Corinthian flair, circa 1895 (US Department of the Interior/National Park Service, 1986)

26 "almost like fairy land" (Besson, 1875)

27 "colored masonry," . . . became a thing in Alabama only in 1867 (Grand Lodge History, 2015)

27 an 1845 cottage orné (Eufaula Chamber of Commerce)

27 "beautiful historic homes, built in the days when 'cotton was king'" (Alabama Fairs and Festivals)

29 "the belly of the segregated beast" (Lewis and D'Orso, 1998)

THE GEOGRAPHY OF HOPE

30 Tuskegee, Alabama, the poorest place in the state (Stebbins et al., 2015)

30 digging out the material from the ground . . . (Slade, 2014; South Carolina College)

31 "I was born a slave on a plantation in Franklin County, Virginia . . ." (Washington, 1901)

34   black student acceptance rates at the top-tier colleges and universities have dropped over the past decades (McGill, 2015)

34   "main artery connecting to the heart of black America" (Nazaryan, 2015)

35   Most of the people who had lived there then were poor sharecroppers, tenant farmers, or hired workers for white landowners ... (Deria, 2006)

36   "We walked from Woodville to Scrabble School ..." (Scrabble School, 2010)

36   "There was a school about a hundred yards from my house ... to the black school" (Scrabble School, 2010)

36   the state might give two million dollars to white schools per year, and $350,000 to black schools ... (Deutsch, 2011)

36   a man who had grown up in a house across from Abraham Lincoln's home in Springfield, Illinois, and whose uncles had clothed Lincoln and escorted Lincoln's casket back to Springfield (Kempner, 2015)

36   offering matching grants to build black YMCAs (Kempner, 2015)

36   "The horrors that are due to race prejudice come home to the Jew more forcefully than to others ..." (Deutsch, 2011)

36   "the well-being of mankind" (Sears Archives, 2012)

37   "schools of hope" (Alabama Tourism Department and Town of Notasulga, 2010)

37   by 1928 one in every five rural schools in the South was a Rosenwald school (Hoffschwelle, 2012)

37   There was a Rosenwald school in every county in the South with significant black population (Deutsch, 2011)

37   the schools educated one-third of the region's rural black children: 663,625 students in all (Hoffschwelle, 2012)

37   after a Washington, DC, viewing of a documentary film *Rosenwald* (Kempner, 2015)

39   "I loved school," "I wasn't the only one" (Lewis and D'Orso, 1998)

40   "root and branch" (Teaching Tolerance, 2004)

40 five hundred to six hundred left in the country (National Trust for Historic Preservation)

42 "what most Negroes could only dream of in terms of medical care . . ." (Tuskegee University)

42 "Tuskegee Institute gets its full share of the credit" (Centers for Disease Control and Prevention [hereafter CDC], 2016)

43 prevented them from using the Public Health Service's Rapid Treatment Centers, established in 1947 to treat syphilis (CDC, 2016)

43 The study continued year after year, decade after decade, with various reputable groups like the American Medical Association and the National Medical Association approving it along the way (CDC, 2016)

43 "ethically unjustified," (CDC, 2016)

43 When it ended, only 74 of the 399 test subjects were alive (Jones, 1993)

43 Forty of their wives had been infected, and 19 of their children were born with the disease (AllPolitics CNN Time, 1997)

44 Another participant told of having to stay in bed for ten days after that procedure (Eagle, 1972)

45 "our first black president" (Morrison, 1998)

45 "a time when our nation failed to live up to its ideals . . . equality for all our citizens" (CDC, 2013)

46 In fact, they were treated worse than the Germans treated those they shot down and took as prisoners of war (National Public Radio, 2006)

46 "The slave went free; stood a brief moment in the sun . . ." (Levine, 2013)

DEFENDERS OF SELMA

50 "the Jew store" (Suberman, 2001)

51 Dallas County landowners had enslaved 76.8 percent of their population (Graham, 1861)

51 a low-level white worker in charge of voter registration could impose a fee at will (Berman, 2015)

51 or demand that blacks undergo some kind of demonstration of literacy . . . (Loewen, 2016)

51 Sometimes the literacy test meant having to recite the preamble of the Constitution (Rutenberg, 2015)

51 having to name all sixty-seven county judges in the state (Berman, 2015)

52 legal and illegal restrictions that county officials and the (White) Citizens' Council imposed on black people to keep them from voting (Payne, 2007)

52 "pursuing the agenda of the Klan with the demeanor of the Rotary Club" (Baker, 2016)

52 "coat-and-tie version of the Ku Klux Klan" (Lewis and D'Orso, 1998)

52 cut off access to a federal program that supplied surplus food to poor people (Lewis and D'Orso, 1998)

52 denied people loans, increased their rents, unleashed violence against those trying to register to vote, and sometimes killed them with direct attacks (Lewis and D'Orso, 1998)

53 "young folks with bedrolls and backpacks . . ." (Obama, 2015)

53 "one of the Big Six leaders of the Civil Rights Movement" (John Lewis)

53 "I remember at one time I had 400 state troopers, conservation officers, and game and wildlife . . ." (Smitherman, 1985)

54 Not only were eventually about 90 percent of the civil rights lawyers in Mississippi northern Jews (Sachar)

54 northern Jews made up a third to a half of the young activists who went South during Freedom Summer 1964 (Religious Action Center of Reform Judaism; Bush, 2016)

55 "It is rare for a Jew to support publicly controversial issues for fear of exciting latent bigotry" (Tedlow, 1979)

55 a 1966 survey of Selma's Jews by student Marshall Bloom (Bloom, "A Participant Observation Study of the Attitudes of Selma Jews Towards Integration," 1966)

55 In terms of business risks, if Jews sided with their white, racist neighbors and customers, and their many black customers boycotted white stores . . . business could go down substantially (Wisenberg, 2015)

55 "willingness to concede whatever is necessary to the Negroes to insure that business conditions are not upset" (Bloom, "A Participant Observation Study of the Attitudes of Selma Jews Towards Integration," 1966)

55 "those relations may have been less solid than had been acknowledged . . ." (Whitfield, 1979)

55 One southern Jewish couple in Selma voiced their support for voting rights to people they knew, and the Citizens' Council got word of it and launched a boycott of their business (Wisenberg, 2015)

56 "I would feel more free to speak by mind if I knew it wouldn't jeopardize my father's position in the community" (Bloom, "Women," 1965–1966)

56 "avoid intervening in affairs outside of the Jewish community, particularly on the issue of civil rights" (Institute of Southern Jewish Life, Selma, Alabama, 2017)

57 "It is hard to know how the Jewish people really feel . . ." (Bloom, "Women," 1965–1966)

57 John Lewis said the same thing in the 1960s about northern students . . . as did . . . Medgar Evers about activists like John Lewis . . . "We didn't want them to come" (Lewis and D'Orso, 1998)

57 He believed in leveling the playing field, according to his brother, David Goodman ("L'Chayim: David Goodman (Andrew Goodman's Brother)")

57 "who dared, who had the courage to go to the lion's den and try to scrub the lion's teeth" (Angelou, 2014)

58 "I hate northern Jews" (Wisenberg, 2015)

58 "Andy didn't go to Mississippi expecting to die" (Goodman and Herzog, 2014)

58 "We had Jewish Rabbis from up East . . ." (Smitherman, 1985)

58 National Refugee Service, based in New York City (Puckett, 2014)

58 Others covertly made financial contributions to civil rights organizations (Dreier, 2015)

59 the earliest Jews came to Alabama in 1785 (Puckett, 2014)

59 "the first chief executive on the North American continent to appoint a Jew to his cabinet . . ." (Evans, 1988)

59 "prominent figure" (American Battlefield Trust, "Nathan Bedford Forrest")

59 "Come on boys, if you want a heap of fun and to kill some Yankees" (American Battlefield Trust, "Nathan Bedford Forrest")

59 "avowedly hostile to the domestic institutions . . ." (University of North Carolina Chapel Hill, *Ordinances*)

60 "dastardly Yankee reporters" (Levine, 2013)

60 "That devil Forrest must be hunted down and killed . . ." (American Battlefield Trust, "Nathan Bedford Forrest")

60 Forrest was also the man who eventually ordered the dissolution of the first iteration of the KKK in 1869 (American Battlefield Trust, "Nathan Bedford Forrest"; Library of Virginia, "Jim Crow"; Mississippi Civil Rights Project)

60 volunteered to help "exterminate" the men responsible for continued violence against blacks (Tures, 2015)

61 "Jews would not tolerate a statue of Hitler in their neighborhood . . ." (Associated Press, 2012)

61 attacked it with cinder blocks (Brown, 2012)

61 "Our country will never, ever be the same because of what happened on this bridge" (Berman, 2015)

61 nineteen other rabbis (nearly all northern, midwestern, or western—not southern) (Dreier, 2015)

62 a thousand military policemen and two thousand army troops (Harmon, 2015)

62 less than 50 percent of the population is connected to a municipal sewer line, meaning some people have to drain their toilet waste out into their yard (Tavernise, 2016)

62 Soon after the march, in retaliation for her support of the protestors, her grocery store was burned to the ground (National Civil Rights Museum, 2017)

62 "a soggy mess" (National Geographic, 2015)

63 "three centuries of suffering and hardship" (Reed, 1965)

63 "Picked . . . just like a movie producer would pick a set . . ." (Smitherman, 1985)

63 "the notorious brutality of local law enforcement under Sheriff Jim Clark . . ." (Stanford University, Martin Luther King Jr. Research and Education Institute)

63 the number of registered voters who were black rose from 31 percent to 73 percent in the subsequent decades (Berman, 2015)

63 Section 5 of the act required parts or all of sixteen states (Berman, 2015)

63 "those areas of the country where Congress believed the potential for discrimination to be the greatest" (US Department of Justice, "History of Federal Voting Rights")

64 "no longer need to seek preclearance for new voting changes" (US Department of Justice, "Jurisdictions Previously Covered")

64 this act prohibited more than three thousand discriminatory practices from happening over its lifetime (Berman, 2015)

64 395 voting restrictions were introduced in 49 states (Berman, 2015)

64 From the time of its gutting through May 2017, 31 states introduced at least 99 bills to restrict registration and voting (Williams, 2017)

64 "so that a visitor, Attorney General Robert F. Kennedy, could not put a desecrating Yankee foot atop it" (Raines, 1998)

65 Governor Wallace, who decided to erect the Confederate flag over the Capitol on the day of Kennedy's visit (Carlson, 2015)

A NIGHT IN NATCHEZ

73 Frogmore, still a working cotton plantation and gin from 1815 whose Civil War–era owner was a Union sympathizer and yet owned 159 slaves (LouisianaTravel.com, 2017)

73 "full hands," "prime hands," "three-quarter hands," "half hands," "quarter hands" (Rosenthal, 2013)

73 "Negroes were but pieces of machinery," "the master hand that set them in motion" (Harby, "In the Days When We Were Young, III," 1886)

74 planter families sent their children to boarding schools in Europe or up North; summered in northern spas . . . (Levine, 2013)

75 "unquestionably the state's most active slave trading city" (Barnett and Burkett, 2003)

76 "regional foods that are among the *most* delectable dishes in the world but also the *most* forbidden by Jewish standards" (Ferris, 2005)

76 "the elegant heart of the diet of the lower Mississippi River" (Ferris, 2015)

76 "Jewish food culture in Natchez defies kosher law in a way that dazzles and surprises" (Amer, 2015)

77 "the greatest trayf buffet one could ever imagine" (Ferris, 2015)

77 "treyfa banquet" . . . : "The event turned into a faux pas heard round the Jewish world" (Weisman, 2018)

77 The early twentieth-century revival of the Klan was apparently more anti-Semitic up North than in the South (Webb, 2001)

78 "its members did not bother to boycott the Jewish retailers on Main Street" (Whitfield, 2006)

78 "Who else would have sold Klansmen their denims, their shoes, and even their sheets?" (Whitfield, 2006; Levitas, 2015; McGraw, 2006)

78 Many sources tell the story of southern Jewish storeowners recognizing men under white hoods by the shoes they had sold them
(Bass, 2002; Webb, 2001)

78 "Most of the Klan's anti-Semitism was discharged against the shadowy, imaginary Jew . . ." (Whitfield, 1979)

78 By 2017 anti-Semitic incidents would rise 57 percent in a year, the
largest single-year growth on record, including at least one incident
in each state (Anti-Defamation League, 2017)

79 Vicksburg, Mississippi, . . . where twenty Jewish families lived by
1825 (Ford and Stiefel, 2012)

79 with 650 members and the city's first indoor swimming pool (Southern Jewish Life, 2017)

79 down from nearly five hundred in the 1870s and again in the 1920
(Weissbach, 1997)

79 forty-seven-day siege while residents starved, even eating rats (Wallace, 1998)

79 and shoe leather (McKay, 2011)

79 "Federals were slaughtered in droves" (Edwards, 2014)

80 "with the Mississippi River now firmly in Union hands . . ." (American Battlefield Trust, "Vicksburg")

80 "too beautiful to burn" (Institute of Southern Jewish Life, "Port
Gibson")

81 "That's where we all come from, after all, back to Abraham" (Applebome, 1991)

81 Jews first settled here in 1798 (Ford and Stiefel, 2012)

81 "They stayed open on Saturdays until one or two in the morning . . ." (Moses, "The Lost Tribe of Natchez")

84 even cutting off their ears (Galik, 2016)

84 "ready to do almost anything to keep their negroes in the field"
(Levine, 2013)

ALL MIXED UP IN GUMBO LAND

87 many black people, especially in New Orleans, were free and owned property (Levine, 2013)

88 "one of the most successful plantation owners in Rapides and Natchitoches Parishes" (Louisiana Regional Folklife Program)

88 French "Black Code" from 1685, decreeing that Jews should be expelled from any French territory . . . (Ford and Stiefel, 2012)

88 though the Spanish kicked the Jews out . . . (Ford and Stiefel, 2012)

88 "My mother professed to being a Jew, though not openly . . . (K. Sutton, 2015)

89 "We love our darkies" (Spiro, 1979)

89 Samuel Myers Hyams, the town and parish's surveyor and engineer starting in 1837 (International Jewish Cemetery Project, 2010)

89 In Natchitoches, this plot follows the custom of other Jewish cemeteries . . . (Goldman, 1968)

90 "the mere fact of non-discrimination . . . was a motivating factor for assimilation" (Goldman, 1968)

91 every store was run by Jews (E. Sutton)

91 "dry goods, groceries, boots, shoes, hats, clothing, hardware, and general plantation supplies" (Goldman, 1968)

91 "fancy and staple groceries," "cotton and country produce" (Goldman, 1968)

92 "I am accountable to all citizens who live in our city . . ." (Sharkey, 2015)

92 "rolling store men" (Evans, 1979; Lewis and D'Orso, 1998)

93 "life-saving credit" (Butler, 2015)

93 "pivotal figures in cotton marketing and financing" (Butler, 2013)

93 "to become conduits for funneling some much-needed cash into rural areas" (Butler, 2015)

95 displaced nearly a million people (Bradshaw, 2011)

95 when the river rose to its highest point ever and stayed that way for 153 days (Bradshaw, 2011)

95 "the worst flood in the history of the United States" (Ambrose, 2001)

95 overflowing the Mississippi River in eleven states (Nowell, 2017)

95 "Towns became deserts. Plantations became inland lakes" (Cohn, 1967)

96 "unprecedented" (Yan, 2016)

96 "deadly, record-setting flood" (Emamdjomeh and Krishnakumar, 2016)

96 a once-in-a-thousand-year event (Samenow, 2016)

96 the Baton Rouge gauge was up to almost eighteen feet (US Geological Survey, 2016)

98 Julius Rosenwald had built the black residents a school (Butler, 2004)

99 "It was an hour of rejoicing" (Butler, 2015)

100 "Everywhere thickly peopled by sugar planters..." (Louisiana Division of Historic Preservation)

101 "Gold Coast" (Louisiana Division of Historic Preservation)

101 home to five hundred plantations and two-thirds of the known millionaires in the United States in the decades prior to the Civil War (Butler, 2004; Louisiana Division of Historic Preservation)

101 St. Charles, 81.5 percent enslaved; Iberville, 73.8 percent; West Baton Rouge, 74.2 percent; West Feliciana, 83.5 percent and Concordia, 91 percent (Graham, 1861)

101 "in all the history of America, it is doubtful that..." (Rosen, 1997)

101 slave owners fell into several categories (Levine, 2013)

101 Those soldiers were some of the two-thirds to three-quarters of white southerners who were slaveless (Levine, 2013)

101 "Poor fellows... [who] did not understand in the least what they were fighting about" (Starobin, 2017)

102   A grass, a reed, a crop that produces honey without bees, as the Persians once said many centuries ago (Food and Agriculture Organization of the United Nations, 2009)

102   more than half the slaves died during childbirth (Levine, 2013)

103   Scalding burns could disfigure or kill a person, fingers could be ground off, and arms could become trapped and have to be chopped off (International Slavery Museum)

103   "left an appalling legacy of death in its wake" (Whitney Plantation)

103   First-offender runaway slaves could have their ears cut off and be branded; second offenders were hamstrung . . . (Galik, 2016)

103   George Washington's Mount Vernon (317 slaves at the time of his death) (George Washington's Mount Vernon)

103   Thomas Jefferson's Monticello (607 slaves) (Bates, 2012)

103   James Madison's Montpelier (100 slaves) (James Madison's Montpelier, "The Life of James Madison")

103   Oatlands (133 slaves) (Oatlands Historic House and Gardens)

103   Sully Plantation (40 slaves) (Fairfax County Park Authority)

103   Arlington House (200 slaves) (National Park Service, 2017)

105   Slavery drove banking, insurance, railroads, shipping—everything in the economy was powered by it (Mitchell, 2018)

105   "the human machines that worked to build the honor of someone else" (Mitchell, 2018)

107   "A small cairn of stones, pine cones and flowers at the edge of the trees . . ." (Beck, 2014)

107   "The Senators could not persist in this polite debate over the future dignity . . ." (Andrew Goodman Foundation)

107   "voodoo math" (Schwartz and Schleifstein, 2018)

107   By 5:00 p.m., the Baton Rouge gage was at twenty feet (US Geological Survey, 2016)

108   "horror movie" (Premack, 2016)

TRUE SOUTH

111   "the deepest South" (Cobb, 1992)

111   "the South's South" (Wilson, 2004)

111   "Mississippi's Mississippi" (Willis, 2000)

111   "the most southern place on earth" (Cobb, 1992)

111   byproduct of milling rice—once relegated to slaves (Twitty, 2017)

112   "horizontalness" (Gatewood, 1996)

113   "recent delta" (Delta Cultural Center)

113   "long silky fiber" (Cohn, 1967)

113   "nothing less than the answer to a cotton planter's prayers . . ." (Cobb, 1992)

113   about the size of New Jersey (Willis, 2000)

113   when the river floods, it actually backs up into the Yazoo River (Hudson, 2016)

113   nearly completely forested . . . (Willis, 2000)

114   "the Yazoo Delta's millions of undrained acres . . ." (Hudson, 2016)

114   wolves, panthers, and alligators (Willis, 2000)

114   the Delta is where the blues was born (Christine Wilson)

114   "one-of-a-kind, they-broke-the-mold, real-deal Delta blues" (Devi, 2013)

114   "Blues, as almost any Mississippian will tell you, came 'from the cotton patch'" (Palmer, 1981)

114   "created not just by black people but by the poorest, most marginal . . ." (Palmer, 1981)

114   "an elaboration on work chants, 'sorrow' slave songs . . . 'field hollers'" (Christine Wilson)

115   today there are 1.4 million Jews in the South (Sheskin and Dashefsky, 2016)

115 their locations have changed; 85 percent of all US Jews live in twenty metropolitan areas (Levere, 2010)

115 Atlanta, New Orleans, Memphis, Dallas, Charleston, and even Birmingham (Sheskin and Dashefsky, 2016)

116 "darling of the burgeoning folk music movement . . ." (Mississippi John Hurt Foundation).

116 a Choctaw chief who negotiated ceding Choctaw lands (Wilson, 2004)

117 "Our position is thoroughly identified with the institution of slavery. . . ." ("Confederate States of America: Mississippi Secession")

117 "There ain't nowhere in this whole world where a Negro has got it as bad" (Cobb, 1992)

117 "Blacks live in a 'reign of terror'" (Cobb, 1992)

117 "Greenwood is growing rapidly . . ." (Welcome to Greenwood, MS "Klein Building")

118 "the Delta's premier shoe store" (Main Street Greenwood)

118 "one of the . . . highest class shoe stores" (Welcome to Greenwood, MS "Goldberg's Shoes")

119 Hopson Planation—formerly about 3,500 acres (Hopson Commissary)

119 While Eli Whitney's cotton gin of 1793 had increased the speed of cotton processing by 4,900 percent . . . (National Museum of African American History and Culture, 2018)

120 Tenant farmers and sharecroppers ran 87 percent of farms in the Delta by 1910 (Wilson, 2004)

120 "It was never enough . . . I could see that from the beginning. Even a six-year-old . . . bottomless pit" (Lewis and D'Orso, 1998)

121 "excite a festive atmosphere" (Zangrando)

121 There were around four thousand lynchings officially recorded throughout the South between 1877 and 1968 (NAACP, 2018; Robertson, 2015; Robertson, 2018)

121 with the highest number (581) in Mississippi (NAACP, 2018)

121 "believed they had fulfilled their obligation to former slaves by fighting for the Union" and "only grudgingly endorsed black voting rights" (Egerton, 2014)

121 "sundown towns," often with signs saying "Nigger, don't let the sun go down on you here" (Loewen, 2005)

121 Also from the 1930s to the 1960s, the home-mortgage market and the Federal Housing Administration . . . (Coates, 2014)

121 "In the North, legislatures, mayors, civic associations . . ." (Coates, 2014)

122 "the most potent legend in the blues" (Christine Wilson)

122 down from about four hundred Jewish people at the end of the 1930s (Institute of Southern Jewish Life, "Clarksdale")

123 full of black customers (Shankman, 1979)

123 "The Jew was the merchant who said 'mister' to blacks" (Shankman, 1979)

123 Jews allowed blacks to try on ready-to-wear clothes without being required to buy them (Shankman, 1979)

123 "to teach them the skills that they would need to open their own businesses" (Shankman, 1979)

123 "patched-up sharecropper shack" (Eckholm, 2007)

124 "a Negro pleasure house" (Eckholm, 2007)

124 Willie "Po' Monkey" Seaberry died of a heart attack (Threadgill, 2016)

124 received seventeen Blues Music Award nominations (Homans, 2015)

125 "ingeniously systematic musical language" (Palmer, 1981)

125 "a fusion of music and poetry accomplished at a very high emotional temperature" (Palmer, 1981)

125 "Instead of funding skills training and providing programs for the vulnerable . . ." (Harlan, 2015)

125 African Americans, who when enslaved made up 79.8 percent of the population in 1860 (Graham, 1861)

125   The article cites Tunica's poverty rate of 30 percent . . . ; the public
       high school's 97 percent black student population and 57 percent
       graduation rate . . . ; the fact that one in four people does not have
       a bank account; and that the average life span in Tunica is sixty-
       seven for men and seventy-three for women . . . (Harlan, 2015)

126   "You can't out-poor the Delta" ("Scratching a Living," 2013)

126   "some of the nation's richest white farmers" and "distracts visitors
       from . . . rural poor" (Willis, 2000)

127   "sea of water in the commercial and residential areas of downtown
       Greenville . . . canals" (Nowell, 2017)

127   even threatening to withhold the food that the Red Cross was
       bringing in . . . (Nowell, 2017)

127   "bring back to life the city of Greenville during a period of his-
       tory . . . 'the golden years'" (Greenville History Museum)

127   "Queen City of the Mississippi Delta" (Greenville History
       Museum)

128   "a third cousin once removed of the Mexican tamale" (Trillin, 2014)

128   "naturally" separate all-white and all-black middle and high
       schools . . . (Hauser, 2016)

128   "the heart and soul of the Delta" (Trillin, 2014)

129   "the effect of locking minority and poor children . . ." (Southern
       Poverty Law Center, 2016)

130   "plantation empire" (Willis, 2000)

130   "Cotton is more than a crop in the Delta . . ." (Cohn, 1967)

130   "the largest public ball we have ever had" (Cobb, 1992)

131   some Chinese are buried in the Jewish section (Institute of South-
       ern Jewish Life, Greenville, 2017)

131   "Work hard, send your kids to college, watch them move away"
       (Block, 2017)

131   As it turns out, Jewish people in the Delta love Chinese food too;
       some even hold a Seder on the second night of Passover at a Chi-
       nese restaurant. (Pomerance, 2002)

131 "was the Delta's liveliest blues center," "a little Chicago" (Palmer, 1981)

131 Arkansas, too, was settled by a variety of enterprising European Jews, beginning in 1825 (Rockoff, 2016)

131 "the deepest of the Deep South" (Gatewood, 1996)

131 Helena is also now the poorest town in the second-poorest state in the country (Stebbins et al., 2015)

134 "He simply views it as things having come full circle," "The Delta Jews, after all . . ." (Nelson, 2016)

136 The state of Mississippi had to take over large tracts . . . (Hudson, 2016)

136 Railroad companies purchasing land and completing a railroad line for cotton commerce from Memphis to New Orleans in 1884 (Hudson, 2016)

137 "strange and detached fragment thrown off by the whirling comet that is America" (Cohn, 1967)

138 more casualties on both sides than in all other previous US wars combined (National Park Service, 2018)

138 "beating down so hard you'd give everything you owned . . ." (Lewis and D'Orso, 1998)

WHERE IT BEGINS AND WHERE IT ENDS

141 oldest surviving Jewish burial ground in the South (Kahal Kadosh Beth Elohim, "Coming Street Cemetery")

141 one of the oldest Jewish sites in the entire New World (Gruber, 2015)

141 second-oldest synagogue building in the country and the oldest in continuous use (Kahal Kadosh Beth Elohim, "History," 2019)

142 "Jews, heathens, and other dissenters from the purity of Christian religion" (Carolina Fundamental Constitutions, Amendment I, 1669)

142   fled again, often eventually to islands in the Caribbean such as
      Curaçao, Barbados, Saint Thomas, Jamaica, and Trinidad (Hagy,
      1993)

142   one of the few Confederate companies named for a Jewish Confed-
      erate (Rosen, 2000)

142   "religious revolution" (Sarna, 2004)

142   "transform and revitalize" (Sarna, 2004)

142   "to make Judaism more suitable to its new American setting" and
      to encourage new members at synagogue (Sarna, 2004)

143   "Most rabbis believed that the destruction of the First Temple . . ."
      (Clare, 2014)

143   "Under the influence of the spirit of the age" (Hagy, 1993)

144   "inheritance" from the Barbados, where many of its slaveholder
      founders were from (Robertson, 1999)

145   like Marks Lazarus, her Revolutionary War relative (Rosefield,
      1959)

145   "worst defeat of the revolution" (History.com, "1780")

146   the first poetry volume by a Jewish American woman (Gruber, 2015)

146   sung across the country for more than a century (Gruber, 2015)

146   "increasing hostility on the part of the non-slaveholding States to
      the institution of slavery," "have denounced as sinful the institu-
      tion of slavery" (South Carolina, 1860)

147   "It was the first time we were seeing other Vulcans . . ." (Ohlheiser,
      2015)

147   "Most people don't know what it's all about . . ." (Ohlheiser, 2015)

147   "to exist as a slave-society: a society whose economy could not
      exist . . ." (Kynor, 2016)

147   "the most thoroughly Africanized urban center in the United
      States . . ." (Robertson, 1999)

147   According to the 1860 census, about 8 percent of the entire US
      population owned slaves (Civil War Home page, 2018)

147 as did 25 percent of the population in the South (Mintz)

147 In the state of South Carolina, however, overall slave ownership was much higher—46 percent (Littlefield, 2016)

148 slave ownership was at more than 74 percent in 1850 (Clare, 2014)

148 urban Charleston—the central port of entry for most slaves in the state (Powers)

148 for nearly half of those transported to the United States (Roberts and Kytle, 2015)

148 87 percent of whites owned slaves (Ashton, "Slaves of Charleston," 2014)

148 Jews . . . were accountants, tailors, clerks, owners of clothing stores, grocers, and merchants of various sorts (Hagy, 1993)

148 very few owned plantations (Korn, 2010)

148 Jews in Charleston were slave owners at a rate of 83 percent (Moore, 2002; Ashton, "Slaves of Charleston")

148 Although generally not much involved with the Atlantic slave trade from abroad (Rosengarten, 2002)

148 which was abolished in 1808 after whites brought over nine million to thirteen million people from Africa (James Madison's Montpelier, 2018)

148 Jews were involved in less than 1 percent of the African trade to America (Drescher, 2010)

148 as merchants and auctioneers who sold all kinds of goods, some Jews participated in the sale of people once they arrived on American soil (Rosengarten, 2002)

148 one of the richest men in Charleston and all of South Carolina (Clare, 2014)

148 the first public orphanage in the United States, whose cornerstone was laid by George Washington (Starobin, 2017)

148 "the auctioning, mortgaging, and leasing of [slave] babies, parents, and families" (Ashton, "Slaves of Charleston")

149   19 to 50 slaves in Goose Creek (Heitzler, 2005; Shanks, 2011; Rosengarten and Rosengarten, 2002)

149   He had always wanted to become a planter because in his native Hanover, Germany . . . (Shanks, 2011)

150   "the first Jew to break through the barriers of bigotry . . ." (Evans, 1988)

150   "How dare you denounce slaveholding as a sin? . . . and became sinful?" (Raphall, 1861)

151   "I am no friend to slavery in the abstract . . ." (Raphall, 1861)

151   "might not only jeopardize the well-being . . ." (Moise, 1829)

151   "tells the history of what was once America's largest and most prosperous Jewish settlement" (Gruber, 2015)

153   1784 map reveals this spot to be an old rice field and salt marsh, as the Ashley River is tidal . . . pastureland with a settlement (Purcell, 1784)

153   He had the slaves cultivate rice mostly for the Cohens' and slaves' domestic needs (Clare, 2014)

153   brown, gray, and red (Clare, 2014)

153   Marx's best customer for this material . . . (Clare, 2014)

153   who supplied building materials to other contractors (Stiefel, 2012)

153   first Jewish builder of a synagogue in America (Stiefel, 2012)

153   built that structure with slave labor (Stiefel, 2012)

153   was built with some of Jewish slave owner Marx E. Cohen's slave-made bricks (Clare, 2014)

153   "Carolina Grey Bricks," used in the walls and the arches (Waddell, 1997)

153   painted white . . . to look like stone (US Department of the Interior, National Park Service, 1980)

154   The proof of their labor, like in other bricks across South Carolina and the South, is in the fingerprints stamped in the clay (Mitchell, 2018; Price, 2019)

154 "I-never-owned-any-slaves syndrome" (Mulholland, 2016)

154 "splendid days of [her] childhood" (Harby, "In the Days When We Were Young, I," 1886)

154 "there were games of all kinds, singing and dancing . . ." "old folks . . . days of their early life" (Harby, "In the Days When We Were Young, IV," 1886)

155 "a circle of dusky faces, with gleaming eyes and teeth . . ." "so naturally joyous . . . the whole negro race" (Harby, "In the Days When We Were Young, IV," 1886)

155 an enslaved man named Jim—likely James Matthews (Ashton, "Re-collecting Jim")

155 "I have often wished that I was a dog; they seemed so much better off than we" (Matthews, 1838)

155 "assembled at 'the bank' and received their sweet potatoes . . ." (Harby, "In the Days When We Were Young, I," 1886)

156 "I did not think it was wrong to steal enough to eat," "I have sometimes been so faint . . ." (Matthews, 1838)

156 Although David Cohen raised hogs, he didn't eat them—possibly due to keeping kosher . . . ("Mapping Jewish Charleston: Mordecai Cohen")

156 Then they'd get "a dose of salts" or be "washed down with brine" and put "in the stocks" (Matthews, 1838)

156 "when their skin is so cut up they have to keep all the time pulling their clothes away . . ." (Matthews, 1838)

156 "the worst thing to whip with of anything they have," "has two lashes . . ." "it makes a hole where it strikes . . ." (Ashton, "Re-collecting Jim")

156 "like walking upstairs for hours on end" (Lienhard)

156 "The truth was . . . the sugar house was worse than the plantation . . ." (Matthews, 1838)

157 considered a tenement then ("Mapping Jewish Charleston: Mordecai Cohen.")

157 became the largest phosphate processing facility in the world (Historic Charleston Foundation, 2014)

158 "Her name might be generally unknown today" (Lewis and D'Orso, 1998)

158 "because of the drastic change in conditions" (Clare, 2014)

158 which could mean his bereavement over losing his son in the war, the emancipation of his slaves (Clare, 2014)

159 "a bitter pill to try to swallow" (Moses, Interview, August 16, 2013)

160 "The Jews in Sumter were loved to death by the non-Jewish people" (Moses, Interview, August 16, 2013)

160 "made merry . . . for weeks" (Harby, "Old Christmas Times in the South")

161 Robert doesn't remember his father having two dimes to rub together (Moses, Interview, August 16, 2013)

161 "there were Murphys buried in the Jewish cemetery and Weinbergs buried in the Catholic cemetery" (Moses, Interview August 17, 2013)

162 "the light at the end of the tunnel," "utter sadness" (Moses, Interview, 2018)

162 "villain, war criminal, [and] devil" (Sullivan, 2014)

162 carpet bag suitcase that was a popular style at the time (National Constitution Center, 2019)

162 Franklin J. Moses "Jewnier" (Ginsberg, 2010)

163 in his earlier life he was a devoted Confederate who raised the Confederate flag over Fort Sumter at the start of the war (Rosengarten, 2002)

163 "If Moses was a robber, what he stole was not so much white South Carolinians' money as their sense of racial exclusivity" (Ginsberg, 2010)

163 Apparently, many of his relatives in Sumter felt so disgraced by the man that they changed their last name to DeLeon or Harby (Rosen, 2000)

163   "I was completely empathetic with the plight of the blacks . . ."
       "No blacks, dogs, or Jews allowed," "protect the children . . ."
       (Moses, Interview, August 16, 2013)

164   "It can with safety be said that Moses's associations with the negro
       on a basis of equality . . ." (Buxton, 1950)

164   "White supremacy has been their most effective weapon . . ." (Bux-
       ton, 1950)

165   apparent dislike of black people and his belief that blacks and
       whites were not equal (Levine, 2013)

THE LONGEST MEMORY

166   "just as Rabbi Heschel marched with Dr. King" in Selma (Jewish
       Federation of Charleston, 2018)

169   only large city south of Philadelphia . . . (Rosen, 1997)

169   and the wealthiest one in the original thirteen colonies (Powers)

169   "a more hedonistic, pleasure-oriented society never lived on the
       North American continent" (Rosen, 1997)

169   "has been fatally compromised" (Kogan et al., 2017)

170   "a positive good" (Waters, 2017)

170   "slavery's greatest champion" (Kytle and Roberts, 2018)

170   When Calhoun died in Charleston in 1850, it is said that white
       Charlestonians draped public buildings and private homes in black
       and wore black arm bands (Starobin, 2017)

170   "It is the most difficult process in the world to make two people of
       one" (Starobin, 2017)

170   "single-mindedly fixated on secession" (Starobin, 2017)

171   "had for years been agitating for war and discord" (Starobin,
       2017)

171   "Nullification and secession, so often confounded, are indeed
       antagonistic principles . . . *within* the Union," "advocated the doc-
       trine . . ." (Davis, 1861)

172   "This statue is a relic and a powerful reminder of the crime against humanity which was slavery" (Waters, 2017)

173   "There is no nullification. There is no secession. Federal law is the supreme law of the land" (Young, 2018)

173   "not quite firing on Fort Sumter, but . . . [an] all-out legal war" (Epps, 2018)

175   "If I could save the union without freeing any slave, I would do it . . ." (Lincoln, 1862)

176   "Jewish national sport" (MJL, "Conversation and Debate")

177   "remained so chaotic and because some white southerners remained so hostile to the US government" (Downs and Masur, 2017)

177   "the most dynamic, inspiring, heart-rending, and transformative periods in American history" (Downs and Masur, 2017)

177   "abandonment of the Negro as a ward . . ." (Woodward, 1957)

178   established originally as a training school for white militia, including teenage boys, to contain slave rebellions (Fordham)

178   "convicted for his crimes against humanity" (Kynor, 2016)

178   "hundreds of newly emancipated men, women and children rejoiced . . ." (Kytle, 2015)

179   land that Vesey may have once walked (Kytle and Roberts, 2018)

179   and it was where the more than ten thousand members of the black population of Charleston initiated the first Memorial Day (Egerton, 2014)

179   "As you passed by, here was Calhoun looking you in the face and telling you, 'Nigger, you may not be a slave, but I am back to see you stay in your place'" (Fields and Fields, 2012)

179   one expert likens to a synagogue, a prison, or even a gas chamber (Gruber, 2017)

182   Even Abraham Lincoln knew "Dixie" by heart (*New York Times*, 1909)

183   "the Hellhole of Secession" (Kytle and Roberts, 2018)

183 "our father" (Rosen, 2000)

183 ten Jewish Confederates killed at Shiloh, five at Second Manas-
     sas, seven in Antietam, six at Vicksburg, six at Gettysburg (Rosen,
     2000)

186 "more terribly punished" (Starobin, 2017)

186 "like the rubble of ancient Rome or Athens" (Starobin, 2017)

186 "ruin, ruin, ruin, everywhere and always" (Starobin, 2017)

186 "prey for Yankee spoils" (Starobin, 2017)

ROAD TO JERUSALEM

188 "old Jerusalem" (Culler, 1931)

188 "intended for some great purpose" (Turner and Gray, 1831)

188 "remarked that I had too much sense to be raised . . . as a slave,"
     "fasting and prayer" (Turner and Gray, 1831)

189 "the Spirit appeared to me and said I had my wishes directed to the
     things of this world, and not to the kingdom of Heaven" (Turner
     and Gray, 1831)

189 "White spirits and black spirits engaged in battle, and the sun was
     darkened . . ." (Turner and Gray, 1831)

189 "I should arise and prepare myself, and slay my enemies with their
     own weapons" (Turner and Gray, 1831)

189 "thinly settled," "large expanse of forest" (Drewry, 1900)

189 "rural, lethargic, slipshod" (Higginson, "Nat Turner," 1861)

189 "due allotment of mansion-houses and log-huts, tobacco fields and
     'old-fields,' horses, dogs, [and] negroes" (Higginson, "Nat Turner,"
     1861)

190 6,500 whites to 9,500 blacks (Boney, 1974)

190 only about one-third of the whites owned slaves, usually no more
     than ten (Wagner, 2000)

190   "poor white folks" (Higginson, "Nat Turner," 1861)

190   "Will, the executioner" (Turner and Gray, 1831)

191   "1 m. 7 days after insurrection" (Wagner, 2000)

191   Mrs. Vaughn's niece was murdered in the yard (Archaeological Consultants of Carolinas, Inc.)

191   "Southampton brandy" (Drewry, 1900)

192   one was decapitated, likely a man named Alfred (Brophy, 2015)

192   "neither age nor sex was to be spared" "the work of death and pillage" (Turner and Gray, 1831)

192   "'twas my object to carry terror and devastation wherever we went" (Turner and Gray, 1831)

192   "nits turn into lice" (Wagner, 2000)

193   "almost devoured by yellow flies, chiggers and ticks" (Bartel, 2010)

193   "horrible desart [sic]" (Tidwell, 2002)

194   As early as about 1680, escaped slaves fled to the dismal swamp (Grant, 2016)

194   "These people performed a critique of a brutal capitalistic enslavement system . . ." (Grant, 2016)

194   "car-boy in the Dismal swamp; I had to drive lumber" (Grandy, 1843)

194   "Captain Grandy" (Grandy, 1843)

194   "sold some cargoes" (Grandy, 1843)

195   "The labour there was very severe . . ." (Grandy, 1843)

195   "undertook the lightening of the shingles or boards out of the Dismal Swamp" (Grandy, 1843)

195   they would help the "shingle gatherers" meet their daily quotas (US Fish and Wildlife Service)

195   "among snakes, bears, and panthers," "a little hut," "further said I was one of their old war captains . . ." (Grandy, 1843)

196   "the continued misery" (Grandy, 1843)

196 Tourist information from 1911, a Charleston newspaper in 1930, and the Charleston Historical Society in 1936, claimed that there was no record that the Old Slave Mart was ever used for slave trading. (Kytle and Roberts, 2018)

197 "the buying and selling of human chattel was actually an everyday feature . . ." (Kytle and Roberts, 2018)

197 Obituaries of slave traders didn't mention their work (Kytle and Roberts, 2018)

197 "Few things troubled white southerners more . . ." (Kytle and Roberts, 2018)

197 "were at least forthright in their assumption that the slave population would murder its masters . . ." "by the fifth generation of masters and slaves . . ." (Robertson, 1999)

197 "By the time Lincoln was elected . . ." (Kelly, 2013)

197 "domestic charade," "Magnolia Curtain" (Robertson, 1999)

197 "instill in white children a reverence . . ." (Cox, 2003)

198 The Daughters monitored, wrote or rewrote textbooks . . . (Cox, 2003)

198 hung portraits of Lee throughout southern classrooms, often next to George Washington (Cox, 2003)

198 "Why not talk about witchcraft if slavery was not the cause of the war . . ." (Egerton, 2014)

198 "It is impossible to conceive of a greater mistake . . ." (Douglass, 1999)

198 "for with his hardest labour, he often cannot save her from being flogged . . ." (Grandy, 1843)

199 "in danger from snakes . . . I have seen a large snake found coiled round the neck . . ." (Grandy, 1843)

199 "give offence," "at every hole comes a blister" (Grandy, 1843)

199 "One of my sisters was so severely punished in this way . . ." (Grandy, 1843)

199 "the exposed and helpless," "put the sufferer to extreme torture," "till their entrails . . ." (Grandy, 1843)

199 "My wife's brother Isaac was a coloured preacher . . ." (Grandy, 1843)

199 1.5 million to 2 million Africans who died en route from their native countries (WNET/PBS, 2013)

199 Roughly 3.2 million enslaved people lived in the United States in terror (WNET/PBS, 2013)

199 in 1831 Virginia was the state with the highest population of enslaved people (Breen, 2015)

200 "inexcusable insurrection" (Blight, 2001)

200 620,000 to 850,000 dead on both sides (American Battlefield Trust, "Civil War Facts")

200 "inexpedient for the present to make any legislative enactments for the abolition of slavery" (Ahrens, 1994)

201 branded and butchered—ears cut off, skin whipped into ribbons, hamstrings cut, and where more than two thousand enslaved people ended their lives in suicide each year (Kynor, 2016)

201 "messianic leader" (Robertson, 1999)

201 to ready perhaps nine thousand slaves (Robertson, 1999)

201 "browns" (Egerton, 2014)

201 "themselves as God's chosen people, and Charleston as Jerusalem being ransacked for becoming ungodly" (Robertson, 1999)

201 he planned to lead a violent rejection of slavery (Robertson, 1999)

202 "Vesey believed that as God had delivered the Jews from Egypt so He would liberate the Negroes of Charleston" (Kynor, 2016)

202 Vesey and thirty-four others were hanged (Kynor, 2016)

202 "that a free black man treated kindly would revolt" (Robertson, 1999)

202 "we should also hang portraits of Hitler, Attila the Hun, and Herod the murderer of babies" (Robertson, 1999)

202   an area known today as Young's Spring (Virginia Department of Historic Resources, 2002)

202   "Gabriel the General of the Rebel Army" (Virginia Humanities)

203   "Death or Liberty" (DeFord, 2000)

203   "his devotion to the ideals of the American Revolution . . ." (Associated Press, 2007)

203   "Gabriel's cause—the end of slavery . . ." (Associated Press, 2007)

204   "The crimes of this guilty land will never be purged away but with blood" (Library of Virginia, "John Brown's Raid")

205   "may be the least Jewish place in America . . . ," "The Jewish population . . ." (Ringle, 1994)

205   the Tidewater region, Fredericksburg, Richmond, Petersburg, and Albemarle County/Charlottesville . . . as early as 1757 (Urofsky, 1997)

205   the first Jewish American residents in the Norfolk region in 1787 (Institute of Southern Jewish Life, "Norfolk")

205   they made up that area's entire Jewish population for more than a decade (Chrysler Museum of Art)

206   They held public positions such as turnkeys of the jail, constables, city marshals . . . (Korn, 2010)

206   Jewish members of the Richmond Light Infantry Blues . . . (Rosen, 2010)

206   "An account of all the horrid transactions we have heard of . . ." (Mordecai, 1831)

206   "deserved to be punished in the most severe manner warranted by civilized society" (Mordecai, 1831)

207   "It is a sickening state of things, one to which we are always, in a more or less degree, liable . . ." (Lazarus, 1831)

207   some Jews believed that safeguarding the rights of blacks would help ensure their own rights and safety (Sokolow, 2010)

207   no southern Jews considered themselves "abolitionists" (Korn, 2010)

207 "drew motivation and inspiration from their evangelic Protestant convictions," "moved in circles . . ." (Sarna and Mendelsohn, 2010)

207 Isaiah Isaacs in Charlottesville, Virginia, freed his slaves in his will in 1806 (Korn, 2010)

207 some left money, land, or homes to their slaves (Korn, 2010)

207 "the obvious intention of emancipating her," as did Solomon Raphael of Richmond in the same year (Korn, 2010)

207 Moses Myers of Norfolk, one of the most important people . . . (Moses Myers House, 2009)

207 when he was told he could avoid debtor's prison by trafficking in slaves, he refused to do so (Touro Synagogue)

207 "the greatest misfortune and curse that could have befallen us" (Korn, 2010)

207 He resigned his forty-year post as an officer with the US Army and refused to take up arms for the Confederacy (Falk, 2010)

208 "the earliest and most important antislavery document . . ." (Monaco, 2005)

211 red clay soil of the plantation as well as shells from the nearby Potomac River (National Park Service, 2017)

212 a 50 percent increase in documented hate crimes in 2017 (Anti-Defamation League, 2018)

213 four thousand people gathered to sing "The Star-Spangled Banner" . . . (Robertson, 1999)

213 "That means nigger citizenship" (Lepore, 2015)

213 "We have lost our Moses" (Lepore, 2015)

213 the four-hundred-year history of "the preferential treatment of white people" (Coates, 2014)

214 "the world's oldest Emancipation ritual" (Twitty, 2012)

SOURCES

All population and demographic figures in the manuscript come from: US Census Bureau. (2017). 2017 ACS (American Community Survey) 5-Year Survey. https://www.census.gov/acs/www/data/data-tables-and -tools/data-profiles/2017/. Numbers used in this document are rounded and derive from this survey's collection of information about and terminology of one race, including white and black or African American. The "other" referred to in this document includes all other census categories: American Indian and Alaska Native, Asian, Native Hawaiian and Other Pacific Islander, some other race, or two or more races.

Ahrens, Frank. "The Slave Revolt That Shook Virginia." *Washington Post,* December 14, 1994. https://www.washingtonpost.com/ archive/politics/1994/12/14/the-slave-revolt-that-shook -virginia/ae4f51c9-cd04-43fc-98f8-9e8a0d36f97c/?utm_term= .f188c7433a6e.

Alabama Fairs and Festivals. "Eufaula Pilgrimage." Accessed July 9, 2019. http://www.alabamafairsandfestivals.com/410019-eufaula-pilgrimage -eufaula-alabama-april-2014.html#.WNlbooWcHSE.

Alabama Tourism Department and Town of Notasulga. Shiloh Rosen- wald School. Historical marker, April 2010.

AllPolitics CNN Time. "Clinton Apologizes to Tuskegee Experiement Victims." May 16, 1997. http://www.cnn.com/ALLPOLITICS/1997 /05/16/tuskegee.apology/index.html.

Ambrose, Stephen. "Man vs. Nature: The Great Mississippi Flood of 1927." *National Geographic,* May 1, 2001. http://news .nationalgeographic.com/news/2001/05/0501_river4.html.

Amer, Robin. "The Last Jews of Natchez." Gravy, Southern Foodways Alliance. May 21, 2015. https://www.southernfoodways.org/gravy /the-last-jews-of-natchez-gravy-ep-14/.

American Battlefield Trust. "The Battle of Vicksburg." Accessed July 8, 2019. https://www.battlefields.org/learn/articles/vicksburg.

———. "Civil War Facts." Accessed July 8, 2019. https://www.battle fields.org/learn/articles/civil-war-facts.

———. "The Cost of War: Killed, Wounded, Captured, and Missing." Accessed July 8, 2019. https://www.battlefields.org/learn/articles /civil-war-casualties.

———. "Nathan Bedford Forrest." Accessed July 8, 2019. https://www .battlefields.org/learn/biographies/nathan-bedford-forrest.

———. "Vicksburg." Accessed July 8, 2019. https://www.battlefields.org /learn/civil-war/battles/vicksburg?tab=facts.

American Jewish Archives: The Jacob Rader Marcus Center of the American Jewish Archives. "Timeline in American Jewish History." Accessed July 8, 2019. http://americanjewisharchives.org/education /timeline.php.

Andrew Goodman Foundation. Historical Archives. Accessed July 9, 2019. https://andrewgoodman.org/historical-archives/.

Angelou, Maya. Foreword. In Goodman and Herzog, *My Mantlepiece.*

Anti-Defamation League. "2017 Audit of Anti-Semitic Incidents." Accessed July 8, 2019. https://www.adl.org/resources/reports/2017 -audit-of-anti-semitic-incidents.

———. "ADL Alarmed by Rise in Reported Hate Crimes in Virginia." June 6, 2018. http://dc.adl.org/news/adl-alarmed-by-rise-in-reported -hate-crimes-in-virginia/.

Applebome, Peter. "Small-Town South Clings to Jewish History." *New York Times,* September 29, 1991. http://www.nytimes.com/1991/09 /29/us/small-town-south-clings-to-jewish-history.html.

Archaeological Consultants of Carolinas. "The Rebecca Vaughn House." Accessed July 8, 2019. http://archcon.org/investigations/the-rebecca -vaughan-house/.

Ashton, Susanna. "Re-collecting Jim." *Common-Place: Tales from the Vault* 15, no. 1 (Fall 2014). http://www.common-place-archives.org /vol-15/no-01/tales/#.Wny-wOZzI2w.

———. "Slaves of Charleston." *The Forward*, September 15, 2014. https://forward.com/culture/205455/slaves-of-charleston/.

Associated Press. "Bust of Gen. Nathan Bedford Forrest Missing in Selma." AL.com. March 26, 2012. http://blog.al.com/wire/2012/03 /bust_of_confederate_gen_nathan.html.

———. "Slave Who Led Failed Revolt in 1800 'Pardoned.'" NBC-news.com. June 31, 2007. http://www.nbcnews.com/id/20536296 /ns/us_news-life/t/slave-who-led-failed-revolt-pardoned/# .WxVqvY6n82w.

Baker, Kelly. J. "White-Collar Supremacy." *New York Times,* November 25, 2016. https://www.nytimes.com/2016/11/25/opinion/white -collar-supremacy.html.

Barnett, J., and H. Clark Burkett. "The Forks of the Road Slave Market at Natchez." Mississippi History Now. February 2003. http:// mshistorynow.mdah.state.ms.us/articles/47/the-forks-of-the-road -slave-market-at-natchez.

Bartel, Bill. "What's in a Name? Great Dismal Swamp." *Virginian-Pilot,* July 26, 2010. https://pilotonline.com/news/local/history/article _3d4bd87c-37cc-5f66-9462-ad14c9859102.html.

Bass, Jack. "Just Like One of Us." In Rosengarten and Rosengarten, *A Portion of the People.*

Bates, Karen G. "Life at Jefferson's Monticello, as His Slaves Saw It." *National Public Radio.* March 11, 2012. http://www.npr.org/2012 /03/11/148305319/life-at-jeffersons-monticello-as-his-slaves-saw-it.

Beck, Richard. "Remembering James Chaney, Michael Schwerner, and Andrew Goodman." *Experimental Theology,* August 4, 2014. http:// experimentaltheology.blogspot.com/2014/08/remembering-james -chaney-michael.html.

Berger, Julia. P. "Jews and the Civil Rights Movement: There's More to It Than You Might Think." *Jewish Women's Archive*, January 20, 2010. https://jwa.org/blog/jews-in-civil-rights-movement.

Berman, Ari. *Give Us the Ballot.* New York: Farrar, Straus and Giroux, 2015.

Besson, J. A. B. *History of Eufaula, Alabama: the Bluff City of the Chattahoochee.* Atlanta, GA: Franklin Steam Printing House, Jas P. Harrison & Company, 1875. https://ia802609.us.archive.org/30/items /historyofeufaulaoobessiala/historyofeufaulaoobessiala.pdf.

Biography.com. "George C. Wallace Biography: 'Segregation Forever'" (video). https://www.biography.com/video/george-wallace-segregation -forever-141276227943.

Blight, David W. *Race and Reunion: The Civil War in American Memory.* Cambridge: Harvard University Press, 2001.

Block, Melissa. "The Legacy of the Mississippi Delta Chinese." *National Public Radio,* March 18, 2017. http://www.npr.org/2017/03/18 /519017287/the-legacy-of-the-mississippi-delta-chinese.

Bloom, Marshall. "A Participant Observation Study of the Attitudes of Selma Jews Towards Integration." Senior honors thesis, Amherst College, 1966. Marshall Bloom Papers, box 5, folder 8, Amherst College Archives and Special Collections, Amherst College Library.

————. Selma Survey "Women." Thesis, Amherst College, 1965–66. Marshall Bloom Papers, box 5, folder 13, Amherst College Archives and Special Collections, Amherst College Library.

Boney, F. N. "Nathaniel Francis, Representative Antebellum Southerner." *Proceedings of the American Philosophical Society,* October 15, 1974.

Bradshaw, Jim. "Great Flood of 1927." *64 Parishes,* May 13, 2011. https://64parishes.org/entry/great-flood-of-1927.

Breen, Patrick H. *The Land Shall Be Deluged in Blood.* Cambridge: Oxford University Press, 2015.

Brophy, Alfred. "Blackhead Signpost Road Needs Another Sign." *Tidewater News,* August 15, 2015. https://www.tidewaternews.com /2015/08/15/blackhead-signpost-road-needs-another-sign/.

Brown, Robbie. "Bust of Civil War General Stirs Anger in Alabama." *New York Times,* August 24, 2012. http://www.nytimes.com/2012 /08/25/us/fight-rages-in-selma-ala-over-a-civil-war-monument.html ?_r=0.

Bush, Lawrence. "Freedom Summer: June 29-Stokely Carmichael and the Jews." *Jewish Currents,* June 28, 2016. https://jewishcurrents.org /june-29-stokely-carmichael-and-the-jews/.

Butler, Anne. "Jewish Heritage in St. Francisville." *Country Roads Magazine,* March 28, 2013. http://countryroadsmagazine.com/art-and -culture/history/jewish-heritage-in-st-francisville/.

———. "Restoration of Old Temple Gives St. Francisville New Cultural Venue." March 28, 2013. Freyhan Foundation. http:// www.freyhanfoundation.org/restoration-of-old-temple-gives-st -francisville-new-cultural-venue/.

———. *Three Generous Generations.* St. Francisville, LA: West Feliciana Historical Society, 2004.

Buxton, Julian. T. "Franklin J. Moses, Jr.: 'The Scalawag Governor of South Carolina,'" Thesis, Princeton University, 1950. College of Charleston Special Collections, Julian T. Buxton Papers, 1950, MSS 1034–016.

Cane River National Heritage Area. "American Cemetery Walking Tour." Brochure, n.d. Natchitoches, LA.

Carlson, Morgan. "History of the Confederate Flag on Alabama Capitol Grounds." WSFA 12 News. July 22, 2015. http://www.wsfa.com /story/29380544/history-of-the-confederate-flag-on-alabama-capitol -grounds.

Carolina Fundamental Constitutions: Amendment I, 1669. University of Chicago. http://press-pubs.uchicago.edu/founders/print_documents /amendI_religions7.html.

Centers for Disease Control and Prevention. "Presidential Apology, May 16, 1997." US Public Health Service Syphilis Study at Tuskegee. September 24, 2013. http://www.cdc.gov/tuskegee/clintonp.htm.

———. "Tuskegee Timeline." US Public Health Service Study at Tuskegee. February 19, 2016. http://www.cdc.gov/tuskegee/timeline.htm.

Chrysler Museum of Art. "The Moses Myers House." Accessed July 8, 2019. https://chrysler.org/historic-houses/the-moses-myers-house/.

Chyet, Stanley F. "Reflections on Southern-Jewish Historiography." In Kaganoff and Urofsky, *Turn to the South.*

Civil War Home Page. Results from the 1860 Census. 2018. http://www
.civil-war.net/pages/1860_census.html.

Clare, Seth R. "Marx Cohen and Clear Springs Plantation." *Southern
Jewish History* 14, (2014).

Coates, Ta-Nehisi. "The Case for Reparations." *Atlantic,* June 2014.
https://www.theatlantic.com/magazine/archive/2014/06/the-case-for
-reparations/361631/.

Cobb, James C. *The Most Southern Place on Earth: The Mississippi
Delta and the Roots of Regional Identity.* Oxford: Oxford University Press, 1992.

Cohn, David L. *Where I Was Born and Raised.* London: University of
Notre Dame Press, 1967.

"Confederate States of America: Mississippi Secession." Yale Law School.
Avalon Project. 2008. http://avalon.law.yale.edu/19th_century/csa
_missec.asp.

Cox, Karen L. *Dixie's Daughters: The United Daughters of the Confederacy and the Preservation of Confederate Culture.* Gainesville:
University Press of Florida, 2003.

Davis, Jefferson. "Jefferson Davis' Farewell Address." Papers of Jefferson
Davis. Rice University. January 21, 1861. https://jeffersondavis.rice
.edu/archives/documents/jefferson-davis-farewell-address.

DeFord, Susan. "Gabriel's Rebellion." *Washington Post,* February 6,
2000. https://www.washingtonpost.com/archive/lifestyle/2000/02/06
/gabriels-rebellion/33c9061a-e33d-4f18-bf02-fe3cd294f5df/.

Delta Cultural Center. "The Delta Is . . ." Accessed July 9, 2019. http://
www.deltaculturalcenter.com/Learn/the-delta-is.

Deria, M. "Protecting the Vulnerable: The Tuskegee Syphilis Study and
the Evolution of Informed Consent in the Twentieth Century." PhD
thesis, University of Ottawa, 2006.

Deutsch, Stephanie. *You Need a Schoolhouse.* Evanston, IL: Northwestern University Press, 2011.

Devi, Debra. "Can the Blues Rescue the Mississippi Delta, Part 3." *Huffington Post,* March 26, 2013. http://www.huffingtonpost.com/debra
-devi/can-the-blues-rescue-the-mississippi-delta_b_2949064.html.

Douglass, Frederick. *Narrative of the Life of Frederick Douglass.* Oxford: Oxford University Press, 1999.

Downs, Gregory P., and Kate Masur. "The Era of Reconstruction, 1861–1900." National Park Service. 2017. http://www.npshistory .com/publications/nhl/theme-studies/reconstruction-era.pdf.

Dreier, Peter. "Selma's Missing Rabbi." *Huffington Post,* January 17, 2015. http://www.huffingtonpost.com/peter-dreier/selmas-missing -rabbi_b_6491368.html.

Drescher, Seymour. "Jews and New Christians in the Atlantic Slave Trade." In Sarna and Mendelsohn, *Jews and the Civil War.*

Drewry, William S. *The Southampton Insurrection.* Washington, DC: Neale Co., 1900.

Du Bois, W. E. B. *The Souls of Black Folk.* Oxford: Oxford University Press, 1903.

Eagle, J. "Tuskegee Syphilis Study Administrative Records, 1929–1972 Record Group 442: Records for the Centers for Disease Control and Prevention, 1921–2006." National Archives and Records Administration. November 1, 1972. https://research.archives.gov/id /650715.

Eckholm, Erik. "At Night, Farmer Trades His Tractor for the Blues." *New York Times,* March 2, 2007. http://www.nytimes.com/2007/03 /02/us/02jukejoint.html.

Edwards, Josh. "As Numbers Fall, Jews Hope to Save the Cemetery." *Vicksburg Post,* July 12, 2014. http://www.vicksburgpost.com/2014 /07/12/as-numbers-fall-jews-hope-to-save-cemetery/.

Egerton, Douglas R. *The Wars of Reconstruction.* New York: Blooms- bury Press, 2014.

Emamdjomeh, Armand, and Priya Krishnakumar. "A Before-and-After Look at the Deadly, Record-Setting Flooding in Louisiana." *Los Angeles Times,* August 22, 2016. http://www.latimes.com/projects/la -na-louisiana-flooding/.

Epps, Garrett. "When Republicans Attack States Rights." *Atlantic,* March 13, 2018. https://www.theatlantic.com/politics/archive/2018 /03/when-republicans-become-anti-states-rights/555362/.

Eufaula Chamber of Commerce. "Walking-Driving Tour, Eufaula, Alabama." Brochure, n.d.

Evans, Eli N. "An Interview with Eli N. Evans, Author of Judah P. Benjamin: The Jewish Confederate." *American Jewish History*, December, 1988.

———. Preface. In Rosengarten and Rosengarten, *A Portion of the People*.

———. *The Provincials*. Chapel Hill: University of North Carolina Press, 2005.

———. "Southern-Jewish History: Alive and Unfolding." In Kaganoff and Urofksy, *Turn to the South*.

Fairfax County Park Authority. "From the Ground Up: The Sully Slave Quarter." Video, 2001. https://www.discoveryvirginia.org/islandora /object/islandora%3A11046.

Falk, Stanley L. "Divided Loyalties in 1861: The Decision of Major Alfred Mordecai." In Sarna and Mendelsohn, *Jews and the Civil War*.

Feldberg, Michael. "Passover Seders during the Civil War." *My Jewish Learning*. Accessed July 8, 2019. https://www.myjewishlearning.com /article/passover-seders-during-the-civil-war/.

Ferris, Marcie C., and Mark I. Greenberg, eds. *Jewish Roots in Southern Soil: A New History*. Waltham, MA: Brandeis University Press, 2006.

———. "The Last Jews of Natchez." Gravy, Southern Foodways Alliance. May 21, 2015. https://www.southernfoodways.org/gravy/the -last-jews-of-natchez-gravy-ep-14/.

———. *Matzoh Ball Gumbo: Culinary Tales of the Jewish South*. Chapel Hill: University of North Carolina Press, 2005.

Fields, Karen E., and Barbara J. Fields. (2012). *Racecraft: The Soul of Inequality in American Life*. New York: Verso, 2014.

Food and Agriculture Organization of the United Nations. *Sugar Beet White Sugar Agribusiness Handbook*. 2009.

Foote, Shelby. *The Civil War: A Narrative (Fort Sumpter to Perryville)*. New York: Vintage Books, 1958.

Ford, Emily, and Barry Stiefel. *The Jews of New Orleans and the Mississippi Delta.* Charleston: History Press, 2012.

Fordham, Damon. "Charleston's African American Heritage: A Port of Entry for Enslaved Africans." *Charleston Chronicle,* March 4, 2016. https://www.charlestonchronicle.net/2016/03/04/charlestons-african -american-heritage-a-port-of-entry-for-enslaved-africans/.

Freemark, Samara, and Joe Richman. "'Segregation Forever': A Fiery Pledge Forgiven, But Not Forgotten." *National Public Radio,* January 10, 2013. https://www.npr.org/2013/01/14/169080969 /segregation-forever-a-fiery-pledge-forgiven-but-not-forgotten.

Fritz, Angela. "How Over 2 Feet of Rain Caused Historic Flooding in Louisiana in Less Than 72 Hours." *Washington Post,* August 15, 2016. https://www.washingtonpost.com/news/capital-weather-gang /wp/2016/08/15/how-over-2-feet-of-rain-caused-historic-flooding-in -louisiana-in-less-than-72-hours/.

Galik, Emily. "Slave Punishment in French Louisiana." Media Nola. Tulane University. June 10, 2016. http://medianola.org/discover /place/985/Slave-Punishment-in-French-Louisiana.

Gatewood, Willard B. "The Arkansas Delta: The Deepest of the Deep South." In Willard B. Gatewood Jr., and Jeannie M. Whayne, eds. *The Arkansas Delta: Land of Paradox,* Fayetteville: The University of Arkansas Press, 1996.

George Washington's Mount Vernon. "Ten Facts About Washington and Slavery." George Washington's Mount Vernon. Accessed July 8, 2019. http://www.mountvernon.org/george-washington/slavery/ten -facts-about-washington-slavery/.

Ginsberg, Benjamin. *Moses of South Carolina: A Jewish Scalawag During Radical Reconstruction.* Baltimore: Johns Hopkins University, 2010.

Goldman, E. "The Jewish Community of Natchitoches Parish." Master's thesis, Northwestern State College of Louisiana, 1968.

Goodman, Carolyn and Brad Herzog. *My Mantelpiece.* Pacific Grove, CA: Why Not Books, 2014.

Graham, Henry S. "Map Showing the Distribution of the Slave Population of the Southern States of the United States. Compiled from the

Census of 1860." Census Office, Department of the Interior. 1861. https://www.loc.gov/resource/g3861e.cw0013200/.

Grand Lodge History. Most Worshipful Prince Hall Grand Lodge of Alabama Free and Accepted Masons. 2015. http://mwphglofal.com /glhistory.html#.

Grandy, Moses. *Narrative of the Life of Moses Grandy; Late a Slave in the United States of America.* London: C. Gilpin, 1843. http:// docsouth.unc.edu/fpn/grandy/grandy.html.

Grant, Richard. "Deep in the Swamps, Archaeologists Are Finding How Fugitive Slaves Kept Their Freedom." Smithsonian.com. September 2016. https://www.smithsonianmag.com/history/ deep-swamps-archaeologists-fugitive-slaves-kept-freedom -180960122/.

Gray, Fred D. *The Tuskegee Syphilis Study.* Montgomery, AL: NewSouth Books, 2013.

Green Mountain Post Films. "No Success Like Failure." Accessed July 8, 2019. http://www.gmpfilms.com/NLF.html.

Greenville History Museum. (n.d.). *Historic Downtown Greenville, Mississippi.*

Gruber, Samuel. "USA: Charleston, SC, Congregation Maintains Historic Jewish Cemetery One Stone (and One Wall) at a Time." *Samuel Gruber's Jewish Art and Monuments* (blog). January 26, 2015. https://samgrubersjewishartmonuments.blogspot.com/2015/01 /charleston-congregation-works-to.html.

———. "Charleston's Holocaust Memorial in Shadow of Calhoun Monument." *Samuel Gruber's Jewish Art and Monuments* (blog). February 26, 2017. https://samgrubersjewishartmonuments .blogspot.com/2017/02/usa-charlestons-holocaust-memorial-in .html.

Hagy, James W. *This Happy Land.* Tuscaloosa: University of Alabama Press, 1993.

Hamm, Sara. *Reeves Peanut Company* (video). Chattahoochee Heritage Project. March 27, 2012. http://www.chattahoocheeheritage.org /2012/03/reeves-peanut/.

Harby, Lee C. "In the Days When We Were Young, I—In Quarters." *Jewish Messenger,* May 21, 1886. College of Charleston Special Collections, Lee Cohen Harby Papers, 1859–1911, MSS 1019.

———. "In the Days When We Were Young, III—The Planter's Household." *Jewish Messenger,* June 11, 1886. College of Charleston Special Collections, Lee Cohen Harby Papers, 1859–1911, MSS 1019.

———. "In the Days When We Were Young, IV—Old Plantation Life." *Jewish Messenger,* June 11, 1886. College of Charleston Special Collections, Lee Cohen Harby Papers, 1859–1911, MSS 1019.

———. "Old Christmas Times in the South." *Weekly Magazine: The Jewish Messenger,* n.d. College of Charleston Special Collections, Lee Cohen Harby Papers, , 1859–1911, MSS 1019.

Harlan, Chico. "An Opportunity Gamed Away." *Washington Post,* July 11, 2015. http://www.washingtonpost.com/sf/business/2015/07/11/an-opportunity-gamed-away/.

Harmon, Rick. "Timeline: The Selma-to-Montgomery Marches." *USA Today,* March 6, 2015. https://eu.usatoday.com/story/news/nation/2015/03/05/black-history-bloody-sunday-timeline/24463923/.

Hauser, Christine. "Mississipi District Ordered to Desegregate Its Schools." *New York Times,* May 17, 2016. https://www.nytimes.com/2016/05/18/us/cleveland-mississippi-school-district-desegregate.html?_r=0.

Heitzler, Michael J. *Goose Creek: A Definitive History.* Charleston, SC: History Press, 2005.

Hennessey, John. "Civilians Endure the Battle of Fredericksburg." American Battlefield Trust. Accessed July 8, 2019. https://www.battlefields.org/learn/articles/voices-storm-0.

Higginson, Thomas W. "Nat Turner's Insurrection." *Atlantic,* August 1861. https://www.theatlantic.com/magazine/archive/1861/08/nat-turners-insurrection/308736/.

———. "The Story of Denmark Vesey." *Atlantic,* June 1861. https://www.theatlantic.com/magazine/archive/1861/06/denmark-vesey/396239/.

Historic Charleston Foundation. "Lambs Phosphate Mining Facility."
Ashley River Historic Corridor. 2014. http://ashleyriverhistoriccor-
ridor.org/sites/lambs-phosphate-mining-facility/.

History.com. "1780: Americans Suffer Worst Defeat of Revolution at
Charleston." November 13, 2009. https://www.history.com/this-day
-in-history/americans-suffer-worst-defeat-of-revolution-at-charleston.

Hoffschwelle, Mary S. *Preserving Rosenwald Schools*. Washington, DC:
National Trust for Historic Preservation, 2012.

Homans, Bill. "Watermelon Slim." "Artist Biography." Accessed July 8,
2019. http://www.watermelonslim.com/bio/.

Hopson Commissary. "History." Accessed July 8, 2019. http://www
.hopsonplantation.com/index.php/history.html.

Hopson Plantation. "Sunflower Plantation." Accessed July 8, 2019.
http://www.sunflowerplantation.org/hopson.html.

Hudson, John C. "The Yazoo-Mississippi Delta as Plantation Country."
*Tall Timbers Research Station and Land Conservancy/Fire Ecology
Conference Proceedings* 16 (March 28, 2016). http://talltimbers.org
/wp-content/uploads/2014/03/Hudson1979_op.pdf.

Institute of Southern Jewish Life. "Clarksdale: A Historical Overview."
Encyclopedia of Southern Jewish Communities. 2017. http://www
.isjl.org/mississippi-clarksdale-encyclopedia.html.

———. "Eufaula, Alabama." *Encyclopedia of Southern Jewish Communities*. 2017. http://www.isjl.org/alabama-eufaula-encyclopedia.html.

———. "Greenville, Mississippi." *Encyclopedia of Southern Jewish
Communities*. 2017. https://www.isjl.org/mississippi-greenville
-encyclopedia.html.

———. "Norfolk: A Historical Overview." *Encyclopedia of Southern
Jewish Communities*. 2017. http://www.isjl.org/virginia-norfolk
-encyclopedia.html.

———. "Port Gibson: Historical Overview." *Encyclopedia of Southern
Jewish Communities*. 2017. http://www.isjl.org/mississippi-port
-gibson-encyclopedia.html.

———. "Selma, Alabama." *Encyclopedia of Southern Jewish Communities*.
2017. http://www.isjl.org/alabama-selma-encyclopedia.html.

———. "Temple Beth Israel—Clarksdale, Mississippi." *Encyclopedia of Southern Jewish Communities.* 2017. http://www.isjl.org/mississippi -clarksdale-temple-beth-israel-encyclopedia.html.

International Jewish Cemetery Project. "Natchitoches (Natchi- toches Parish)." Updated April 17, 2010. http://www .iajgsjewishcemeteryproject.org/louisiana-la/nachitoches-nachitoches -parish.html.

International Slavery Museum. "Conditions in the Sugar Works." Accessed July 8, 2019. http://www.liverpoolmuseums.org.uk/ism/slavery /archaeology/caribbean/plantations/caribbean35.aspx.

James Madison's Montpelier. "The Life of James Madison." Accessed July 8, 2019. http://www.montpelier.org/learn/the-life-of-james -madison.

———. Tour and Exhibit, April 17, 2018. Jewish Federation of Charles- ton, SC. "Jewish Community Marches in Annual MLK Day Parade." January 15, 2018. https://www.jewishcharleston.org/events-in -charleston/jewish-community-marches-in-annual-mlk-day-parade.

John Lewis. Congressman John Lewis (website). Accessed July 8, 2019. https://johnlewis.house.gov/john-lewis.

Jones, James H. *Bad Blood: The Tuskegee Syphilis Study.* New York: Free Press, 1993.

Kaganoff, Nathan M., and Melvin I. Urofsky, eds. *Turn to the South: Essays on Southern Jewry.* Charlottesville: University Press of Virginia, 1979.

Kahal Kadosh Beth Elohim. "Coming Street Cemetery." 2019. https:// www.kkbe.org/cemetries.

———. "History." 2019. https://www.kkbe.org/visit.

Kelly, Joseph. *America's Longest Siege.* New York: Overlook Press, 2013.

Kempner, Aviva, dir. *Rosenwald: The Remarkable Story of a Jewish Part- nership with African American Communities.* Produced by Ciesla Foundation. 2015.

Kogan, Michael S., et al. "Confederate Honor and Sacrifice Are Still Worth Defending." *Post and Courier,* December 8, 2017. https://

www.postandcourier.com/opinion/commentary/confederate-honor
-and-sacrifice-are-still-worth-defending/article_d4adf340-db98-11e7
-9e46-5bfeoab82e44.html.

Korn, Bertram W. "Jews and Negro Slavery in the Old South, 1789–1865." In Sarna and Mendelsohn, *Jews and the Civil War.*

Kynor, S. "The Moses of Charleston: Denmark Vesey." *Undergraduate Research Journal—University of Colorado at Colorado Springs* 10, no. 1 (2016). http://ojs.uccs.edu/index.php/urj/article/view/250/155.

Kytle, Ethan. J., and Blain Roberts. *Denmark Vesey's Garden: Slavery and Memory in the Cradle of the Confederacy.* New York: New Press, 2018.

Lazarus, Rachel M. Letter to Ellen Mordecai. October 9, 1831. Mordecai Family Papers, 1649–1947, no. 847. Southern Historical Collection. Wilson Special Collections Library. University of North Carolina.

"L'Chayim: David Goodman (Andrew Goodman's Brother)." YouTube video posted by JBS. July 7, 2016. https://www.youtube.com/watch ?v=oxG3zDbL4U8.

Leibman, Laura A. "The Crossroads of American History: Jews in the Colonial Americas." In *By Dawn's Early Light.* Princeton: Princeton University Library, 2016.

Lemann, Nicholas. "The Price of Union." *New Yorker,* November 2, 2015.

Lepore, Jill. "'Mourning Lincoln' and 'Lincoln's Body.'" *New York Times,* February 4, 2015. https://www.nytimes.com/2015/02/08 /books/review/mourning-lincoln-and-lincolns-body.html.

Levere, Jane L. "Small-City Congregations Try to Preserve Rituals of Jewish Life." *New York Times,* December 1, 2010.

Levine, Bruce. *The Fall of the House of Dixie.* New York: Random House, 2013.

Levitas, Susan. "Gefilte Fish in the Land of the Kingfish: Jewish Life in Louisiana." Folklife in Louisiana. Accessed July 8, 2019. http://www .louisianafolklife.org/LT/Articles_Essays/jewsinla.html.

Lewis, John, and Michael D'Orso. *Walking With the Wind.* New York: Simon and Schuster, 1998.

Library of Virginia. "Jim Crow and the KKK." Accessed July 9, 2019. http://www.lva.virginia.gov/exhibits/mitchell/jimcro.htm.

———. "John Brown's Raid." Accessed July 9, 2019. http://www.lva.virginia.gov/exhibits/DeathLiberty/johnbrown/index.htm.

Lienhard, John H. "Prison Treadmills." Houston Public Radio. Engines of Our Ingenuity. Accessed July 8, 2019. https://www.uh.edu/engines/epi374.htm.

Lincoln, Abraham. "A Letter from President Lincoln; Reply to Horace Greeley; Slavery and the Union the Restoration of the Union the Paramount Object." *New York Times,* August 24, 1862. https://www.nytimes.com/1862/08/24/archives/a-letter-from-president-lincoln-reply-to-horace-greeley-slavery-and.html.

Littlefield, Daniel C. "Slavery." University of South Carolina. South Carolina Encyclopedia. 2016. http://www.scencyclopedia.org/sce/entries/slavery/.

Loewen, J. W. "Reconstruction." *Washington Post,* January 24, 2016. https://www.washingtonpost.com/opinions/five-myths-about-reconstruction/2016/01/21/0719b324-bfc5-11e5-83d4-42e3bceea902_story.html?utm_term=.d99b1778d6c0.

———. *Sundown Towns.* New York: New Press, 2005.

Louisiana Division of Historic Preservation. "The River Road." National Park Service, Southeastern Louisiana. Accessed July 8, 2019. https://www.nps.gov/nr/travel/louisiana/riverroad.htm.

Louisiana Regional Folklife Program. "Carroll Jones House." Accessed August 10, 2019. https://folklife.nsula.edu/crcc/CarrollJones.html.

LouisianaTravel.com. "Making History at Frogmore Plantation." Louisiana Office of Tourism. 2017. http://www.louisianatravel.com/articles/making-history-frogmore-plantation.

Main Street Greenwood. "Historic Downtown Greenwood Walking Tour." Brochure, n.d.

"Mapping Jewish Charleston: Mordecai Cohen." College of Charleston Libraries, Special Collections. 2019. https://mappingjewishcharleston.cofc.edu/1833/map.php?id=1004.

Matthews, J. (1838). "Recollections of Slavery by a Runaway Slave."
The Emancipator, August 23, 1838. National Anti-Slavery Society,
University of North Carolina at Chapel Hill. University of North
Carolina at Chapel Hill. http://docsouth.unc.edu/neh/runaway
/runaway.html.

McCabe, Daniel, and Paul Stekler, dirs. *George Wallace: Settin' the
Woods on Fire* (Film). PBS American Experience, 2000.

McGill, Andrew. "The Missing Black Students at Elite American Universities." *Atlantic,* November 23, 2015. https://www.theatlantic.com
/politics/archive/2015/11/black-college-student-body/417189/.

McGraw, Eliza R. L. "An 'Intense Heritage': Southern Jewishness in Literature and Film." In Ferris and Greenberg, *Jewish Roots in Southern Soil.*

McKay, Gretchen. "Civil War Victory in Vicksburg Costly for Both
Sides, As a Tour of the National Military Park Shows." *Pittsburgh
Post-Gazette,* May 29, 2011. https://www.post-gazette.com/life
/travel/2011/05/29/Civil-War-victory-in-Vicksburg-costly-for
-both-sides-as-a-tour-of-the-National-Military-Park-shows/stories
/201105290231.

Mintz, Steven. "Historical Context: Facts About the Slave Trade and
Slavery." Gilder Lehrman Institute of American History. Accessed
July 8, 2019. https://www.gilderlehrman.org/content/historical
-context-facts-about-slave-trade-and-slavery.

Mississippi Blues Commission. "Mississippi John Hurt." Mississippi
Blues Trail. Accessed July 8, 2019. http://www.msbluestrail.org/blues
-trail-markers/mississippi-john-hurt.

———. "Po' Monkey's." Mississippi Blues Trail. Accessed July 8, 2019.
http://www.msbluestrail.org/blues-trail-markers/po-monkeys.

Mississippi Civil Rights Project. "Forrest, Nathan Bedford." Accessed
July 8, 2019. https://mscivilrightsproject.org/forrest/person-forrest
/nathan-bedford-forrest/.

Mississippi John Hurt Foundation. "MJH Bio." Accessed July 9, 2019.
http://mississippijohnhurtfoundation.org/bio.html.

Mitchell, Christine K. Monuments of Marion Square. Presentation at the
Jewish Historical Society of South Carolina: Memory, Monuments,

and Memorials. April 28, 2018. http://jhssc.org/2018/05/01/jhssc
-spring-2018-meeting/.

MJL, "Conversation and Debate." My Jewish Learning. Accessed July 8,
2019. https://www.myjewishlearning.com/article/conversation
-debate/.

Moise, Abraham. *A Selection from the Miscellaneous Writings of the
Late Isaac Harby.* Charleston, SC: James S. Burges, 1829.

Monaco, C. S. *Moses Levy of Florida: Jewish Utopian and Antebellum
Reformer.* Baton Rouge: Louisiana State University Press, 2005.

Moore, Deborah D. "Freedom's Fruits." In Rosengarten and Rosengarten,
A Portion of the People.

Mordecai, Ellen. Letter to Rachel Mordecai Lazarus. September 1831.
Mordecai Family Papers, 1649–1947, no. 847. Southern Historical
Collection. Wilson Special Collections Library. University of North
Carolina.

Morrison, Toni. "Comment." *New Yorker,* October 5, 1998. http://www
.newyorker.com/magazine/1998/10/05/comment-6543.

Moses, Jennifer. "The Lost Tribe of Natchez." *New York Times,* September 20, 1998. http://www.nytimes.com/1998/09/20/travel/the-lost
-tribe-of-natchez.html?_r=0.

Moses, Robert A. Interview by Elizabeth Moses and Dale Rosengarten.
August 16, 2013. College of Charleston, Special Collections, Jewish Heritage Collection, MSS 1035-375. http://fedora.library.cofc
.edu:8080/fedora/objects/lcdl:64127/datastreams/PDF1/content.

———. Interview by Elizabeth Moses and Dale Rosengarten. August 17,
2013. College of Charleston, Special Collections, MSS 1035-376.
http://fedora.library.cofc.edu:8080/fedora/objects/lcdl:64128
/datastreams/PDF1/content.

———. Interview by Elizabeth Moses, transmitted by email. February 25, 2018.

Moses Myers House. National Register of Historic Places Registra-
tion Form. 2009. https://www.dhr.virginia.gov/VLR_to_transfer
/PDFNoms/122-0017_Moses_Myers_House_1969_Final
_Nomination.pdf.

Mulholland, Loki. *The Uncomfortable Truth* (Film). Taylor Street Films, 2016.

NAACP. "History of Lynchings." 2018. http://www.naacp.org/history-of -lynchings/.

National Civil Rights Museum. Exhibit. 2017. Memphis, TN.

National Constitution Center. "Civil War and Reconstruction: The Battle for Freedom and Equality." Exhibit. 2019. Philadelphia, PA.

National Geographic. "Selma to Montgomery March." 2015. Accesssed August 1, 2018. http://www.nationalgeographic.com/selma-to -montgomery-photo-gallery/#/brown-chapelame-990-60152_16967 _600x450.jpg.

National Museum of African American History and Culture. "The Expansion of Slavery." Exhibit. 2018. Washington, DC.

National Park Service. "The Anti-Secessionist Jefferson Davis." National Park Service. September 4, 2015. https://www.nps.gov/bost/the-anti -secessionist-jefferson-davis.htm.

———. "An Epic Contest." Shiloh National Military Park. February 14, 2018. https://www.nps.gov/shil/index.htm.

———. "Slavery at Arlington." Arlington House: The Robert E. Lee Memorial. January 27, 2017. https://www.nps.gov/arho/learn/history culture/slavery.htm.

National Public Radio. "A Tuskegee Airman's Harrowing WWII Tale." November 10, 2006. https://www.npr.org/templates/story/story.php ?storyId=6467779.

National Trust for Historic Preservation. "Rosenwald Schools." National Trust for Historic Preservation. Accessed July 9, 2019. https://savingplaces.org/places/rosenwald-schools#.VzNnM4-cHOZ.

Nazaryan, Alexander. "Black Colleges Matter." *Newsweek,* August 18, 2015. http://www.newsweek.com/black-colleges-matter-363667.

Nelson, Rex. "David Solomon at 100." *Southern Fried,* July 26, 2016. http://www.rexnelsonsouthernfried.com/?p=8035.

New York Historical Society. "The First Jewish Americans: Freedom and Culture in the New World." Exhibit. March 11, 2017. New York, NY.

New York Times. "Lincoln Called for Dixie," February 7, 1909. https://
timesmachine.nytimes.com/timesmachine/1909/02/07/106116509
.html?emc=eta1&pageNumber=10.

Nowell, Princella W. "The Flood of 1927 and Its Impact in Greenville,
Mississippi." Mississippi History Now/Mississippi Historical Society.
2017. http://www.mshistorynow.mdah.ms.gov/articles/230/the-flood
-of-1927-and-its-impact-in-greenville-mississippi.

Oatlands. "Slavery at Oatlands." Oatlands Historic House and Gardens.
https://www.oatlands.org/slavery/.

Obama, Barack. "Remarks by the President at the 50th Anniversary
of the Selma to Montgomery Marches." White House. March 7,
2015. https://obamawhitehouse.archives.gov/the-press-office/2015
/03/07/remarks-president-50th-anniversary-selma-montgomery
-marches.

Ohlheiser, Abby. "The Jewish Roots of Leonard Nimoy and 'Live Long
and Prosper.'" *Washington Post,* February 27, 2015. https://www
.washingtonpost.com/news/arts-and-entertainment/wp/2015/02/27
/the-jewish-roots-of-leonard-nimoy-and-live-long-and-prosper/?utm
_term=.6cb03e4d4544.

Ollstein, Alice M.. "The Dark Side of Selma the Mainstream Media
Ignored." ThinkProgress. March 10, 2015. http://thinkprogress.org
/economy/2015/03/10/3631364/thousands-depart-selma-leaving
-deep-poverty-behind/.

Palmer, Robert. *Deep Blues.* New York: Penguin, 1981.

Payne, Charles M. *I've Got the Light of Freedom.* Oakland: University
of California Press, 2007.

Pearson, Richard. "Former Ala. Gov. George C. Wallace Dies." *Washington Post,* September 14, 1998. https://www.washingtonpost.com/wp
-srv/politics/daily/sept98/wallace.htm.

Pomerance, Rachel. "If It's Matzah Balls with Gravy, It Must Be Seder
Time Down South." *InterfaithFamily,* March 2002.

Powers, Bernard E. "African Americans in 19th-Century Charleston."
Charleston's African-American Heritage. http://www.africanamerican
charleston.com/19thcentury.html.

Premack, Rachel. "A 'Horror Movie': Fast-Rising Floodwaters in Louisiana Spark a State of Emergency." *Washington Post,* August 13, 2016. https://www.washingtonpost.com/news/post-nation/wp/2016/08/13/a-horror-movie-louisiana-is-in-a-state-of-emergency-because-of-record-flooding/?utm_term=.476acba67cc3.

Preserve America. "Port Gibson, Mississippi." March 10, 2009. https://www.achp.gov/preserve-america/community/port-gibson-mississippi.

Price, Mark. "Historians Find Fingerprints of Long-Forgotten South Carolina Slaves in 200-Year-Old Bricks." *Charlotte Observer,* February 24, 2019. https://www.charlotteobserver.com/news/local/article226335430.html.

Puckett, Dan J. *In the Shadow of Hitler: Alabama's Jews, the Second World War, and the Holocaust.* Tuscaloosa: University of Alabama Press, 2004.

Puckett, Susan. "10 Things to Know About the Mississippi Delta." CNN. May 1, 2015. http://www.cnn.com/2014/05/15/travel/mississippi-delta-10-things-bourdain/index.html.

Purcell, S. J. Plat, Soldier's Retreat Plantation, 1784. College of Charleston Special Collections, Inventory of the Drayton Family Papers After 1970, Land and Legal, MSS 0152, box 14, folder 4.

Raines, Howell. "George Wallace, Segregation Symbol, Dies at 79." *New York Times,* September 14, 1998. https://www.nytimes.com/1998/09/14/us/george-wallace-segregation-symbol-dies-at-79.html.

Raphall, M. J. "The Bible View of Slavery." 1861. Jewish American History Foundation. http://www.jewish-history.com/civilwar/raphall.html.

Reed, Roy. "25,000 Go to Alabama's Capitol: Wallace Rebuffs Petitioners; White Rights Worker Is Slain." *New York Times,* March 25, 1965. http://www.nytimes.com/learning/general/onthisday/big/0325.html#article.

Religious Action Center of Reform Judaism. "Jews in the Civil Rights Movement." Accessed July 9, 2019. http://www.rac.org/jews-and-civil-rights-movement.

Ringle, Ken. "The Real Life and Death of Nat Turner." *Washington Post,* April 24, 1994. https://www.washingtonpost.com/archive/opinions /1994/04/24/the-real-life-and-death-of-nat-turner/568cfa77-9963 -4642-807c-436e36d12fe5/?utm_term=.8cdf7f179b04.

Roberts, Blain, and Ethan J. Kytle. "When Freedom Came to Charleston." *New York Times,* February 19, 2015. https://opinionator.blogs .nytimes.com/2015/02/19/when-freedom-came-to-charleston/.

Robertson, Campbell. "History of Lynchings in the South Documents Nearly 4,000 Names." *New York Times,* February 10, 2015. https:// www.nytimes.com/2015/02/10/us/history-of-lynchings-in-the-south -documents-nearly-4000-names.html.

———. "A Lynching Memorial Is Opening. The Country Has Never Seen Anything Like It." *New York Times,* April 25, 2018. https:// www.nytimes.com/2018/04/25/us/lynching-memorial-alabama.html.

Robertson, David. *Denmark Vesey: The Buried History of America's Largest Slave Rebellion and the Man Who Led It.* New York: Alfred A. Knopf, 1999.

Rockoff, Stuart. "Jews." Encyclopedia of Arkansas History and Culture. July 12, 2016. http://www.encyclopediaofarkansas.net/encyclopedia /entry-detail.aspx?entryID=2297.

Rosefield, V. M. Application for Membership to the National Society of the Daughters of the American Revolution. January 22, 1959. College of Charleston Special Collections, Jewish Heritage Collection, MSS 1034–033.

Rosen, Robert N. *A Short History of Charleston.* University of South Carolina Press, 1997.

———. *The Jewish Confederates.* Columbia: University of South Carolina Press, 2000.

———. "Jewish Confederates." In Ferris and Greenberg, *Jewish Roots in Southern Soil.*

———. "Jewish Confederates." In Sarna and Mendelsohn, *Jews and the Civil War.*

Rosengarten, Dale. "A Call for Candlesticks." In Rosengarten and Rosengarten, *A Portion of the People.*

Rosengarten, Theodore. Introduction. In Rosengarten and Rosengarten, *A Portion of the People.*

Rosengarten, Theodore, and Dale Rosengarten, eds. *A Portion of the People: Three Hundred Years of Southern Jewish Life.* Columbia: University of South Carolina Press, 2002.

Rosenthal, Caitlin. "Plantations Practiced Modern Management." *Harvard Business Review,* September 2013. https://hbr.org/2013/09/plantations-practiced-modern-management.

Ruchames, Louis. "The Abolitionists and the Jews." In Sarna and Mendelsohn, *Jews and the Civil War.*

RuralSWAlabama. "Temple Mishkan Israel at Selma, AL." Welcome to Rural Southwest Alabama. 2017. http://www.ruralswalabama.org/attraction/temple-mishkan-israel-selma-al1899/.

Rutenberg, Jim. "A Dream Undone." *New York Times,* July 29, 2015.

Sachar, Howard. "Jews in the Civil Rights Movement." My Jewish Learning. Accessed July 9, 2019. https://www.myjewishlearning.com/article/jews-in-the-civil-rights-movement/.

Samenow, Jason. "No-Name Storm Dumped Three Times as Much Rain in Louisiana as Hurricane Katrina." *Washington Post,* August 19, 2016. https://www.washingtonpost.com/news/capital-weather-gang/wp/2016/08/19/no-name-storm-dumped-three-times-as-much-rain-in-louisiana-as-hurricane-katrina/.

Sarna, Jonathan. D. *American Judaism.* New Haven, CT: Yale University Press, 2004.

Sarna, Jonathan. D., and Adam Mendelsohn. "Jews and Abolition." In Sarna and Mendelsohn, *Jews and the Civil War.*

———, eds. *Jews and the Civil War.* New York: New York University Press, 2010.

Schnugg, Alyssa. "Hundreds Gather to Meet their Muslim Neighbors in Oxford." *Oxford Eagle,* February 20, 2017. http://www.oxfordeagle.com/2017/02/20/hundreds-gather-to-meet-their-muslim-neighbors-in-oxford/.

Schwartz, John, and Mark Schleifstein. "Fortified But Still in Peril." *New York Times,* February 25, 2018.

Scrabble School. Scrabble School Preservation Foundation. Accessed July 9, 2019. http://scrabbleschool.org/.

"Scratching a Living." *Economist,* June 8, 2013. http://www.economist .com/news/united-states/21579025-shocking-rate-depopulation -rural-south-scratching-living.

Sears Archives. "The Rosenwald School Program." March 21, 2012. http://www.searsarchives.com/history/questions/rosenwald.htm.

Shankman, Arnold. "Friend or Foe? Southern Blacks View the Jew, 1880–1935." In Kaganoff and Urofksy, *Turn to the South.*

Shanks, Judith A. W. *Old Family Things: An Affectionate Look Back.* Self-published, CreateSpace, 2011.

Sharkey, Richard. "Natchitoches Mayor Defends Confederate Flag Ban." *Town Talk,* November 17, 2015. http://www.thetowntalk.com/story /news/local/2015/11/16/natchitoches-mayor-defends-confederate -flag-decision/75881574/.

Sheskin, Ira M., and Arnold Dashefsky. "United States Jewish Population, 2016." Berman Jewish DataBank. 2016. http://www.jewishdatabank .org/Studies/downloadFile.cfm?FileID=3557.

Slade, Suzanne. *With Books and Bricks: How Booker T. Washington Built a School.* Chicago: Albert Whitman and Company, 2014.

Smitherman, Joseph. "Eyes on the Prize: America's Civil Rights Years 1954–1965; Interviews: Mayor Joseph Smitherman." Washington University Digital Gateway Texts. December 5, 1985. http://digital .wustl.edu/e/eop/eopweb/smi0015.0712.099mayorjosephsmither man.html.

Sokolow, Jayme A. "Revolution and Reform: The Antebellum Jewish Abolitionists." In Sarna and Mendelsohn, *Jews and the Civil War.*

South Carolina. "Confederate States of America—Declaration of the Immediate Causes Which Induce and Justify the Secession of South Carolina from the Federal Union." December 24, 1860. Yale Law School. Avalon Project. http://avalon.law.yale.edu/19th_century/csa _scarsec.asp.

South Carolina College. "Slavery at South Carolina College, 1801– 1865." Introduction to Historic Brickmaking. Historic Wall of South

Carolina College. https://delphi.tcl.sc.edu/library/digital/slaveryscc
/introduction-to-historic-brickmaking.html.

Southern Jewish Life. "Centennial Gala Planned for Vicksburg's B'nai
B'rith Literary Club." *Southern Jewish Life,* March 9, 2017. http://
www.sjlmag.com/2017/03/centennial-gala-planned-for-vicksburgs
.html.

Southern Poverty Law Center. "*Brown v. Board*: Timeline of School Integration in the US Teaching Tolerance." 2016. http://www.tolerance
.org/magazine/number-25-spring-2004/feature/brown-v-board
-timeline-school-integration-us.

———. "Whose Heritage? Public Symbols of the Confederacy." June 4,
2018. https://www.splcenter.org/20180604/whose-heritage-public
-symbols-confederacy.

Spiro, Jack D. "Rabbi in the South: A Personal View." In Kaganoff and
Urofsky, *Turn to the South.*

Stanford University. Martin Luther King Jr. Research and Education
Institute. "Selma to Montgomery March." Accessed July 9, 2019.
http://kingencyclopedia.stanford.edu/encyclopedia/encyclopedia/enc
_selma_to_montgomery_march/.

Starobin, Paul. *Madness Rules the Hour.* New York: Public Affairs,
2017.

Stebbins, Sam, et al. "America's Poorest Towns, State by State." *MSN,*
June 10, 2015. https://www.msn.com/en-us/money/generalmoney
/americas-poorest-towns-state-by-state/ar-BBkW5UI#image
=BBkTdDOl48.

Stiefel, Barry. "David Lopez, Jr.: Builder, Industrialist, and Defender of
the Confederacy." *The American Jewish Archives Journal* 64, nos.
1–2 (2012).

Suberman, Stella. *The Jew Store.* Chapel Hill, NC: Algonquin Books,
2001.

Sullivan, Christopher. "South Will Never Forget Sherman's 'March to the
Sea.'" *Daily Herald,* November 15, 2014. http://www.dailyherald.com
/article/20141115/news/141118831/.

Sutton, E. Interview transcript provided by Mark Sutton, n.d.

Sutton, Kerlin. "Jew Boy." Unpublished paper, 2015. Natchitoches, LA.

Tavernise, Sabrina. "A Pipe to the Woods." *New York Times,* September 27, 2016.

Teaching Tolerance. "*Brown v. Board*: Timeline of School Integration in the US." Teaching Tolerance. Southern Poverty Law Center. Spring 2004. http://www.tolerance.org/magazine/number-25-spring-2004 /feature/brown-v-board-timeline-school-integration-us.

Tedlow, Richard S. "Judah P. Benjamin." In Kaganoff and Urofksy, *Turn to the South.*

Threadgill, Jacob. "Fate of Po' Monkey's in Flux; Seaberry Funeral Saturday." *Clarion-Ledger,* July 21, 2016. http://www.clarionledger.com /story/magnolia/entertainment/2016/07/21/fate-po-monkeys-flux -seaberry-funeral-saturday/87360230/.

Tidwell, John. "The Great Dismal Swamp." *American Heritage.* April/ May 2002. https://www.americanheritage.com/content/great-dismal -swamp.

Touro Synagogue. "From Inquisition to Freedom." Accessed July 9, 2019. http://www.tourosynagogue.org/history-learning/jews-in-colonies.

Trillin, Calvin. "Tamales on the Delta." *New Yorker,* January 6, 2014. http://www.newyorker.com/magazine/2014/01/06/tamales-on-the -delta.

Tures, John A. "General Nathan Bedford Forrest Versus the Ku Klux Klan." *Huffington Post.* July 6, 2015. http://www.huffingtonpost .com/john-a-tures/general-nathan-bedford-fo_b_7734444.html.

Turner, Nat, and Thomas R. Gray. *The Confessions of Nat Turner, The Leader of the Late Insurrection in Southampton, VA.* November 5, 1831. University of North Carolina–Chapel Hill. http://docsouth .unc.edu/neh/turner/turner.html.

Tuskegee University. "About the USPHS Syphilis Study." Accessed July 9, 2019. https://www.tuskegee.edu/about-us/centers-of-excellence /bioethics-center/about-the-usphs-syphilis-study.

Twitty, M. *The Cooking Gene: A Journey Through African-American Culinary History in the Old South.* New York: HarperCollins Publishing, 2017.

———. "I'm Dreaming of . . . an African American . . . Passover." Afroculinaria. April 6, 2012. https://afroculinaria.com/2012/04/06 /im-dreaming-of-an-african-american-passover/.

University of North Carolina Chapel Hill. *Ordinances and Constitution of the State of Alabama, with the Constitution of the Provisional Government and of the Confederate States of America. In Documenting the American South.* 1861. https://docsouth.unc.edu/imls /alabama/alabama.html.

Urofsky, Melvin I. *Commonwealth and Community: The Jewish Experience in Virginia.* Richmond: Virginia Historical Society, 1997.

———. Preface. In Kaganoff and Urofsky, *Turn to the South.*

US Department of Justice. "History of Federal Voting Rights." August 8, 2015. http://www.justice.gov/crt/history-federal-voting -rights-laws.

———. "Jurisdictions Previously Covered by Section 5." August 6, 2015. http://www.justice.gov/crt/jurisdictions-previously-covered -section-5.

US Department of the Interior/National Park Service. National Registry of Historic Places Inventory Nomination Form for Kahal Kadosh Beth Elohim. April 1980. https://npgallery.nps.gov/NRHP/GetAsset /NHLS/78002499_text.

———. National Register of Historic Places Inventory Nomination Form for Seth Lore and Irwington Historic District. August 14, 1986. https://npgallery.nps.gov/pdfhost/docs/NRHP/Text/86001534 .pdf.

US Fish and Wildlife Service. "The Great Dismal Swamp and the Underground Railroad" (brochure). Great Dismal Swamp National Wildlife Refuge.

US Geological Survey. Mississippi River at Baton Rouge, LA. National Water Information System. August 2016. http://waterdata.usgs.gov /usa/nwis/uv?site_no=07374000.

Virginia Department of Historic Resources. Joseph Bryan Park. National Register of Historic Places Registration Form. 2002. https://www .dhr.virginia.gov/VLR_to_transfer/PDFNoms/127-5677_Joseph _Bryan_Park_2002_Final_Nomination.pdf.

Virginia Humanities. "Young's Spring and Spring Park Historic Site." AfroVirginia. Accessed July 9, 2019. http://www.aahistoricsitesva .org/items/show/494.

Waddell, Gene. "An Architectural History of Kahal Kadosh Beth Elohim, Charleston." *South Carolina Historical Magazine* 98, no. 1 (January 1997).

Wagner, Lon. "Nat Turner's Trail Is Personal Quest." *Virginian-Pilot,* March 26, 2000. https://pilotonline.com/news/local/history/article _10db165f-5bb9-51b6-927d-ba19b92112e5.html.

Wallace, Rich. "Vicksburg." Shelby County Historical Society. July 1998. http://www.shelbycountyhistory.org/schs/civilwar/siegevicksburg .htm.

Washington, Booker T. *Up From Slavery.* New York: Dover Publications, Inc., 1901.

Waters, Dustin. "Looking Back at the Origins of Charleston's Most Controversial Monument." *Charleston City Paper,* October 10, 2017. https://www.charlestoncitypaper.com/TheBattery/archives/2017/10 /10/the-day-calhoun-rose-in-charleston.

Webb, Clive. *Fight Against Fear.* Athens: University of Georgia Press, 2001.

Weisman, Steven R. *The Chosen Wars: How Judaism Became an American Religion.* NY: Simon and Schuster, 2018.

Weissbach, Lee Shai. "East European Immigrants and the Image of Jews in the Small-Town South." *American Jewish History* 85, no. 3 (1997). http://www.jstor.org/stable/23885564.

Welcome to Greenwood, MS: This Is Our History (website). "Goldberg's Shoes." Accessed July 9, 2019. http://aboutgreenwoodmississippi .com/goldbergs-shoe-store.html.

―――. "Klein Building." Accessed July 9, 2019. http://aboutgreenwood mississippi.com/klein-building.html.

West Feliciana Historic Society Museum and Tourist Information Center. "A Walk Through History." Brochure, 2016.

Whitfield, Stephen J. "Jews and Other Southerners: Counterpoint and Paradox." In Kaganoff and Urofksy, *Turn to the South.*

————. "Jewish Fates, Altered States." In Ferris and Greenberg, *Jewish Roots in Southern Soil*.

Whitman, James Q. *Hitler's American Model*. Princeton University Press, 2017.

Whitney Plantation. "Slavery in Louisiana." Accessed July 9, 2019. http://www.whitneyplantation.com/slavery-in-louisiana.html.

"Why America Needs a Slavery Museum." YouTube video posted by *The Atlantic*. August 27, 2015. https://www.youtube.com/watch?v =NToQ3iwz7LQ.

Williams, Vanessa. "Activist Says Voter Suppression Is a 'Greater Threat to US Democracy Than Russian Election Tampering.'" *Washington Post*, June 23, 2017. https://www.washingtonpost .com/news/post-nation/wp/2017/06/23/activist-says-voter -suppression-is-a-greater-threat-to-u-s-democracy-than-russian -election-tampering/.

Willis, John C. *Forgotten Time: The Yazoo-Mississippi Delta After the Civil War*. Charlottesville: University Press of Virginia, 2000.

Wilson, Charles Reagan. "Mississippi Delta." *Southern Spaces*, April 4, 2004. http://southernspaces.org/2004/mississippi-delta.

Wilson, Christine. "Mississippi Blues." Mississippi History Now. Mississipi Historical Society. Accessed July 9, 2019. http://mshistorynow .mdah.state.ms.us/articles/41/mississippi-blues.

Wisenberg, Sandi. "What Was on the Minds of Selma's Jews?" *Tablet*, March 6, 2015. http://www.tabletmag.com/scroll/189454/what-was -on-the-minds-of-selmas-jews.

WNET/PBS. "The African-Americans: Many Rivers to Cross." With Henry Louis Gates Jr. African-American Migration Story. 2013. http://www.pbs.org/wnet/african-americans-many-rivers-to-cross /history/on-african-american-migrations/.

Woodward, C. Vann. *The Strange Career of Jim Crow*. New York: Oxford University Press, 1957.

Yan, Holly. "Louisiana's Mammouth Flooding: By the Numbers." *CNN*, August 22, 2016. http://www.cnn.com/2016/08/16/us/louisiana -flooding-by-the-numbers/.

Young, Allen, M. Zapotsky, and E. O'Keefe. "'There Is No Secession': Sessions Blasts California for 'Sanctuary' Policies, Says He Will Use His Power to Stop Them." *Washington Post,* March 8, 2018. https://www.washingtonpost.com/world/national-security/there-is-no-secession-sessions-blasts-california-for-sanctuary-policies-says-he-will-use-his-power-to-stop-them/2018/03/07/7aee6890-2219-11e8-86f6-54bfff693d2b_story.html?utm_term=.e467696b343c.

Zangrando, Robert L. "About Lynching." Modern American Poetry. University of Illinois. http://www.english.illinois.edu/maps/poets/g_l/lynching/lynching.htm.

AUTHOR INTERVIEWS

Berger, H., January 13, 2016.

Chandler, F., August 7, 2015.

Egerton, D., June 7 and 10, 2018.

Finkelstein, N., June 7, 2017.

Francis, R., April 21 and 23, 2018.

Genet, A., August 9, 2016.

Ginsberg, B., February 22, 2018.

Goodman, D., February 4, 2016.

Greene, H., January 15 and 21, 2018.

Gulledge, S., August 6, 2015.

Hamm, S., August 6, October 16, and November 13, 2015.

Hart, M., December 8, 2016.

Himelstein, A., February 17, 2017.

Johnson, S., August 7, 2015, and May 11, 2016.

Kogan, M., November 29 and 30 and December 5 and 7, 2017; January 11 and 21, 2018.

Leet, R., August 9, 2015, January 6, 2016, and January 24, 2018.

Levasseur, B., August 11, 2016.

Moses, E., January 19 and February 27, 2018.

Nachman, L., July 31, 2016.

Nelken, B., August 16, 2015.

Powers, B., February 20, 2018.

Rhoden, L., February 17, 2017.

Risen, C., June 1, 2017.

Rosen, R., January 17, 2018.

Rosenberg, A. M., April 17, 2014, and January 16, 2018.

Rosengarten, D., December 18, 2014, and November 17, 2017.

Senturia, P., January 10, 2018.

Serrins, R., February 9, 2018.

Solomon, L., February 18, 2017.

Sutton, K., August 14, 2016.

Sutton, M., August 14, 2016.